I'll Grant You That

A Step-by-Step Guide to Finding Funds,
Designing Winning Projects,
and Writing Powerful Grant Proposals

Jim Burke *&* Carol Ann Prater

HEINEMANN
Portsmouth, NH

Heinemann
A division of Reed Elsevier Inc.
361 Hanover Street
Portsmouth, NH 03801–3912
www.heinemann.com

Offices and agents throughout the world

Library of Congress Cataloging-in-Publication Data
Burke, Jim, 1961–
    I'll grant you that : a step-by-step guide to finding funds, designing winning projects, and writing powerful grant proposals / Jim Burke, Carol Ann Prater.
        p.   cm.
    Includes bibliographical references and index.
    ISBN 0-325-00197-9
    1. Proposal writing for grants.   2. Fund raising.   I. Title: Guide to finding funds, designing winning projects, and writing powerful grant proposals.   II. Prater, Carol Ann.   III. Title.
HG177.B868   2000
658.15′224—dc21   00-022502

Editor: Lois Bridges
Technology Project Manager: Dan Breslin
Production: Abigail M. Heim
Interior design: Joni Doherty Design
Cover design: Jenny Jensen Greenleaf
Manufacturing: Deanna Richardson

Printed in the United States of America on acid-free paper

04   03   02   01   00   RRD   1   2   3   4   5

JIM

To my mother,
Judy Burke,
who taught me the importance of persuasion,
persistence, and professionalism

CAROL

To my father and mother, Fred and Jean
Horton, and sister Diane,
who taught me that everyone deserves a dream

To my precious daughters, Hannah and Jessica,
who taught me that miracles happen every day

To my patient and loving husband, Doy,
who taught me to "Celebrate Life"

And to God,
who taught me to believe in order to see

Thanksgiving and Praise

Contents

Appendices

Acknowledgments

We wish to thank the following grant makers, nonprofit organizations, educators, and consultants for the time, resources, and valuable insights they provided us during the writing of this book:

Dr. James Aven, founder/director, National Diffusion Network

Joe Becerra, Rich Foley, and Ruth Goldhammer, San Mateo County Office of Education

Robert Beuthel, superintendent, Burlingame School District

John and Ruthmary Cradler, Educational Support Systems

Lynn Dennis, Literacy Project, Couer d'Alene School District

Richard Drew, head master, Eric Temple, director of studies, and John Draper, educational outreach, Crystal Springs Uplands School

The Foundation Center, New York City

Andrea Hamilton, Development Office, Sacred Heart Academy

Fred Heron, principal, Roosevelt School, Burlingame School District

Diana Hernandez, director, ESL/Project MORE, Los Angeles Unified School District

Sam Intrator, Stanford University School of Education

Carol Maero-Fetzer, director, Education Programs, Walt Disney World Company

Ann McCrow, director, Schools Plus Foundation

Georgia W. McDaniel, Peninsula Nonprofit Center

Peter and Aneta Murphy, directors, National League of High Schools and California League of Middle Schools

Kevin Nelson, Jerry Arrigoni, Jim Ryan, Burlingame High School

Mary Ann Overton, director, Middle Schools Partnership, Carnegie Project

Portia Wakuzawa, Honolulu District Office

Sandra Rawls, Washington State University

Bill Sommerville, director, Philanthropic Ventures Foundation

Claire Schooley, director, Alameda County Office of Education Grants Resource Center

Ron Temple, director, Specialized Secondary Schools, California Department of Education

Kate Warziniack, North West Regional Labs

Westinghouse Corporation—SAT on CD

Amherst H. Wilder Foundation

In addition to these colleagues, foundations, and organizations, we wish to thank the following people at Heinemann for their constant and generous support throughout the creation of this book and the CD-ROM: Abby Heim, Dan Breslin, Maura Sullivan, Bill Varner, Leigh Peake, Lisa Luedeke, and Mike Gibbons. We are especially grateful to our editor, Lois Bridges, for her remarkable support, insightful advice, and friendship.

Thanks also to Janice Wolfe for her thoughtful illustrations and amazing graphic layouts, and to Darren Patterson for his assistance in developing the Web site.

Finally, we wish to thank our families for their patience and encouragement throughout the writing of this book, which celebrates all that each of our families contributed to this project.

Jim Burke
Carol Ann Prater

Introduction

Look with favor on a bold beginning.
—Virgil

Mighty things from small beginnings grow.
—John Dryden

Why Seek Grant Support?

People don't seek grants to get money. They seek to improve lives, neighborhoods, communities, and ultimately society in general. They accomplish these changes by writing proposals to an ever expanding network of philanthropic organizations and people committed to helping others. This is, after all, the meaning of the word *philanthropy* (*phil* = love + *anthropo* = man), a word that translates into billions of dollars invested in nonprofit organizations, schools, public agencies, and individual talent annually. This book is designed to walk you through this process so that you, too, can get the resources you need to meet your goals, expand your program, train your staff, or create your project. In the end, this book is not about money; it is about the people you work with, the products you are trying to develop, the communities you endeavor to improve.

Who Seeks Grant Support?

Those most commonly eligible to seek grant support include:

- nonprofit agencies
- schools
- public agencies
- churches
- individuals (e.g., scientists, artists, writers)

More and more, people find themselves, regardless of their profession, forced to compete for funding. Teachers, despite growing investment in education from all sectors, are asked to compete for state or federal funding to create literacy programs or get the training they need to integrate technology into their classrooms. Instead of conducting their research, graduate students spend their precious time writing National Science Foundation grant applications. In San Francisco, a coalition of children wrote—and drew, and painted, and sang!—a proposal that earned them $1.1 million dollars to create what we all agree should already exist: a safe neighborhood park where kids can get outside and play. This particular grant embodies much of what we hope will grow out of your own efforts to write proposals. Young people felt empowered by the possibility that they could change their world. The neighborhood was forced—by these persistent little kids!—to ask itself some hard questions about the life it offered its children. Through such questions people began to wake up to their larger responsibilities to themselves and those around them.

Not everyone wants to build a park or create a new education program, however. Some people, teachers for example, need help writing grant proposals that will enable them to study via a sabbatical or summer institute available through the National Endowment for the Humanities or the Fulbright Scholar Program. This book will help you win those opportunities, providing specific examples and useful tips to give your proposal the winning edge it needs in the increasingly competitive realm of grant seeking.

Gandhi once said, "We must be the change we wish to see in the world." This book strives to help you answer and stay focused on a set of essential questions that will, we hope, result in such change:

1. Who will your proposal target? (*Introduce yourself*)

2. What are their needs/concerns? (*Define focus areas*)

3. What do you want to accomplish? (*Develop goals and objectives*)

4. Why do you want to accomplish this? (*Establish benefits*)

5. How will you accomplish it? (*Describe methods and activities*)

6. What assets and strengths do you bring to this project? (*Establish organizational capability*)

7. What obstacles do you foresee? (*Identify liabilities and weaknesses*)

8. How will you measure your progress? (*Design assessment/evaluation strategies*)

9. What financial resources are available and needed? (*Design budget*)

10. How will this project fit in with what you have done before, are doing now, and plan to do in the future? (*Discuss implementation and dissemination*)

11. Why should a funder choose you? (*Describe systematic efforts and resources*)

This book is designed to help you answer these questions in a number of different ways. It offers examples from winning proposals and specific analysis of why they were successful. This insight into the process and, specifically, the mind of the evaluator comes from our experience of reading and scoring thousands of proposals and knowing what wins and what does not. Our backgrounds provide a solid foundation for our teaching throughout the book. One or the other of us has extensive experience in technical writing, strategic planning, leadership, organizational skills, presenting, marketing, and facilitating. Our experience writing large federal and foundation proposals combined with our personal experience of pursuing sabbaticals, summer institutes, and scholarships, gives you a complete course in persuasive writing to help you get the resources and opportunities you seek.

This book and its CD are not so much about improving education or a specific program as helping you to develop what Tom Peters calls "Wow Projects," projects that will "add value, projects that matter, projects that make a difference, projects that leave a legacy—and, yes, projects that make you a star" (Peters 1999). We provide you the tools and strategies not only to come up with an idea that wows people, but to translate that idea into documents, designs, and presentations that carry the day and get you the support you need to do the things you want.

These tools come in various forms and media. The book itself offers you everything you need to write a successful proposal. Not only does it take you step-by-step through the process of writing a powerful proposal, it provides you with a series of workshops in those areas—writing, organizing, presenting, being creative—in which you might need a little extra help along the way. On the CD-ROM you will find additional workshops, as well as samples of winning grants to help you promote your projects, and evaluation tools you can print out to help finish your proposal in style. In addition to these resources, the CD-ROM includes a point-by-point evaluation of a winning technology grant that we, the authors (along with a group of amazing teachers from Roosevelt Elementary School), wrote. Finally, the book provides further resources on its accompanying Web site (www.grantwriterstoolkit.com). Among these resources you will find an extensive and current directory of organizations that either offer grants or support.

If you follow the steps laid out in this book, they will lead you to what you seek. Our own efforts have led not only to millions of dollars but, more importantly, improved education for our students, better communities, and richer lives for ourselves through opportunities for study abroad. This book will help you do the same. We wish you luck and will be by your side the rest of the way to help you get the money and other resources you need to do the things you want.

How to Use This Book

For the student there is no better companion than a good oar.
    —*Francis Parkman*

This book is designed to be read several ways. Most importantly, we organized the book to take you through each stage of the writing process for any proposal. One word in the book's subtitle—*guide*—describes the role we hope to play for you during this process. Not everyone, however, will want or need to go from A to Z. Whether you are writing a simple letter proposal or are responsible for only a portion of a larger proposal being written by a team, you should be able to navigate your way to the information you need by several different routes.

- *Table of Contents*: The table of contents is designed to serve as a checklist and quick reference sheet for the entire proposal-writing process. We suggest you make a copy of it and use it as a map to guide you through the process.

- *Sidebars*: There are a variety of types of sidebars, all designed to offer tips, additional information, or directions to other resources within the book or on the CD that will help you with specific steps. Sidebars appear with the portion of the text they complement. Look for the icons to signal if a particular sidebar offers expert advice or links to other parts of the book or the CD-ROM.

- *Words to Know:* Each chapter begins with a list of terms readers should know if they are to read the chapter knowledgeably. The definitions of these words are in the glossary, which is located in the appendix.

- *Examples:* Examples are set off from the text to help you identify them quickly. They can also be found by referring to the table of contents and appendices.

- *CD Connections:* Throughout the book you will encounter the CD Connection feature, which directs you to specific resources on the CD-ROM. In addition to the assessment tool and resource directory, the CD includes three complete grant applications; you might want to consult these examples in addition to those in the book to provide more continuity as you learn about the different stages of developing and implementing a proposal.

- *Workshops:* The workshop chapters offer readers and team members a variety of help in areas crucial to your proposal's success. These areas—which include presenting, writing, creating, and organizing—often pose particular challenges to people. You might not need to read them at all, if you are experienced in the proposal-writing process; however, most readers will find these workshops, if nothing else, a useful reference point as they move through the different stages. These workshops represent a summary of the best writing and thinking in each of these areas, all presented to you in helpful checklists. We offer suggestions of when to consult these workshops at different points along the way. They are there, in short, to help you give your proposed ideas, presentation, or writing the extra edge.

- *Appendices:* You can quickly refer to the glossary in the appendix to define most words you encounter but do not fully understand. Aside from this one interactive element of the appendix, you should not need to refer to it while reading.

We assume that you are working under pressure and need to find information fast. This book—from its table of contents to its index, its headers and subheaders—was designed to meet your needs as a reader and grant seeker. We have also worked hard to make the structure and look of the book reflect the design concepts that should be incorporated into your proposal to make it easy to read and as compelling as possible.

*Academic
enrichment
and tutorials*

1

Conduct a
Strategic
Assessment

*If you always do what you've done, you'll always
get what you've always got.*

—*Anonymous*

**WORDS
TO KNOW**

assessment

evaluation

mission

stakeholders

vision

As individuals or institutions, we should constantly reflect on and assess our performance to determine our progress toward our goals. Such habits of thought, such ongoing feedback, consistently distinguish those people and institutions in the education and business worlds. "Visionary companies do not ask, 'What should we value?' They ask, 'What do we *actually* value deep down in our toes?'" (Collins and Porras 1994, 8). In a world of constant change, the most effective companies, those "built to last," respond to change by asking not "How should we change?" but rather "What do we stand for and why do we exist?" (ibid., xiv). This last question clarifies the entire process: just as your school exists, for example, to prepare students to succeed in and contribute to the adult world, the agency to which you are applying for support exists to sponsor growth and innovation in a particular area (e.g., Apple Computer preparing students to use a variety of technological tools). In short, what you propose must always be consistent with your stated mission and that of the agency to which you apply for assistance.

Ask the Essential Questions

Review the list of questions in the Introduction (pages xvi–xvii). These will help you complete your strategic assessment.

Use Data to Support Your Assessment

Swimmers and runners love data: they are constantly checking the stopwatch to find out how well they performed and consulting with their coaches to determine how they can improve their performance the next time around. As individuals and organizations, we can gather a range of data to help us better understand and communicate to others what we need to more effectively do our work. Data comes in two forms—quantitative (numbers) and anecdotal (stories)—both of which have their place. Most individuals and programs, depending on their needs, should consider the following information to help them evaluate their current performance:

- enrollment in specific programs
- frequency of participation
- number of units (e.g., classes, computers, instruments) you currently possess
- current level of performance as measured by a reliable instrument/ process

- alternative means of assessing performance (e.g., portfolios, projects, products)
- surveys, questionnaires, or interviews

Anecdotal data can yield profound insights into the vision and needs of people or programs. One school, as part of its accreditation process, amassed abundant data about how successful its students were as measured by college entrance rates, SAT scores, and AP pass rates. However, when it began interviewing students, another picture quickly surfaced: many students complained of feeling dehumanized by the school, saying, "They only care about us because our scores make the property values go up."

Institutional introspection helped the school to identify needs it did not know it had. In the wake of such revelations, it surveyed students to find out what they wanted. Involving primary stakeholders in the development of a vision or the evaluation of needs provides a powerful starting point for any proposal process, as it shows the potential funding agencies that there is genuine support for the proposed changes.

See Chapter 23 (Workshop 7), "Managing the Change Process: Planning, Implementing, Sustaining" for more practical advice in this area.

LEARNING LINKS

Needs—as opposed to ideas and solutions, which we will consider further on in this section—come in a variety of sizes and shapes. When evaluating where you are versus where you want to be, it is crucial to know "which ball to keep your eye on." Here is a helpful list that you can use to determine those areas you need to improve or change:

- structural
- cultural
- social
- facilities
- products
- programs and services
- material
- technological
- emotional/personal
- intellectual
- curricular

Sample Strategic Assessment: Drug and Safety Grant

TO: ABC Middle Schools
FROM: Carol Prater
SUBJECT: Safe and Drug-Free School Program OMB# 1234-XYZ

A Brief Introduction: The Safe and Drug-Free Schools and Communities Act (SDFSCA) oversees the federal government's largest single source of funding for drug and violence programs in our nation's schools. The SDFSCA offers grant programs which develop innovative programs that provide models of proven effective practices that will assist schools and communities around the nation to improve their programs in drug prevention and school safety.

Our district is in the process of identifying four to seven middle schools to participate in an SDFSCA grant application, the focus of which is to generate funds for a three-year period to employ one to two full-time drug and safety coordinator(s). The coordinators will help funded schools select prevention programs of demonstrated effectiveness. Nineteen model programs are suggested for review in the application guidelines. Coordinator(s) will devote a significant amount of time assessing site needs, identify research-based drug and violence prevention strategies, and assist middle schools in adopting the "best practices" for their site. Program coordinators will train teachers, staff, and relevant partners as needed.

If you are interested in being considered for one of these spots, please complete the following questionnaire in as much detail as possible and return to our office by Friday, May 20th.

On a separate, attached sheet(s) of paper please respond to the following questions. If at all possible, use a word processor and submit both the hard and disk copy to expedite our writing process. We would prefer that you use a Macintosh computer and ClarisWorks or Microsoft Word.

Include: school name, school address, phone and fax numbers, e-mail address, contact persons, and if possible any drug/safety plans or grants your school has developed. We also need school size and demographic and socioeconomic information.

1. Describe the drug, violence, and/or safety problems in your middle school.

2. Explain how a coordinator will make a difference in the drug prevention and safety problems at your school.

3. What specific gaps or weaknesses in services, infrastructure, or opportunities have been identified at your middle school site that should be addressed in this project?

4. Provide data on the number of students in grades 6–9 who were suspended, expelled, or transferred to alternative settings during the past twelve months. Mark N/A for not applicable.

Grade	Expelled	Suspended	Transferred
6			
7			
8			
9			

5. Complete this discrepancy model with a description of your present condition and your dream plan (vision) for your community.

What IS	What SHOULD BE	Proposed Solution

6. What funding sources are used to implement your present drug/safety efforts?

7. What budget items besides the coordinator are necessary to implement your future drug and safety program efforts?

8. What evaluation strategies are in place and what needs data is available to justify your assessment of your present drug and safety program and your future needs?

9. Describe your student population, their needs and their strengths.

Please Note: Our timeline is very tight and the information submitted will be the only basis for our selection. Please make every effort to provide as detailed a description of your school and community as possible so that we can create a competitive application. Thank you.

Clarify Your Thinking

The following questions are designed to help you refine your plan and vision. Not all questions help you identify actual needs; some, instead, help you consider important related concerns.

- Who else believes that this need is crucial and should be addressed now?

- Who needs it: you, your organization, the community, the administration, parents? (All of these?)

- What evidence can you provide to support the urgency or credibility of this need?

- Why is your request reasonable and appropriate?

- How can this problem be fixed?

- Who is the appropriate person or agency to approach for help in this particular area?

- Is this need ongoing or situational?

- What will help you best address this need (e.g., material goods, expertise, professional development)?

- What is the underlying cause of this problem?
- Of the different factors responsible for this problem, which are you able to actually control?
- Is there a way for you to involve (e.g., through focus groups) the "problem" (e.g., troubled adolescents) in the solution?

Define Your Vision, Mission, and Values

Through these questions and others posed in this chapter there runs a theme that is very important for you to address in your grant proposal; it has to do with your purpose, your values as an individual and an organization. The words used most commonly to describe this subject are vision, mission, and values. While they share many elements, they are different in the following ways:

- *Vision*: Your vision answers the question "What are you committed to?" Whether it is the safety of the neighborhood or the preparation of children for the demands of the future, you must have a clear answer to this question, one that you emphasize throughout the proposal.
- *Mission*: Your mission answers the question "What is your business?" There is a large difference between being in the business of "teaching math" and preparing children to meet the demands of the future.
- *Values*: What you value comes from answering the question "What do you believe in?" Do you believe that *all* kids can learn? Do you believe that the environment and all its creatures are crucial to our survival? The proposal must reflect and be an expression of these values.

Accentuate the Positive

It is easy, when writing a proposal, to emphasize the needs, the problems, the challenges that you or your constituents face. It is crucial to your proposal's success, however, that you do not whine or complain, that you avoid the negative and speak, instead, in terms of "opportunities," and "expanding access" or past and future success. You don't want to say that your students need to "learn how to read," since this would imply that you had not been able to teach them; such a message would destroy your credibility and sink your proposal. You want to make bold, affirmative statements which imply that you are doing something and want only to do more or do it better: For example, you might say that your plan will:

- develop our students' research skills by expanding access
- expand access to the latest technologies
- expand parent involvement in their child's education, taking advantage of last year's progress through the English Learners

Community Picnic, which recently won a Brent Award for educational innovation

- increase academic accountability by providing after-hours enrichment and proficiency courses that target all interests and levels of need

- provide intensive remediation for those incoming struggling readers in an effort to help them succeed in their mainstream classes

One can easily get lost in the labyrinth of needs and begin confusing them with solutions. Students don't "need" books; rather they need to be able to read successfully. Nor do students "need" technology; they do, however, need to have the skills and knowledge necessary to compete and succeed in the world for which schools are preparing them.

CHECKPOINT

Answer these questions before moving on.

- Is your vision clearly articulated and compelling?

- Is your vision reasonable in light of other constraints?

- Is the stated need clearly aligned with the goals, programs, and services of your organization and the agency to which you are applying?

- Does your proposal speak in terms of what your clients need? (e.g., students need to know how to use computers)

- Are you thinking systemically—i.e., are your ideas sustainable, integrated, flexible?

- Are your proposed objectives/outcomes measurable and consistent with your needs/goals?

- If we asked your colleagues, the community, or your clients if this need was a priority, what would they say?

See Chapter 22 (Workshop 6), "Making Room for Creativity" and Chapter 23 (Workshop 7), "Managing the Change Process: Planning, Implementing, Sustaining," for more guidance during this stage of the process.

LEARNING LINKS

2

Explore the Philanthropic Network

We must dare to think "unthinkable" thoughts. We must learn to explore all the options and possibilities that confront us in a complex and rapidly changing world.
—James William Fulbright

Consider the following facts, all of which come from the Foundation Center's 1999 report on philanthropy in the United States:

- Funding for education remains the top priority for America's top one thousand foundations.
- During 1997, $19.5 billion dollars were donated, 25 percent of which went to education.
- Philanthropic donations to education consistently increase every year.
- Recent efforts to fund educational programs have focused on teacher-quality programs and partnerships between schools and organizations. (*Education Week* 1999)

What Should I Ask For?

Grants exist to help people much like yourself to accomplish their goals and, through such investment, to help companies and foundations achieve *their* goals. As previously mentioned, the word *philanthropy* reflects the ideals behind investing in people, communities, and ideas: *philo* = love + *anthropo* = man. Of course, people tend to direct their love of mankind in specific directions, most often toward those ideas or issues most important to themselves or their organization's interests: reading, technology, scientific research, the arts, community programs, or a community facility that will benefit everyone.

Two obvious questions arise, questions so important that we will return to them throughout this book: What does a particular agency want to invest in? What are the values or goals that guide its investment strategy? You must do all you can to find out these answers; without such vital information it will be nearly impossible to write effectively since, in essence, you will not know what the funding agency wants to hear.

Aside from these two crucial questions, several others arise:

- Are you eligible?
- What are the stated goals of the funding agency?
- Are the funder's goals consistent with your institution's vision and needs?
- What types of proposals have been successful (i.e., grants awarded) in the past?
- What is the likelihood that the grantor will fund your idea?

Types of Grants, Awards, and Opportunities

What you write for will be defined by what you request (time, materials, capital, opportunity) and what the grantor has to offer (money, expertise, a fellowship, materials). The following list gives you some sense of the types of opportunities available to you; keep the previously mentioned

---

WORDS TO KNOW

alliance

bidders' conference

in-kind support

Request for Application (RFA)

Request for Proposal (RFP)

questions in mind when considering which is right for you. We have included samples to illustrate each example, taking them from actual proposals we have written or with which we are familiar.

Funding Levels
- *Full funding*: You request money to cover all costs for your proposed districtwide program to help meet the needs of struggling readers.

- *Matching funds*: You invite potential funders to match (e.g., dollar for dollar) all investments in your Reading Buddies program, which seeks to buy a new book for every student in the school to take home and keep as their own.

- *Partial funding*: You ask a service club to support the installation of a sprinkler system for the youth center's garden. All the plants and labor will be donated by the kids, their families, community volunteers, and local businesses.

Types of Grants
- *Planning grant*: You apply to the state for funding to purchase release time for one or more staff members so that they can devote their full attention to creating and preparing to teach a new program the following fall.

- *Start-up (aka "seed") funding*: You approach a local foundation for money to start a Service Learning program at your school, requesting money to pay the part-time salary of the coordinator for a three-year period after which (you propose) long-term funding will be sought through the school district as part of a School-to-Work program whose funding will be increased to meet such needs.

- *Fellowship*: You write to the professor who is running a National Endowment for the Humanities summer institute, explaining what you have to offer, why you want to participate in this particular institute, and how the experience will benefit your teaching of American poetry the following year.

- *Sabbatical*: You apply to your district office for a paid semester leave to spend a semester studying reading difficulties, promising to offer a series of workshops and publish a newsletter to teachers throughout the district during that semester.

- *Mentorship*: You propose to mentor the six new teachers at your school or train staff in the strategies of computer-assisted learning.

- *Professional development*: Your math department, in order to align itself with the new state standards, asks for paid release time to meet outside of school during the school year and throughout the summer.

- *Accreditation*: You are asking not for money but for recognition. You propose that yours is an excellent school as measured by a particular accreditation agency's criteria.

- *Award*: Your school considers itself worthy of and ready to apply for a National Blue Ribbon Award for school excellence. Though you are not requesting money, the process described here is much the same.

- *Continuation*: You request funding to sustain your award-winning Service Learning program, which was initially funded by a grant from a foundation. The program should be continued by the district or organization so as to represent local, sustainable commitment to maintaining the program.

- *Facilities*: Your school solicits help from the surrounding community to help renovate the school's football stadium track, describing it as a multiuse facility designed to meet the needs of both the school and the community.

- *Staffing*: Your agency applies for federal grants to pay the salary of a School-to-Work coordinator so that you can meet the needs of those non-college-bound students at the neighborhood school who need more career guidance. (Such collaborative grants are very attractive to funders.)

- *Restructuring*: Your junior college applies to the state for a newly available grant that will create integrated curricular paths into its program to better prepare students for the demands of the workplace.

- *Technology*: A coalition of schools, senior citizen centers, and regional environmental agencies apply for an Apple Technology Grant in which they propose to create a virtual community called "Our Town" where they can create and foster on-line mentorships between elementary school students and senior citizens to help students learn about the environment.

Whom Should I Ask?

Government

The United States government offers billions of dollars each year for research and development, facilities improvement, and a broad range of educational and social reforms. Competition for these grants is often intense, since they are usually multiple-year grants for large sums of money. The 21st Century Technology Challenge Grants for 1998, for example, offered as much as $2 million annually for a period of five years. Over four hundred proposals were submitted from all fifty states, twenty of which were ultimately funded. Because government grants are often linked to legislation or political issues, it is essential that applicants study the context in which the specific grant is offered (i.e., what values and assumptions does the funding agency reflect through the legislation or the guidelines?). In 1999, for example, many grants were available through both federal and state departments of education to improve reading. By looking at the legislation you can get a better idea of what it is they want to achieve through this grant or, to put it another way, *how* they want to achieve it. Competition for state grants tends to be more severe than federal grants because people are more familiar with their local agency and can often solicit help from local school or government offices. The state capitol's proximity also makes attending bidders' conferences (i.e., training sessions sponsored by the government agency) easier. When applying for government grants, find out the answer to the following questions:

- Who is eligible to apply for this grant?
- When and where is the bidders' conference?
- Is there an electronic bulletin board, Web site, or other support system in place?
- Is this grant linked to any particular government initiatives (e.g., Goals 2000, America Reads, School-to-Work) and are there related support documents to help (e.g., official reports that inspired the legislation)?
- What support, if any, can my legislators offer?
- Who will read and score these applications (teachers, administrators, legislatively convened committees)?

CD   H O T

TOOL   TIPS

Learn more about what the government and foundations are offering by visiting their Web sites, which are listed on the CD-ROM. These sites usually offer a range of opportunities and helpful information to guide you through the process.

Nonprofit Foundations—501(c)3

Private foundations invest billions of dollars each year to help schools, communities, and nonprofit organizations achieve their goals. It is important to realize that foundations exist to support specific ideals that inspired the creation of the foundation. The Lila Wallace–Reader's Digest Fund, for example, understandably exists to support the teaching of reading. The Getty Foundation for the Arts was created, obviously, to support and expand the role of the arts in society and education. Foundations often provide applicants with abundant resources through actual and virtual libraries. In addition, most foundations offer workshops to help applicants better understand what they expect in a successful grant proposal. When applying for foundation grants, find out the answer to the following questions:

- What is the stated mission of the foundation and how does this particular grant relate to that?
- Does the foundation provide workshops to help applicants assess their needs, develop their plans, or write their proposals?
- Does the foundation publish a newsletter or annual report to help me understand its values and mission?
- Does the foundation have a Web site, bulletin board, or listserv that might help me gather valuable information throughout the application process?
- Does the foundation employ a program officer or resource librarian who can help me during the application process?
- Are examples of past grant applications that were funded as well as those that were rejected made available?
- Who will read and score the applications?

The Foundation Center (www.fdncenter.org) offers the most extensive resources about nonprofit foundations that offer money specific to their interests (e.g., literacy). It is the best place to begin your search. It also offers abundant support resources to help you give your application the edge it needs to win. For further information, see Appendix F and the resource directory on the CD-ROM.

Corporations

Corporations offer not only money but partnerships, material resources, expertise, and adult mentors to local schools and nonprofit organizations. Corporations see such investment as vital to their future success, since a hardworking, educated, ethical community means hardworking, educated, ethical employees. Such investments also provide high-profile exposure for the company when, for example, the press comes to cover the ribbon-cutting ceremony at the youth center or school with the corporation's CEO, mayor, and students sitting down to work in their new computer lab. While there are many multinational corporations that offer money and other resources, it is your regional or local corporations that are easier to target. They are looking to establish their name and a relationship within their community. Ben and Jerry's, for example, commits substantial resources to support local initiatives, especially in such areas as reading. Corporations differ from foundations and government agencies in that they are commercial enterprises; their philanthropy is often driven by their desire for public recognition. Tapping corporate or commercial interests has become increasingly common, even as it has grown more controversial in some communities. Stakeholders might want a new scoreboard at the high school, but not everyone thinks schools or recreation facilities should be used as advertisements for products. When applying for corporate grants, find out the answer to the following questions:

- Does the corporation have a local or regional site in our area?
- Does it issue an annual report or other documents that detail its affiliations, mission statement, past philanthropic investments, and core values?
- Do we need money or personnel? Might a couple of experts be better used than funding to support our school goal of improving students' research skills using the Internet?
- Will the corporation require us, if we are selected, to display any logos or other commercial signs in our school?
- Will the school or community permit a commercial presence in the facility or on organization's items (e.g., student planners, dedication plaques)?
- What can we offer the funders by way of publicity to show our appreciation of their investment in our program?
- Who will be reading and scoring this application?

H O T

T I P S

Your chances of receiving corporate funding are dramatically increased if the company has a store or division in your area. Remember: Corporations see investments in the community as an investment in their own future employees.

Local Organizations and Individuals

Local groups such as the Rotary Club International and individuals provide substantial support for local projects and programs—more, in fact, than any other source. Such organizations and individuals are motivated to help improve their own communities, and they do so through service, materials, and financial investment. Through fund-raisers, auctions, dues, and solicitations, these groups and individuals accumulate funds that are often targeted for specific local needs (e.g., playground improvement, scholarships, library books, or the medical needs of people in need). When applying to organizations or individuals for grants, find out the answer to the following questions:

- What is their stated mission (e.g., to "serve the community")?
- Do they offer support or examples of past projects that they have funded?
- What would they be willing to invest in?
- How can we best create and nurture our relationship with the funder so that we might approach them about future projects?
- If we are running a large campaign—e.g., we need $300,000 for a new multipurpose track facility—how can we inform the community of our progress toward that goal?
- Who will read and score this application?
- How is our proposed project connected to other work that the organization is currently supporting?
- Which of the different funding agencies would be most appropriate to approach?
- How can we recognize and thank them for their contribution to our program?

If you need more guidance on how to explore the philanthropic network, consult the helpful guide in the appendix or the resource directory on the CD-ROM; otherwise, use the checkpoint questions at the end of each chapter to check your work before moving to the next chapter.

How Much Should I Ask For?

Grants come in different amounts. You should rarely ask for the maximum, but always request at least the minimum if the guidelines identify one. Small grants (e.g., under $1,000) tend to come from local agencies or individuals committed to improving their own community. Small grants often go to sponsor a single event, such as "Renaissance Day" or "Art in the Park," or a historical reenactment. If you are arranging a field trip, you might ask for transportation help in lieu of money from a provider. Dryers Ice Cream Company, for example, "grants" a bus and driver to nonprofit organizations and schools to help them get where they need to go.

The tendency, of course, is to ask for the maximum amount offered. However, this approach does not always pay off. If the funding agency limits the grant to $12,000, many applicants will ask for

$11,999, a figure that distracts the reader from your idea and implies that your emphasis is on the money. Better to learn from the Gold Feather Union School District, where teachers and community members applied for a grant from Bank of America. This small community proposed that a portion of the town's general store be set aside to create a library. Its humble request for $750 to buy lumber and brackets earned it $10,000 and a note to "buy some books, too!" to supplement the used copies community members offered to donate.

CHECKPOINT
Answer these questions before moving on.

- Why write a grant proposal at this time?
- Why does this funding agency seem like the best one for us to apply to?
- Am I eligible to apply to this agency?
- How are both the funder and our organization likely to benefit from this grant?
- Are we competitive in light of the others who are likely to apply to this agency for this grant?
- Would creating or establishing a systematic alliance improve our chances of getting funded?
- Is it possible to talk with someone at the agency before proceeding to be sure we are a good match for each other?

Community service and outreach

3

Seek Support for Your Proposal

There is but one unconditional commandment, which is that we should seek incessantly . . . to bring about the very largest total universe of good which we can see.

—William James

Throughout the proposal process you need lots of support—and for many different reasons. You need technical support from writers, technology specialists, and strategic planners to get you across the finish line. You need political and personal support both at home and at work, especially when the process winds down and your own energy is on the wane. You need the support of your colleagues and the community at large if your proposal is to generate the momentum and credibility it needs to succeed. Thus you must seek support from those who would be affected by the proposed program or changes, and you must solicit the expertise of those who will actually help you prepare the grant proposal. These different constituents fall into roughly four distinct groups:

1. clients (those who are served)
2. stakeholders/community (those who benefit)
3. alliance/partners (those who support)
4. family/friends (those who inspire and intervene)

Who You Need: Spheres of Influence

If you are applying for a large grant, say $1 million, the funding agency wants to see a coalition, evidence of a network of alliances and partnerships—in short, a team that works systemically. They want to know you have identified and achieved the endorsement if not the help of the different stakeholders. This trend toward collaboration, which some grant makers have also called your "horizontal and vertical slice," requires that you create a more systemic approach to solving the problem by involving all who might play a part in developing and implementing the solution. A proposal to address early literacy might then include a network made up of community volunteers, a community college, local libraries, elementary school students and their parents, high school students (through a Service Learning program), and local area booksellers.

These days your network is considered a necessary means of achieving your goals since it establishes your organizational capacity. Most networks break down into several groups, each of which contributes different capacities and resources than the others:

• *Institutional/organizational alliances*: These include but are not limited to museums, government agencies, local organizations, schools, clubs, corporations, and foundations, all of which have an obvious interest in the success of your grant proposal because it benefits them too.

• *Colleagues and similar agencies*: These include but are not limited to those agencies in your own domain—e.g., other schools in your district—and in your field which stand to benefit from and thus have a sincere interest in your success.

• *Community partnership*: Included here are those local stakeholders who are in a position to both help and hinder the efforts depending on whether they support the proposal. The best example of this group would be students' parents. Their interests are personal, whereas an institution's might be commercial or political.

• *Individual people network*: This group consists of colleagues, mentors, staff, and clients, i.e., those who might potentially implement the proposed changes or be directly affected by the proposal activities. In a school, these would be administrators and teachers, as well as students.

Sample Network:
Community Development/Technology Grant
Desert Without Borders Partnerships

The Desert Without Borders project will benefit greatly from the diverse group of partners who bring a wealth of resources to the consortium. The following partnerships were formed and will contribute to the success of this project. A priority of Desert Without Borders will be to promote the project and build additional partnerships that will serve to strengthen Desert Without Borders and assure that the project will be sustainable beyond the period of the grant:

• *The Imperial County Office of Education, along with the following twelve public school districts that each serve a substantial number of underserved and at-risk students*: Brawley Elementary, Brawley Union High, Calexico Unified, Calipatria Unified, Central Union High School, El Centro, Holtville Unified, McCabe, Meadows Union, Mulberry, Seeley Union, and Westmorland Union will provide equipment to establish local area networks (LANs), staff, and support to establish connectivity and participate in curriculum content and staff development activities.

• *California Technology Assistance Project (CTAP)* will provide staff, professional development resources, and training through the use of the Technology Learning Center and related projects and activities. The two computer training centers and professional training staff will be made available to the project to conduct Technology Academies for consortium partners. A cadre of trainers will be trained and supported to implement project activities, build capacity through a trainee-trainer model, and assist with the identification of professional development needs. CTAP will also contribute a Mobile Investigation Lab to the Desert Without Borders project. The mobile lab is a thirty-foot motor home that has been modified and fitted with twelve computer stations. The lab will be designated entirely (100 percent) to the Desert Without Borders project.

• *Bureau of Land Management (BLM)* will provide staff and resources to assist with environmental-education curriculum development involving conservation and management of natural resources. BLM staff will be available to assist with the implementation of the Mobile Investigation Lab through expertise and resources related to the desert ecosystem and environmental education. BLM staff will also assist with the activities of the interactive Web site.

• *Century Communications* will provide broadband cable access over our local cable television infrastructure to allow professional development and project curriculum to be broadcast to schools, businesses, and homes in Imperial County. Equipment and staff will be made available to provide a reliable channel for distance learning.

• *Imperial National Wildlife Refuge* will provide staff and resources to assist with environmental-education curriculum development involving conservation and management of natural resources. Refuge staff will be available to assist with the implementation of the Mobile Investigation Lab through expertise and resources related to the desert ecosystem and environmental education, and will provide assistance with outreach of project activities via the interactive Web site.

• *Private Industry Council of Imperial County* will serve as liaison between the Desert Without Borders project and the business community of Imperial County. This resource partner will assist with dissemination of information and project activities to the community.

• *Imperial County Historical Society*, through the Pioneers Museum and Historical Center, will provide staff and resources to facilitate access to their archives and exhibits. Their mission includes the charge to advance the knowledge of local history and to facilitate educational and cultural development in the community. The society will assist in the development of project activities and curricula, and will support the activities of the interactive Web site.

• *El Centro Public Library* will provide equipment, staff, and resources to make their library resources available to the project. Staff will also assist with resources and facilitation of the interactive Web site.

• *California Department of Parks and Recreation—Salton Sea Sector* will provide outdoor education, interpretation, and presentation of riparian studies. Park rangers will assist with the implementation of the Mobile Investigation Lab by hosting visits and working with students and teachers in environmental education. Staff and resources will be made available to assist with curriculum development and activities via the interactive Web site.

• *Digital Networks Corporation* will provide consulting services, CAD design services, technology seminars, and session workshops in the areas of wide area network implementation and support; voice, data, and video cabling design, engineering and implementation services; and multimedia delivery systems for education including curriculum lesson-plan development and training.

• *Cisco Systems, Inc.* will provide comprehensive training and network/technical support through its twenty-three local system engineers.

What You Need: Talents and Tasks

From the moment you begin the process of assessing your existing conditions and determining your needs, you need help. The Desert Without Borders proposal above exemplifies this: you just cannot go it alone if your proposal is to succeed. You do not request the same things from everyone, nor do you require assistance every step of the way. Certain alliances or partners might play a crucial role prior to the writing of a proposal by sharing their concerns and ideas with you. Others might have specific skills such as group facilitation or technological expertise which are needed only under certain circumstances; all such expertise eventually gets listed as in-kind contributions to help realize your organization's project.

See Chapter 20 (Workshop 4), "Running Effective Meetings," Chapter 21 (Workshop 5), "Giving Dynamic Presentations," and Chapter 23 (Workshop 7), "Managing the Change Process: Planning, Implementing, Sustaining," for help with the various tasks described in this chapter.

LEARNING **LINKS**

The following list captures the most common problems that must be addressed for any large proposal; smaller, individual proposals, of course, need less of a network, though the projects can also benefit from various types of support. All are clearly present in the example above. John Kotter, in his book *Leading Change* (1996), identifies the following points as essential to any successful program for change, each of which captures the true notion of in-kind contributions:

• *Expertise*: includes but is not limited to skills in the areas of writing, art, computers, facilitation, organization, presentations, and negotiations.

• *Influence* (what Kotter calls "Position Power"): includes but is not limited to the key players in the relevant domains involved in the process. Their influence can create momentum, shift opinions, and increase support for the project.

• *Leadership*: your organization needs someone or a core of people who can keep the alliance focused, motivated, and confident throughout the process while at the same time gathering support within the institutional and communal domains.

- *Credibility*: to gain support you need credibility in the eyes of those whose support you require; this can be achieved by getting key players on your team and by involving all stakeholders in the development process to achieve confidence in your plan and your ability to make it happen.

- *Permission*: resistance to good ideas often lurks in the most unlikely places and must be heard. If you do not get the permission of key stakeholders at all three levels—institutional, communal, and individual—your proposal will inevitably fail, even if you succeed in getting funded. Grant makers are often concerned about this issue and will spend the time to find out if your idea has the support it needs to succeed.

- *Resources*: these might include but are not limited to time, money, food, meeting space, necessary tools, and books or other support personnel.

H O T

TIPS

Remember that your fundability (in the eyes of the reader) relates to your credibility or organizational capability. No one will fund an applicant who has not clearly established their ability to deliver the promised outcomes. Funders want to invest with confidence; it's your job to inspire such confidence in the mind of your potential funder.

Final Words

Sometimes it's better to start small, with a core group of people who truly have a vision, a "Wow Project" (Peters 1999). If you follow the guidelines outlined in this chapter, making sure you have the backing of the right people—e.g., your clients, your community, your administrators—you can lay the foundation for others to follow. You can't expect everyone to jump on the bandwagon right away; in fact, many have found parents in affluent communities, those most supportive of education, to be the most resistant to proposed reforms. By taking time to educate these crucial partners and involve them in the process of developing and implementing our ideas, we will only ensure greater investment in and the long-term success of projects, products, and programs.

As we mentioned in the previous section, bringing these different people, organizations, and resources together, beginning the conversations that will lead to substantial change and subsequent improvement, is already a huge step forward. Too often we think acquiring fiscal resources is the point; sure it is vital to our mission when we seek to launch new programs or improve old ones. However, the changes that grow out of such collaboration are often the seeds from which more lasting and substantial change grows. Furthermore, such new alliances as arise through your proposal development establish the very credibility you require to apply for future and larger grants, showing as they do a history of collaboration that makes you and your organization seem worthy of investment.

We don't mean to close with a discouraging word, but the truth is that even great proposals sometimes don't win. The stakeholders and students do, however, when their teachers, parents, and community members begin to talk, to dream of how things could be better. The proposal that lost last year might need only a few adjustments and a stamp to win this year. Whatever happens, seeking and establishing the necessary support for your proposal and ideas will always pay off.

H O T

T I P S

Remember to involve many different people in this part of the process; many of the ideas generated at this point can always be used in other aspects of the proposal development process to garner expanded support or to generate additional proposals. Specifically, much of the information gathered in Chapter 1 can be used in marketing brochures, Web sites, and other communications with everyone in your strategic network.

CHECKPOINT
Answer these questions before moving on.

- Have we involved all the obvious and essential stakeholders at some point in the design process?

- Do we have the permission of the key stakeholders to proceed?

- If we have been given conditional approval to proceed, what can we do to enhance our credibility in the eyes of these stakeholders?

- Have we—or are we able to—establish our credibility to achieve our stated goals?

- Are there any resources (human, fiscal, or material) lacking in our network at this time?

- Are there any skills or capabilities we might need but currently lack?

- Do we have all the necessary names and contact information for the different members of the alliance so we are able to reach them at any time?

- What can we do throughout the remainder of the development and writing process to take care of the different professional and personal needs of our team members?

4

Choose Grants
That Match
Your Needs
and Values

We must choose to do the things we think we cannot do. The future belongs to those who believe in the beauty of their dreams.
                                    —*Eleanor Roosevelt*

Last Exit: When Not to Proceed with Your Application

This is the crossroads: now you must choose the grant, follow the road of opportunity that seems best suited to your vision and needs or those of your stakeholders and constituency. Of course, you may not be the one to have chosen a particular grant application; someone, say your director or principal, might have left it in your mailbox with a note attached asking you to "see what you can do with this." This is also the moment at which you must determine, honestly, whether your proposal would be competitive in light of the different demographic or philosophical constraints the grant application guidelines impose. Your time is valuable, too valuable to knowingly squander it; thus, if you know you cannot win the grant someone is telling you to seek, this is the point at which you must make your case against applying.

You might offer any of the following explanations as to why you should not apply for a particular grant, so long as they are true. You don't want someone saying you're just trying to get out of doing the work.

1. *You are not eligible.*

   • You do not fit the demographic, socioeconomic, or geographic criteria.

   • Your project does not match the funder's vision and giving guidelines.

2. *You are not able to submit a viable (i.e., competitive) application.*

   • After reviewing annual reports and talking with the funding agency's representatives, it seems unlikely that you can submit a competitive proposal.

   • After reviewing the guidelines and brainstorming with your stakeholders, your coalition is unwilling to adapt or adopt strategies or reforms that are suggested or even required by the funding agency's guidelines.

3. *You cannot reasonably assemble an effective team to do all that is required in the time that remains.*

   • You cannot garner support from key stakeholders.

   • You do not have a team of developers with the necessary skills to proceed efficiently.

   • You cannot secure approval/signatures from designated or required authorities (e.g., trustees) in time for the deadline.

Select the Right Grant

Once you have determined that you *will* proceed, that the grant proposal you'll assemble can meet the funder's criteria, you have to make some decisions. If, for example, there are several grant application packets that interest you, which one do you choose?

Occasionally it is a good idea to submit your grant proposal simultaneously to multiple agencies. You do this to show that you are exploring many avenues for funding. Check to see if this is acceptable to your most desirable funding agency. It may even suggest additional funders. Make sure a cover letter informs each funding agency about your plan to submit elsewhere. No funder wants to take the time to review a grant proposal only to learn later that it was already funded by someone else. This is an ethical issue. As soon as you receive news from one funder that you will be awarded a grant, you must notify the other possible funders who have received your proposal.

The following suggestions should help you narrow your field of possible choices:

• *Ask the grant maker for guidance.* No one wants to waste their time or someone else's in this process. Grant makers typically appoint a program officer to take calls from potential applicants. The officers know both the agency's vision and guidelines, so they can help you determine whether you should apply for a particular grant. They might, for example, suggest you pursue a planning grant from a different agency, but stay in touch. Remember: relationships are the key to lasting success in the grant-seeking world.

When contacting a potential funder, keep the following in mind: phone calls or, better yet, personal visits are the most effective; each time you speak or meet with representatives of the funding agency they are measuring your capability and forming an overall impression of you. Be professional. Reread the application packet carefully prior to calling or visiting the funder. Have your questions written down ahead of time. Ask for the program officer assigned to the particular grant. Ask if there are any workshops or other support materials forthcoming or suggested.

• *Consider your needs.* Return to your work from Chapter 1, during which time your strategic assessment confirmed your vision, identified your performance gaps, and established your needs or those of your stakeholders. Which of the grants best aligns with your mission, vision, and values? Are you sure you have the resources to compete for the $200,000 federal reform grant? Perhaps the best choice is a smaller planning grant offered by your state or a local corporation. This would, for example, prepare you to apply and thus be more competitive for a larger grant next year, by which time your planning work would also have enhanced your organizational capacity.

• *Identify the best match.* Consider the funder's mission and yours; compare the funder's values with yours. Even though you might be eligible to apply for a certain grant, the subsequent constraints might be too restrictive. Furthermore, the constituents and community might not support the required reforms or adoptions, in which case your otherwise wonderful proposal would be undermined. One high school we worked with was rejected for a large restructuring grant; when asked why this happened, they were told that their proclamation of being a "traditional" high school seemed inconsistent with the ideals of reform and change outlined in the application guidelines. When the school changed its mission statement to read "a tradition of innovation and excellence," it positioned itself to win the funding that valued reform. Funders finally believed the school had the resources to implement the necessary changes.

Once you have selected the best grant for your vision and needs, it's still not time to start writing the narrative. Before moving on you should stop and evaluate what and who you will need to help you complete this specific application. Chapter 3 helped you to identify those who would support your ideas and solutions; now that you have chosen, it is time to establish the proposal development team and involve them in the proposal construction process by matching them to appropriate tasks.

H O T

T I P S

This is a good time for you to read some of the workshop chapters to help you set up and manage the process that is about to begin.

CHECKPOINT
Answer these questions before moving on.

Have you:

• identified the agencies that will be involved in the actual project proposed (and designated who will secure their letters of support)?

• written and sent in a letter of inquiry or letter of intent, if one is required? (Look carefully, as the requirements are sometimes hidden in large application packets; see sample in Chapter 6).

- made copies of the application packet and given one to all members of the development team?

- developed possible ideas/solutions to the targeted needs that the proposed project will address?

- secured the necessary permissions from those people (e.g., school board trustees, administrators) whose signatures will be required to continue the process (e.g., to provide evidence of support)?

- registered for any workshops or other support opportunities provided by the funding agency and formulated questions that will reflect the stakeholders' values so that you can validate eligibility and clarify any concerns or confusion about the application guidelines and requirements?

- notified all members of your development team and scheduled the first meeting?

After the first meeting with the funding agency did you:

- contact your network of partners to obtain their support and assistance?

- design an activity chart that outlines tasks, assignments, and timeline for the coming weeks, and aligns tasks with talents and available time? (See Chapter 10.)

- develop a communication plan to engage and update stakeholders as the proposal development process unfolds?

Special events—science fair

5

Review the
Grant Application
Packet

*Books must be read as deliberately as they
were written.*
—Henry David Thoreau

The grant application packet is many things to you at this point: a map, a guide, and an invitation to a relationship with the funder which, if you develop and maintain it, can yield lasting support for your organization. Now that you've accepted this invitation to propose growth, change, and investment, let's get down to work.

If you are working as a development team, each of you was selected for a reason. If you feel that the tasks you have been assigned do not match your talents, now is the time to speak up; otherwise your own struggles will begin to impact the development process. During this process, the following jobs will need to be done:

- conduct assessments
- research solutions
- develop a strategic plan
- facilitate meetings
- write the proposed narrative
- design graphs and charts
- organize logistics (people, places, info, data)
- present updates, ideas, proposals
- attend training meetings and bidders' conferences

Obviously, different grants demand different roles or skills depending on their focus and scale. The thousand dollars you might seek for books and support materials from a local foundation is something you can complete on your own; the million dollars another foundation or corporation wants to give away requires a vision, a plan, a team, and a headquarters. Such collaborative applications allow you to create—even demand—a team made up of diverse people, each with their own specialty, though all must inevitably wear many hats as they learn to "work with intelligence" (Goleman 1998) to not only manage their own work but help others to master theirs. Few people, for example, walk around describing or seeing themselves as "writers." So it is with leaders. But Julia Cameron, in *The Right to Write* (1999), proclaims that "we should write, above all, because we are writers, whether we call ourselves that or not."

If you require additional support in such areas as writing or working with others, consult the appropriate workshop chapters listed in the table of contents.

WORDS TO KNOW

administrative costs

annual report

authorizing signature

demographic data

DUNS number

indirect costs

rubric

LEARNING LINKS

Use the Application Guidelines to Get Organized

Always make copies of the original application packet for each development team member so that they can make notes on their copy. We suggest that you highlight passages or key words. You will use the application guidelines for several essential purposes right off:

- Use the requirements and eligibility sections and any other information from the application packet (i.e., annual report, training documents), to create a checklist of what you must do, get, avoid, and create.

- Identify your needs, ideas, and solutions as they accord with the application's stated goals and objectives.

- Create a master proposal development task/activity chart on butcher paper. Break the application down into its component parts, identifying roles, responsibilities, sections, and so on.

- Identify and create a list of crucial or unique terms (e.g., "horizontal/vertical slice"). Be sure to use the funder's language in the proposal; get used to thinking in their terms from the beginning.

- Note on the application any organization goals, state initiatives, or other guiding values that might help you link your proposal to a larger reform effort; remember that you are the one selling yourself here: the funder is looking for a person or organization that can use this opportunity to achieve their objectives.

- Look for words that signal value, priority, or bias in the funder's mind; use these to develop a scoring rubric. The rubric can be of particular use in helping you read the application critically and effectively, as it shows what the funder assigns the most weight to. If the application packet does not include a reader's score sheet, request one or ask for one from a previous grant cycle. In a pinch, create your own by asking yourself what the criteria could be for scoring the proposal as indicated by its questions and the agency's stated priorities.

- Develop a rubric that scores each question and attachment required by the application so that nothing is missed or insufficiently addressed.

H O T

T I P S

Pay close attention to how the rubric or application guidelines assign "points" to various items; rubrics provide insight into what the agency thinks is most and least important.

In addition to getting yourself or your team set up, you must begin to take care of the following issues at this point:

- Collect evidence to include in your application's accompanying appendices or portfolio (this is especially important if you are applying for arts funding, National Board of Professional Teaching Standards, or accreditation).

You will want to check with the funding agency to be sure that it accepts supplementary materials before you collect and submit them. Also, if you are including multimedia products as part of your application, you should check to see what platform and equipment are available to the readers.

- Make sure your organization will and can sign government or funder's assurances regarding such things as antidiscrimination policies, drug-free status, and animal research. Your proposal is a binding contract, which is why you must always submit the original signature pages with your completed grant proposal application.
- Get necessary permissions and, ideally, required signatures (e.g., from administrators, union representatives, school board officials).

Authorizing signatures can be difficult to obtain due to the mobility of and demands on many of the signatories. There is nothing sadder, however, than to see a team spend a month writing a proposal only to bring it to their governing board and have the board president refuse to sign it because of potential obstacles to forthcoming reforms.

- Gather any necessary information; funders often require certain data. Such information has the added benefit of helping you validate your needs and write with greater precision. The most commonly requested or useful data includes:
  - relevant board minutes (e.g., reflecting the official decision to support this proposal)
  - client data (e.g., demographic information)
  - audit reports
  - performance data (e.g., test scores, accreditation reviews)

More and more education funders want concrete, measurable results from tests, assessment tools, and strategies that are linked to standardized, norm-referenced tests. Find out right away if such information is available—even required—and how you can get it. In California, for example, each public school is required to file a California Basic Education Document (CBED) report each fall. Such reports offer abundant statistical and demographic information.

- demographic data (e.g., socioeconomic information, participation in special programs, ethnicity profile)
- philanthropic history (e.g., record of past grants)
- parent group (or other volunteer) participation information
- current resources (e.g., inventory of computers, equipment)
- in-kind contributions (i.e., evidence of what you will contribute of your own resources toward the proposed project)
- accounting information that might be needed in the budget (e.g., "indirect" or administrative costs which will be taken from the grant if awarded)
- DUNS number (Your Dun and Bradstreet number identifies you as a nonprofit agency and establishes your fiscal solvency and credit rating.)

See the Apple Technology proposal on the CD-ROM for an example that makes good use of school data to support its request.

- federal and state identification numbers (These allow government agencies such as the IRS to identify your site. This and other necessary financial identification information can be obtained through your organization's financial officer.)
- required resumes (Some larger grant applications or those such as the Fulbright Scholarship require resumes from key personnel. These should be presented in a uniform or similar format.)

This is also a good time to solicit letters of support for your proposal. A sabbatical applicant, for example, might ask the principal or department chair to write a letter explaining the value of the proposed sabbatical project to the school's current emphasis on interdisciplinary curriculum.

Overview of the Proposal Process: Common Elements

We strongly encourage you to set up a system of filing with sections—we call them "buckets"—for each part of the proposal so that your team members can keep track of all materials and know where they are, what they need, and where things are located. Most applications include the following components, with some variation.

When setting up your buckets, consider using a portable crate or file box that permits you to use hanging file folders. This allows everyone to find and share things easily, and take the individual files or entire bucket wherever you or your team decide to work. See Chapter 19 (Workshop 3), "Organizing for Success," for more details on this process.

- letter of intent or intent to apply form
- application form
- signed assurances
- table of contents
- project overview
- introduction of stakeholders
- areas of focus, needs, and benefits
- goals and objectives
- plan of operation (methods, activities, and timeline)
- evaluation tools and strategies
- management plan
- budget forms and justification
- appendices (which could include):
  - staff resumes
  - job descriptions
  - letters of support or commitment
  - evidence of previous success
  - test data/statistical data
  - charts/graphs
  - fiscal audit of nonprofit
  - list of proposal support and participant network

- bibliography
- glossary

CHECKPOINT
Answer these questions before moving on.

- Have you set up your buckets? Consider using the following system:

  Bucket 1: necessary resource materials (books, catalogs, resumes, etc.) and research

  Bucket 2: necessary application packets, annual reports

  Bucket 3: necessary samples of proposals: proposals (previous winners *and* losers) obtained from other nonprofit organizations, schools, county offices, government agencies, funders, or colleagues

  Bucket 4: Your response materials for this proposal in progress, separated into folders that match application guideline components (e.g., "Goals," "Evaluation") and reflect the generic components (as listed on page 73) that exemplify a solid, sound grant proposal

How to Read and Use the Grant Application Guidelines

To write a winning proposal you must return to the application guidelines constantly. It should be your Bible during the course of the proposal development process since it is the standard against which your proposal will be measured. Thus it is crucial to assemble a group of people to help you read it closely. You have read it several times already, of course, but now you are reading it to use it, to plan and write by it.

One crucial reason you need to have a team read through the application packet is to help you spot potential obstacles to your success and help determine your eligibility. There are other reasons you need several readers. Effective readers bring to any reading task certain contextual or background information—about the past, other organizational efforts under way, constraints—that will help you read the application with the critical eyes necessary.

The book *Questioning the Author* (Beck 1997) offers several useful tips to help you read for deeper understanding. First of all, good readers *interact* with a text in order to increase comprehension. This is crucial, for one does not merely extract information from a grant application; instead, one "builds understanding," through discussion between informed parties, of what the funder *really* wants, what certain words or phrases *really* mean. Such critical, effective reading demands more than most individual readers can provide on their own. For this reason, we suggest the following strategies to help you better read your application:

• *Have the necessary experts on hand* when you do your initial read-through. Even if the technology coordinator will not be an ongoing part of the team, for example, make sure that he or she is there to lend an informed ear and professional intelligence to this part of the planning. This person may know of other initiatives going on, or similar programs the funder would expect you to know about. He or she may have background information about certain components of the request that only an expert would know about.

• *Prepare for the reading* if at all possible by looking at past winners and losers, talking to others who have applied to this organization, or researching the organization; this will create the necessary context to help you read intelligently.

• *Read through the application together,* stopping to query each other as to the meaning of particular portions of the text. The purpose of such queries is to "make public the messages or ideas presented by an author" (Beck 1997).

• *Use the reading session to brainstorm ideas* as you go through the application. If the application instructs you to "explain how you will use this project to improve instructional practices schoolwide," listen and make a note of someone's sudden observation that the new study skills program could tie in with the proposed project. If someone wonders if you couldn't link your School-to-Work program with the Service Learning Coordinator's position, pay attention.

• *If your development team has a strategic planner or facilitator,* you might consider breaking the application packet into sections for specific teams—by specialty, department, or other focus—to increase reading comprehension and efficiency. You might also look for potential obstacles or questions you can get answered before the group gathers for the read-through. Examples of such obstacles might include requirements, limitations, fiscal constraints, and logistics.

• *Use the bidders' conference and the group's collective intelligence* to establish the difference between what the application says and what it truly means. Do this by asking such questions as:

  • Do the guidelines explain the funding agency's vision, goals, and expectations clearly?

  • What evidence is the funder willing to accept or permit you to offer in the targeted areas?

  • Do all parts of the application packet agree? Are they consistent with the agency's previous ideas and current vision?

- What does this mean?
- Why is it important?
- Why does the funding agency tell us this now?
- What is the funder trying to tell us by including this example, using this word? Why do you think that?

Reading Between the Lines

While the above are helpful questions to use throughout the reading process, there remains one particularly difficult challenge: reading between the lines. There are several key elements that, while not always explicitly requested in the application guidelines and not even on the scoresheet, experienced readers will expect to find. These include:

- your capacity to deliver
- what you or others have done or what you will do to match the requested investment (How invested are *you* in your own project? Or is it something you are *willing* to do only if you get funded?)

Should you find yourself with questions about specific passages and their implications, do not hesitate to consult the funder's program officer for guidance, making a list of concerns ahead of time to keep your discussion focused. If the funder offers any workshops or orientations to help prospective grant seekers, you absolutely should attend; not only will your presence signal commitment and gain you inside information, it will provide an opportunity to establish a relationship, one that transcends the impersonal nature of phones, e-mails, and forms. Whoever attends these meetings should be a strong representative of your organization's ideas and concerns, since they are forming in the funder's mind a substantial impression of the applicant's needs that could contribute to assumptions of credibility and eligibility.

Finally, you should revisit and reread the grant application—or at least relevant sections of it—each time you sit down to work on it again. This helps to orient your mind, but it also accomplishes other essential goals. Certain phrases or requirements which do not, in the early read-throughs, seem important, often begin to reveal their significance the more you read them or the deeper you get into the proposal development process. While no application packet can compare to Shakespeare's texts, the point is nonetheless true that they merit rereading for the same reason the plays do—the more we read them the more they reveal.

The importance of rereading the guidelines in the application cannot be overemphasized. Many English students fail writing competency tests not because they wrote badly but because they wrote about the wrong subject. They glanced at the topic and galloped off, never stopping to look back and check what they were supposed to do. In this respect the application guidelines become, from the beginning, the essential map to which you must return constantly to check your progress, your direction, your accuracy. It can be hard to remember to stop and check yourself; rather like when Americans drive in Europe and forget to pull over and check the maps because they are driving at eighty-five miles an hour (and still honking at people to speed up). When working on some big proposal you don't want to suddenly find yourself, as many do, pulling up to the border of France when you thought you were headed to Amsterdam. Not reading the map—i.e., the application—carefully and frequently is one of the main reasons for not arriving safely at your chosen destination.

How the Funding Agency Will Read *You*

After you're done thinking about how to read *them*, stop to consider in advance how they will read *you*. Throughout the proposal development process consider the following elements:

- rationale for applying
- benefits for funder and clients
- credibility of applicant
- capacity to implement
- appearance and layout of document
- politics of the organization

Know When to Hire a Consultant

Throughout the process there are moments when a paid consultant can offer crucial guidance. But consultants can also be an obstacle if brought in at the wrong time or for the wrong reasons. There are different types of consultants one might consider at different stages, depending on your resources and needs:

- assessment/evaluation consultant
- graphic designer or clerical staff
- proposal development facilitator
- strategic planner
- technology expert
- curriculum or reform specialist
- professional, technical, or grant writer
- budget/financial consultant

Consultants can be very expensive and not always efficient if brought in too early in the development process. For a consultant to be effective, the applicant must have some sense of where they are headed. A writer, for example, will want you to have done all the essential research and thinking, formed outlines in response to the guideline's questions, and collected the necessary data so that they can focus on putting words on the page instead of hunting for facts or orienting themselves to information. Then as they begin to write, they can give your team drafts to edit and refine before the final document is written. Or, if you have able writers, you can hire a professional grant writer later in the process, to add the rhetorical and stylistic polish and identify gaps and clean up the presentation, adding formatting that makes the proposal more powerful.

CHECKPOINT
Answer these questions before moving on.

By the time you finish with the first—of dozens—reading of the application, whether working as a team or an individual, you should be able to respond in the affirmative to the following questions:

- Did you define the activities that are necessary (brainstorm, research, present, write, edit, design)?

- Have you identified your team and defined everyone's roles?

- Did you establish a development timeline and post it for all to see in a centralized location?

- Did you identify the methods of compiling the necessary data and alliances?

- Did you answer any questions that arose during the reading of the application?

6

Write a Concept Paper, a Letter of Inquiry, or a Letter of Intent to Apply

Some people see things as they are and say why. I see things as they could be and say why not.
—Robert Kennedy

WORDS TO KNOW

abstract

acronyms

executive summary

outcomes

partnership

reader

At this point in the process funders ask for different things before you proceed with the writing of the actual proposal. Keep in mind that some funders will also require nothing, in which case you can skip this chapter, although writing a concept paper will prepare you for the work involved in writing the proposal. Government agencies, private foundations, and corporations use a variety of terms differently; thus you must always take the extra minute to figure out what the guidelines are actually requesting. Look at the requirements outlined in the application packet to find out if you must submit any of the following, each of which is briefly defined below:

• *Concept paper*: After thinking about your proposed project, you write up an overview of what you want to do, what is needed, who will benefit, why it should be done, and what support is necessary. This concise overview clarifies your own thinking before you proceed with the application.

• *Letter of inquiry*: You establish contact with the funding agency by introducing yourself and providing a summary (two to three pages) of your project in order to get the funder's reaction to the idea (see sample below).

• *Letter of intent to apply*: This letter does little more than state who you are, where you are located, and that you intend to submit a proposal in response to a particular request for proposals (RFP). It is very short, sometimes a form included in the application packet supplied by the agency as part of the package.

Write a Concept Paper to Clarify Your Ideas

The concept paper resembles an abstract, a project summary, or an executive summary; however, it is different in an important way. It is used as a tool to get you going, to help you clarify your initial plans. The abstract, on the other hand, is best written *after* the proposal is finished, as its job is to effectively summarize what the proposal will examine in detail. Whereas the abstract is written with a specific funder's guidelines in mind, the concept paper is primarily an in-house document used to help your organization get or stay focused. The abstract quickly summarizes your project and helps the funding agency better understand what you are trying to achieve through your proposal.

LEARNING LINKS

You will find an example of a concept paper in Appendix I.

Elements of an Effective Concept Paper

Good concept papers:

• are generally no longer than two to six pages (excluding attachments)

- include a clear statement of the problem, need, and areas of focus the proposal will address
- identify previous efforts to solve this problem—by yourself or other agencies—and explain how this effort will be different (i.e., more effective)
- outline resources needed (e.g., human, physical, or fiscal)
- state goals and objectives
- establish a realistic but ambitious plan of operation
- clearly define the expected outcomes

You won't always have time to develop a concept paper, but it is very helpful if you can. The concept paper allows you to figure out what you really think, to articulate what your vision looks like. The real value here is more for yourself than the funder. In fact, most people will never see this paper; you or your team, however, will have a more immediate sense of what you are doing after scratching out a draft of the big ideas. Such a paper:

- provides you an entry point into the proposal-writing process, one to which everyone can contribute their ideas
- creates something for you to share with others to get useful feedback; no one works well in a vacuum
- helps you develop and refine your initial ideas
- results in a thoughtful piece of work you could show to someone at the funding agency for initial response (i.e., to answer the question "Is this what you are looking for?")

CHECKPOINT
Answer these questions before moving on.

Before moving on to the next stage, stop and ask yourself the following questions—ones very much like those your prospective reader might pose—about your concept paper:

- Who is applying?
- Who will assist?
- What are your areas of concern, your themes, your focus?
- What are your needs/problems?
- What are your goals and objectives?
- What are your proposed methods and major activities?
- Who will manage and implement?
- How will you evaluate the program?
- What will this project cost?

- What resources will you—or members of your support network—contribute?

Composing the Letter of Inquiry

Not all applications require that you submit a letter of inquiry. While some ask for a formal letter, other agencies use a simple questionnaire that typically must be completed weeks or even months before the actual proposal is due.

H O T

T I P S

If, as sometimes happens, you miss the filing deadline for the Intent form, ask the funder to add you to the submission list. Many times it is that simple. Also, be sure to submit your letter of intent on appropriate letterhead, first, to make it a binding, valid entry and, second, to make the best possible impression.

According to Bill Somerville, president of the Philanthropic Ventures Foundation, an effective letter of inquiry will explain:

- *Who you are.* Identify your organization by name (and whether it is a nonprofit, 501(c)3), who it serves, where it's located, and how long it has been in existence.

LEARNING LINKS

See Chapter 17 (Workshop 1), "Writing with Power," to help you write more persuasively.

- *What you are proposing to do.* Briefly describe your project, including the cost, duration, and population served. Emphasize the results, not the means. State why there is a need for the project. Be specific. Explain why the organization is capable of carrying out the proposed idea.

- *What you are asking for.* Attach a dollar amount to your request and ask if you might submit a proposal for your project. State whether you will follow up with a phone call. Thank the funder for his or her time and attention.

Your first opportunity to align your ideas with the funder's is often the letter of inquiry. In this letter—the directions for which can often be hidden within the labyrinth of the application—you must make the best possible first impression, one that conveys competence in all respects, for, perhaps more than anything, a proposal is selling your capacity to accomplish your vision. This letter also confirms your eligibility and serves as your official entry form into the process. Note, however, that not all proposals require such formal letters, and anything you can do to distinguish yourself (in a positive way) from the other candidates is worth considering. If, for example, you are applying to your district office for a mentor position, consider putting in a call to the head of the selection committee to inquire about the process, asking if there is anything in particular that they are looking for. (Make sure you read the guidelines first!) This establishes a personal connection, one that raises your application one notch above the pile to the extent that you create and maintain a relationship with this person.

Realize, as you begin writing your letter of inquiry, that funders use these letters to separate the wheat from the chaff; after all, they can only handle so many interviews, so many visitations, so many applications. Therefore, you want to be sure that your letter contains/establishes the following:

- the breath and depth of your partnerships (or alliances)
- your capacity to accomplish what you propose
- your eligibility
- your availability should they have any questions

Sample Letter of Inquiry

The following example is from a high school drama department.

Carol Ann Prater
Burlingame School District
Burlingame, CA

September 23, 1999

Mr. Glenn Rock
International Brotherhood of Electricians
55 Fillmore Street
Anyplace, Illinois 34567

Dear Mr. Rock:

I am writing you on behalf of the XYZ Drama Club. For many years XYZ High School produced exciting productions but, as budgets got tighter, the theater arts program and the theater itself were much neglected.

Over the past four years a new theater arts director and a dedicated parent support group have worked diligently to create a theater arts program having a level of excellence equal to the talents and needs of the students. The problem that remains is a facility that has been allowed to deteriorate for twenty years.

The rebuilding of the theater arts program began several years ago when the students ambitiously scheduled both a full drama and spring musical, complete with pit orchestra. Students have since played to sold-out crowds due to their improved reputation.

The theater students and their parents have actively worked to help gather the funds to begin the journey of getting the XYZ High School/Community Theater back in shape. The facility does not meet the basic needs of staging the many school and local community productions that the students, parents, and local citizens work so hard on each year.

The lighting system is at the top of the renovation list and needs to be replaced. There are gaps of illumination with the present lighting system and in some areas the wiring is unsafe.

This fall marks our fifth season of fund-raising. It was our dream that for this fifth anniversary a new lighting system could be installed for the fall comedy *You Can't Take It with You*. To this effort the students and parents have raised $22,000, the cost quoted last spring by several companies to be up and running with a new lighting system this fall. Unfortunately, when the contract went out to bid last summer the lowest bid submitted was $9,500 higher due to some electrical complications. It seems we now have enough money to purchase all the lighting equipment but lack the funds needed to pay electricians for installation.

The lighting equipment is destined to sit in boxes for a year or two more until the parents and students can raise the additional funds, by which time costs will no doubt have risen further. The new system could be installed this week if we had the additional $9,500.

The new lighting system will provide students and community groups a beautiful facility for many years to come. It will complete phase one of our theater renovation project and will bring hours of wholesome activity and entertainment to the students and neighboring communities.

We realize you receive many requests; however, we are in need of qualified electricians who would donate their time to erect and install these lights for us. If this is not possible, perhaps you would consider approving a grant to help us secure the labor to complete this job.

Any consideration you may give to help our fine arts students and this community will be greatly appreciated.

Sincerely,

Carol Ann Prater
[telephone number]
[fax number]
wingrant@ix.netcom.com

Sample Letter of Intent to Apply

The letter of intent to apply, more commonly found in large (e.g., million dollar) grant applications, requires little more than contact information and the name of your proposed project. Figure 6.1 is a sample from a government grant application.

Intent-to-Apply Form
Alternative Assessment Pilot Project

Name/Title of Proposed Project   **Date**

<u>COMPASS: Pointing the Way to Alternative Assessment</u>   <u>May 2, 1998</u>

The organization(s) named on this form intend to jointly apply for funding under the provisions of the Alternative Assessment Plan Project (AB 40, Quackenbush, 1990). It is understood that other districts or agencies may later join the original participants in making this application for funding.

Contact Person(s) for **Lead Consortium** Ms. Francis Hawthorne* Curriculum Administrator	Contact Person(s) for **Satellite Consortium** Mr. Jason Perkins Southern Consortium Coordinator
Address Midwest Unified School District 123 Columbus Avenue Middletown, MI 34567	**Address** Western Unified School District 456 Lewis Avenue Clarktown, MI 35677
FAX Numbers (123) 456-7890	**FAX Numbers** (456) 789-1234
Phone Numbers (789) 123-4567	**Phone Numbers** (321) 987-6543

List the Proposed Lead Consortium Participants:

[Place an asterisk(*) next to the district which would serve as the LEA (Lead Education Administrator)]

District   **Name of Superintendent**

This consortium consists of fifty school districts in western St. Louis, Missouri. All XYZ member districts will have access to activities of the Alternative Assessment Collaborative. The following agencies will support field test sites:

ABC Unified School District   Mr. Thomas Moore

DEF Unified School District   Ms. Flannery O'Connor

GHI Unified School District   Mr. Gerald Roberts

FIGURE 6.1   Sample Letter of Intent (aka Letter of Transmittal or Intent to Apply Form)

CHECKPOINT
Answer these questions before moving on.

- Have you avoided using any acronyms (e.g., R and D, CDE, DOE) that might confuse the reader?

- Did you adequately and effectively describe the proposed idea, the methods you will use, and what you hope to accomplish?

- Have you established your credibility and capability to accomplish what you propose?

- Did you establish the proper tone and relationship with the funder in your letter?

H O T

T I P S

This is a perfect time to have others (especially stakeholders and outsiders) read what you have written so far. Their objective eyes might detect as condescension or arrogance what you had intended to portray as pride or confidence.

*New facilities,
renovations,
and repairs*

7

Write the Introduction

Honor the past, challenge the present, look to the future.

—*Walt Disney*

**WORDS
TO KNOW**

exemplar

positioning

qualitative

quantitative

rubric

Etymologically, the word *introduction* means "to bring in" or "a leading into," both of which make the purpose clear: evaluators need help if they are to read your proposal successfully, if they are to remain oriented throughout. Think of the introduction as the gateway to the entire proposal. While your letter of inquiry or your concept paper—if these were required of you—allowed you to make that first impression a strong one, it is your introduction that will make the difference now for the simple reason that from this point on your proposal will be evaluated. From now on you must write with the evaluators in mind, guided by the funder's scoring rubrics, their requirements, values, terminology and suggestions, and the examples of applications.

Your introduction must accomplish the following crucial outcomes, doing so in a rather short space:

- capture the reader's interest
- set the scene (i.e., define how you will approach the situation)
- define your themes or areas of focus
- establish your individual or organizational capability (e.g., your assets and strengths)
- align your ideas with the funding agency's and show your understanding of the problem at hand
- validate your eligibility according to funder's guidelines
- present a sound program design or solution worthy of funding
- stimulate an emotional response
- show logic and reasoning
- exhibit systemic thinking

In addition, you must make several important decisions before writing, any one of which could make the difference between getting funded and getting thanked for your interest. Ask yourself the following questions before you proceed:

- What is the most appropriate style of writing (the one that will be most persuasive) for this particular application?
- Who is evaluating my proposal and what biases, values, and assumptions will influence them?
- What, of all the data available to me, is most important (i.e., will help me persuade my reader) to include at this point?
- How should I organize (i.e., sequence, arrange) the narrative information to achieve the greatest effect on my reader at this point? (*Never* bypass the funder's requested format though, no matter how illogical their sequence seems.)

- What is the best form (e.g., letter, business plan, formal proposal) in which to write this application (if it is not spelled out)?

- How will most other applicants approach this application and how can I make mine different in a powerful way?

H O T

T I P S

> **M**ost of the information in your introduction should come from the preparation work you did in Chapter 1. If your application requires no introduction, work in the essential data—e.g., create a strong profile of your organization and your idea—in the abstract or at the beginning of the needs section to greet and focus the reader. Readers want to know who you are as they score your proposal.

Elements of an Effective Introduction

A winning introduction will communicate information appropriate to the application guidelines. Now is a good time to revisit the foundation's or company's annual report, Web site, and other support documents to help you determine what the funder really wants to hear about or what position best complements their vision and goals. In general, however, a good introduction includes some or all of the following information as required by the guidelines:

- Title
  - What is the name of your project/proposal?
- Mission/vision/values statement
  - What past, current, future directions?
- History/background
  - What are the significant events relating to this proposal (milestones)?
- Current situation (existing conditions)
  - What are your opportunities, threats, innovative reforms, future goals and directions?
- Organizational capabilities/capacity statements
  - What are your major programs or projects/accomplishments/awards that demonstrate your ability/capacity to deliver the goods?
- Description of network/coalition/partners
  - Who will support/collaborate on project (e.g., volunteers, corporations, parent groups, city agencies, other consultants)?
  - What evidence of support or endorsement exists from other institutions?

- Human resources/staff, clients/stakeholders
  - Who is involved in or will benefit from your project?
  - Who is applying for funds?
  - What staff are involved and what are their qualifications?
  - What are the size and characteristics of the target population?
- In-kind resources (e.g., equipment, training, materials)
  - What existing and available resources complement this effort?
- Facilities (physical resources)
  - What is the location of the agency?
  - What is the description of the physical plant?
- Fiscal resources (e.g., matching funds, other grants, other budgeted funds directed toward effort)
  - What is the current operating budget to supplement the effort?
  - What special funds (grants, donations) are available to supplement this effort?
  - What endowments, trusts, or other support efforts are or will be in place?
- Relevant experiences that would motivate or inspire your reader
- Qualitative/quantitative data (e.g., demographics, test scores, survey results, transciency rates, location, size)
  - What are your demographics?
  - What are your test scores?
  - What are your results from program review?
  - What other significant statistics can you offer?
- Summary of management and implementation team/expertise and past achievements
  - Who will manage this project?
  - What is their expertise?
  - What are their past efforts and skills?
  - What special training/degrees do they have?
  - What expert assistance/coaches/consultants exist?

Take a minute to respond to the following items; they will help your team generate some "fast facts" about your organization. If you cannot answer any of them, or feel your answers are hopelessly inadequate, that should not trouble you; it just tells you where to begin, what to do next. Complete the following helpful startup activities:

- Make a list of at least twenty-five facts about your organization or program, using the previous list to help you get started.

- Name all the documents you have access to or should obtain that would contain information relevant to your capacity, capabilities, or needs.

- Identify all the data sources that will assist you in the writing of the introduction; this might include documents or assessments that would provide examples, support, or evidence to help substantiate your stated need(s) and organizational capabilities.

- List those people or departments that would be helpful responders to this section because of their ability or knowledge, identifying people by name if you can.

- Write down what you think the reader's biggest concern is at this point (i.e., what is the question they will expect your introduction to answer?).

LEARNING LINKS

See Chapter 17 (Workshop 1), "Writing with Power," for more detailed guidance in the area of writing style. See also Chapter 22 (Workshop 6), "Making Room for Creativity," to help you brainstorm more ideas here.

Sample Introduction: Technology Grant

Without a doubt, information access and usage is changing the role of today's educators. For example, it is no longer acceptable to confine education to the four walls of a classroom and use the instructor as the only source of information. The vast resources of today's information environment must be made available to all of our nation's students, rural or urban, rich or poor, English speaking or speakers of other languages. Technology must extend to the physically handicapped as well as to those isolated by geographical boundaries. Classrooms and communities everywhere must possess the means to access information for local as well as global connections.

The President's Educational Technology Initiative defines four elements that must be addressed to ensure that every young person is prepared to enter the workforce technologically literate. The four pillars of this technology challenge follow:

1. Appropriate hardware (e.g., computers, modems, scanners) will be accessible to every student.
2. Classrooms will be connected to one another and to the outside world.
3. Educational software will be an integral part of the curriculum—and as engaging as the best video game.
4. Instructors will be ready to use and integrate technology into their curriculum.

There is a clear need to transform today's classrooms into modern communications centers for learning, with an emphasis on quality professional development for teachers and high academic standards and achievement for students. The Desert Without Borders project has a clear vision of how to meet this challenge. The project will meet this challenge through a multitude of technologies, including an interactive Web site for delivery of curricula, a multimedia delivery system (MDS), a CD-ROM resource kit and video series, a mobile investigation lab, and a strong distance learning component using the MDS and broadband cable. (Imperial County Office of Education)

Establish and Develop Themes and Areas of Focus

Just as in a film or novel, themes help to hold the text together as the reader progresses. All the better if the particular theme or focus aligns with the values or emphasis of the funding agency. Writing for an agency devoted to improving communities? You want the funder's values reflected and reinforced in your proposal through images, metaphors, and words. Other themes might convey capability; thus you will look for opportunities to continually reiterate why you have the capacity to make this proposal a success, and thereby make the funder a success.

In addition to organizing your introduction—and the proposal itself—around a theme, it should have a clear, identifiable focus that is powerfully aligned with the values of the prospective funder. Consider the following example, taken from a winning California Department of Education application:

Sample Introduction: Educational Reform Grant

The XYZ project will focus on four main areas and reform goals that target instructional reform for systemic change.

FOCUS AREA ONE: UPGRADE THE INSTRUCTIONAL PROGRAM
Goal 1   All children will come to school ready to learn. (Goals 2000 #1)
Goal 2   All students will meet high expectations for achievement in the core academic subjects. (Goals 2000 #3)
Goal 3   All students will develop knowledge and understanding of diverse cultures and a positive cross-cultural attitude. (Goals 2000 Improving America's Schools Act—IASA)
Goal 4   All students will remain in school to foster lifelong learning. (Goals 2000 IASA)
Goal 5   All students will promote/graduate to an appropriate grade level at the end of each school year. (Goals 2000 #2)

FOCUS AREA TWO: REFORM PARENT EDUCATION, OUTREACH PROGRAMS, AND COMMUNITY COLLABORATION

Goal 6   Parents will become active partners in their children's education. (Goals 2000 #8)

Goal 7   The district will collaborate with community-based organizations (CBOs) to promote successful, safe, disciplined, and drug-free schools and to ensure basic security needs of students including physical and mental health and positive self-concept. (Goals 2000 #7)

FOCUS AREA THREE: RESTRUCTURE THE COORDINATION OF SERVICES TO SERVICE THE WHOLE CHILD (IASA)

Goal 8   All federal, state, and local resources and programs will be coordinated and integrated.

FOCUS AREA FOUR: REFORM THE PROFESSIONAL DEVELOPMENT PROGRAM (IASA)

Goal 9   All staff will acquire and apply the knowledge and skills needed to ensure students' success. (Goals 2000 #4)

CHECKPOINT
Answer these questions before moving on.

- Have you checked your introduction against the guidelines and scoring rubric the funder provided (or from examples of past winners and losers)?

- Have you established your organizational capability in the eyes of the evaluator?

- Have you used any language—jargon, acronyms, names—that might confuse or otherwise frustrate the evaluator?

- Is the focus of your proposal clearly established by the end of your introduction?

8

Identify, Validate, and Align Your Project Needs and Benefits

*The only limit to our realization of tomorrow will
be our doubts of today.*
—Franklin Delano Roosevelt

The needs statement is the most crucial part of your entire proposal. In short, it must answer three fundamental questions put to all proposals:

- What problem does the targeted need address?
- Why should this project be undertaken?
- What are the benefits of addressing this need now?

Other sections of the proposal—the goals and objectives, for example—are also important; however, it is your needs statement that paves the way for everything else. If you do not identify a compelling need—one that is aligned with the funder's vision, one that your community or the funder immediately recognizes the value of—you cannot hope to win. In this sense, your needs statement is, to return to the days of Aristotle, your argument, the point you will spend the rest of the proposal supporting. To support your argument effectively, you will use many types of evidence and data in different ways. This information will "help the funder understand the problem the project will remedy and enable the reader to learn more about the issues" (McNeill and Greever 1999).

Before reading this section, we suggest you revisit Chapter 1, in which you assessed your existing conditions. Chapter 8 is designed to help you adapt one or more of your organizational needs to a particular grant application.

LEARNING LINKS

Elements of an Effective Needs Statement

In an article written for the Grantsmanship Center, Norton Kiritz identifies the four requirements of any effective needs statement:

1. It should be clearly related to the mission, values, and vision of your organization.
2. It should be supported by evidence drawn from your experience, from statistics provided by authoritative sources, and/or from the testimony of persons and organizations known to be knowledgeable about the situation.
3. It should be of reasonable dimensions—a concern that you can realistically do something about over the course of the grant.
4. It should be stated in terms of clients or constituents, rather than the needs or problems of your organization.

In addition to these crucial aspects, there are other important considerations to keep in mind when writing your needs statement. Funders are, remember, overrun by dozens, even hundreds, of applications to wade through; thus you want your needs statement written as concisely and clearly as possible. This can only be achieved if you are clear about what you actually require to solve your problem: leadership, training, expertise, time, materials? Moreover, if you cannot get a hold of an actual copy of the funder's scoring rubric, you can at least try to anticipate the questions that will most likely need to be answered. Consider using this set of focus questions to help guide your writing:

- What are our liabilities, weaknesses, and areas of concern?

- Why do I/we have these problems or concerns?

- Who will be involved (e.g., who is the target group, the client)?

- What evidence can we provide to demonstrate and support these stated problems and needs?

- What have we already done and what else do we plan to do to address these needs (i.e., in addition to what we are proposing)?

- Who else will benefit from the proposal (e.g., constituents, the community, alliances, stakeholders)?

H O T

T I P S

It is always advisable to present your challenges and needs as opportunities (to expand literacy, etc.) instead of complaints (e.g., "the kids cannot read!"). This does not mean that you should omit or downplay bad news; instead, you should explain how you are going to overcome this problem, perhaps by describing how you have overcome such difficulties in the past. Remember, whiners do not win.

In his *Rhetoric*, Aristotle identifies only two parts to any speech: the statement of the case and its proof. His idea is helpful to us as we think about what we are really trying to accomplish in any proposal: state a need and convince others of its importance to such an extent that they will feel compelled to help address it. Aristotle subsequently provides three means by which a person can persuade others to believe, feel, or act in a certain way.

- *Appeal to logic.* Given that the word *philanthropy* means expressing one's concern for fellow human beings, especially through gifts, the obvious logical appeal of most proposals is the benefit to the community at large as well as to the individual nonprofit organization. When applying to a Silicon Valley foundation for a multimillion-dollar grant, we realized that the foundation's primary concern was the ethical and technical capabilities students would bring to the workplace. Thus all needs (e.g., kids need to learn to solve complicated problems collaboratively) were stated according to the logic that, in being answered, they would benefit the community and its corporations.

• *Appeal to emotion.* Aristotle found the appeal to emotion to be one of the most powerful means of persuading people. While they might *know* a particular idea is risky, they can be induced to believe in it if they become emotionally attached to the idea. Roosevelt Elementary School's winning Apple Technology Grant used this approach to get the reader emotionally involved in the lives of senior citizens and hearing-impaired students. In short, the school created a persuasive narrative that emotionally drew Apple's readers into a story they could make come true through their investment.

• *Appeal to ethics.* We might better understand the "appeal to ethics" as integrity. Aristotle believed that the ethical appeal was potentially the strongest of the three approaches. We have alluded throughout this book to the importance of individual or institutional capability. In Aristotle's book, he believed that the outcome of any argument often depended on the intelligence, benevolence, and general capability of a person or institution as perceived by the audience one sought to persuade. It is for this reason that Carol, for example, will do everything she can to get a nationally renowned technology expert like David Thornburg to join her project team for a multimillion-dollar federal technology grant application. The currency of Thornburg's reputation helps to immediately establish the credibility and capability of the proposed idea and the applicant; the reader might be inclined to say, in essence, "Who am I to question the viability of this idea if a recognized expert is willing to put his name and reputation on the line by designing or supporting it?"

Before moving on, let's take a quick look at a portion of a sabbatical proposal that illustrates several of these approaches to argument. Jim's proposal requested that he be given a sabbatical to learn more about reading and to help teachers in all disciplines improve students' reading ability. The items listed below come from a follow-up letter he was asked to write in order to clarify the value of his project. The value of the project depended on the extent to which the sabbatical review committee understood and recognized the urgency of the district's needs. (Jim's analysis appears in italics in the parentheses following each item.)

Sample Needs Analysis

Thank you (and the committee) for your recent invitation to elaborate on my sabbatical plans. While I have responded in some detail to the committee's questions, I wanted to take a moment to point out several developments that make my proposed sabbatical all the more valuable.

• Approximately 37 percent of the incoming Woodbury freshman (1999–2000) tested at the fifth-grade level or lower on the most recent Gates-MacGinitie Reading Test. This represents a dramatic increase in the number of students—and teachers—who will need help in the coming year. (*Appeal to logic: the problem is growing; it makes sense to do this in light of the trend. I use objective data to support and illustrate my argument that this is a real problem.*)

• I was appointed to the California Reads Roundtable (the western region branch of President Clinton's America Reads initiative). This appointment allows me access to some of the state's best reading resources, including WestEd's Strategic Literacy Initiative for the study and aid of struggling high school readers. (*This point appeals not only to logic—I have access to resources others might not—but links the integrity of the proposal to my professional integrity: I am someone whose credibility is already recognized by others.*)

• The district will hire a number of new teachers for the coming year. As part of its new commitment (through the Beginning Teacher Support and Assessment program) to supporting these developing teachers, the district needs expanded support services such as I would provide, particularly in the area of reading, since this is often a weak point in many teacher education programs. (*This is an appeal to emotions—you won't let those new teachers struggle and suffer, will you?—to logic—it's in your best interests to see these new teachers succeed—and to "ethics"—my capacity to help new teachers has been established through past and recent efforts.*)

• I have been asked to help a publisher road test (not as a paid position) some excellent materials for struggling high school readers; I can make these available to the teachers of the Developmental Reading classes.

Sabbatical proposals, just like National Endowment for the Humanities or Fulbright proposals, are no different than million-dollar grant applications in that they all come down to:

• defining the need
• describing what you propose to do to answer it

- demonstrating your capability to remedy it
- explaining why you should be allowed to do what you propose

Problems to Avoid

Throughout the proposal there are crossroad moments when we can get lost or undermine the power of our own proposal. In the needs statement section, several common errors arise, each of which is easily avoided if you keep your eyes open for them. Therefore:

- *Identify problems, not solutions*: You know you do not have it right if your needs statement restricts itself to a solution (e.g., development of a computer lab, days off to design new curriculum, acquisition of new textbooks). Your statement should focus on what you are looking to address; it should be expressed, for example, like this: "to help students meet the needs of the workforce"; "to ensure that all students develop the skills to communicate effectively"; "test data shows that 55 percent of all incoming freshman students need to improve their reading skills in all academic subjects."

- *Identify needs, not wants*: We all have dreams in which we muse "Wouldn't it be nice if. . . . " But grants are not the answer to wish lists. Grants exist to fund visions that are linked to a specific set of goals the funder developed and the applicant is willing to embrace. Your needs must be presented as just that—needs; if you'd like to have a new computer or a new darkroom for your nonprofit organization merely because such an acquisition would be "nice," you will be rejected. (If, however, you ask for a digital camera and a new computer so that you can improve communication between your organization and the surrounding community through a newsletter or Web site, someone will listen!)

- *Focus on the client's needs instead of the organization's*: Funders expect to hear what your clients need first so that they can, through the grant, help you meet these needs. It is therefore a mistake to say that the park needs a new fitness and training center when what the kids really need is a safe place to gather and interact in healthy ways (which can be achieved through the recreation department's systemic plan, one part of which calls for the renovation of the training center). The funder wants to know that clients would actually desire the proposed improvement or product.

- *Look committed, not greedy*: A proposal should never imply that you are willing to do something—expand a program, upgrade facilities, offer additional support groups—only if the funder is willing to pay for it. You can dramatically increase your perceived capability by outlining those things that you are already doing and will do to meet your needs; this establishes more of a partnership: between us, we can make this happen.

• *Use many types of evidence and data to validate the need*: The statement "Everyone says our kids are lazy and not good in math, so we thought we would try something new; we need new textbooks," is not a compelling argument—and such a remark is typical of many losing proposals. It is much more effective to back up your statement with relevant facts, as below.

> Our math program is inadequately addressing our students' needs as evidenced by the following indicators:
>
> • drop in SAT test scores over the past three years
> • drop in enrollment in advanced math classes
> • increased cuts and tardies in math classes
> • drop in grades in math classes at all levels
> • increased frustration level of math teachers in advanced sections
> • comments made by students, staff, and parents to the accreditation committee

The wedding of needs and research emphasizes the link between instruction, professional development, and performance. In this way effective proposals use data to validate and advance their arguments on behalf of their clients' needs.

H O T

T I P S

As mentioned previously, you should always try to anchor your needs in a certain area (e.g., literacy) or theme (e.g., safety, relationships, community). Promoting yourself or your program as a beacon in this specific area often appeals to funders who are looking for models that can be replicated.

Use Data to Support and Illustrate Your Needs Statement

Data to support your needs comes in various forms: numbers, words, and images. Some of the data is formal or quantitative—e.g., state test scores—while other information, which can be just as powerful if used correctly, is more anecdotal—stories, profiles, examples. The challenge is to choose the most current, accurate data that will best illustrate the extent of your needs, doing so in a manner that will help to engage your funder's intelligence (appeal to logic) and heart (appeal to emotions).

In addition to the obvious sources of data—institutional records, test scores, frequency rates—you can gather powerful information from other sources, in other ways, that can be used to persuade the reader. Surveys or interviews, for example, show you involving the community, constituents, or other stakeholders in the process. Such data further enhances your credibility and capability in the eyes of the reader by showing that you are approaching the project collaboratively, publicly, and honestly. Interviews can also provide strong voice to the writing, taking the otherwise bureaucratic voice of the application and warming it up for real people. Consider the following examples of needs statements, noting how each uses data to support its argument.

> The use of drugs, alcohol, and tobacco by youth in our community has steadily increased over the past five years, as has the incidence of teen crime. The ABC community must offer a comprehensive after-school program that meets the needs of our youth and reduces involvement in at-risk activities. The following data validates our stated needs:
>
> - The number of latchkey children in our community has risen 32 percent in the last five years while the number of after-school-hours teen crime has risen 48 percent in the same time period.
>
> - The frequency and number of merchant complaints about youth "hanging out" and creating disturbances have doubled in the last two years.
>
> - The availability of drugs has increased dramatically as evidenced by arrests and increased drug-related activities in the neighborhood.
>
> - The rise in school dropout rates, teen pregnancy, and runaways has continued to climb each year, exceeding the national average by 23 percent last year.
>
> - The reduction in academic enrichment classes offered by schools and recreation departments has continued unabated for the last five years, leaving over 65 percent of those children who apply unable to take a class.
>
> - Geographic isolation and economic hardship have impacted our community to create a serious problem for unemployed adults who lack the skills to take on new jobs.

The major employer in our community has laid off 50 percent of its workforce, forcing parents to commute longer to jobs that earn less.

- The community recreation department has stopped construction of a new youth center due to the reduced tax base, and needed maintenance of existing community parks has been postponed. Several other parks are slated to be closed in the coming year. The absence of facilities for youth to meet or be engaged in constructive activities has begun to signal a growing crisis within the community as seen in the rise in teen crime during after-school hours.

H O T

T I P S

Throughout the application process, you must keep in mind the other uses to which the ideas and data you assemble can be put. Data on school or other program needs, for example, can be easily recycled for use in subsequent proposals, school accreditation reports, or award applications. To this end, agencies should create and update throughout the year a data profile that includes not only demographic but programmatic information. This process will help you remain reflective, but will also keep you prepared and thus able to apply for grant opportunities that arise suddenly or those with short timelines.

Consider the example of the following survey created by parents—students created their own version and had all students in the school complete it—to identify the needs of the school for its accreditation report. The questionnaire accomplishes several objectives.

- It clearly demonstrates a partnership between the different stakeholders; thus any needs identified through the survey will have demonstrable credibility.
- The data gathered through this survey can easily be used in subsequent proposals, applications, or reports.
- The domains of need—e.g., "School Culture," "Communications"— are conspicuously aligned (i.e., in italics, at the top of each section) with those against which they will be measured.
- The data suggests objectivity to the extent that it is gathered anonymously and using a Scan-Tron form for standardized scoring of results, with all respondents limited to the same set of possible answers (e.g., ranging from "strongly agree to "strongly disagree") to guard against any muddled answers.

Sample Data-Gathering Tool: Survey

School Culture
Students respect themselves, the learning environment, the campus, and the community.

1. The school staff and faculty respect students.
2. The students respect the staff and faculty.
3. The students respect each other.
4. Students feel safe at school.
5. This school has clear, consistent rules for student behavior.
6. This school has an effective process for dealing with sexual harassment.
7. This school is neat and clean.
8. Students learn to work with people of different ethnic, social, or educational backgrounds.
9. Students learn to be responsible citizens, demonstrating integrity and honesty.
10. Students learn to maintain good health and physical fitness throughout life.

Communications
Students communicate ideas and information effectively.

11. Students learn to create, perform in, or appreciate the arts.
12. Students effectively communicate ideas and information verbally and in writing.

Preparation for the Future
Students prepare themselves to meet the demands of work, school, and adult life.

13. Students are developing a positive personal work ethic.
14. Students learn to set and accomplish realistic and challenging goals for themselves.
15. Academic and career counseling services are available to both students and parents at appropriate times throughout the students' high school career.
16. Students feel welcome in the counseling office.
17. Academic and career counseling services are available at times that meet the needs of students and parents.

Knowledge
Students produce evidence of knowledge and problem-solving ability by meeting current standards in all subject areas.

18. Students learn to apply complex problem-solving procedures and critical thinking to real-life situations.
19. Students learn to apply mathematical computations and concepts to solve problems.

20. Students reinforce science concepts related to the real world through hands-on activities.

21. Students use technology tools to communicate information to others.

22. Students locate and use a variety of resources to accomplish an assigned project.

Extra and Co-curricular Programs
Students contribute time, energy, and talents to their school and community.

23. A wide range of extracurricular activities are available to students.

24. Males and females have an equal opportunity to participate in extracurricular activities.

Staff Support for Student Learning
Staff (administrators and teachers) support the school's goals.

25. Teachers in this school are dedicated to helping all students learn.

26. The school has high academic standards for students who plan to attend two-year colleges.

27. The school has high academic standards for students who plan to attend four-year colleges.

28. This school has high academic standards for students who enter the work world.

29. Sufficient and meaningful homework is assigned by teachers.

30. Teachers let students know regularly how they are doing in class.

31. Working on group projects outside of class is a valuable learning experience.

32. All students in this school receive appropriate recognition for academic and other achievements (e.g., personal praise, assemblies, special awards, displays of work).

Parent Involvement
Parents contribute to the betterment of the school and its students.

33. Teachers at the school are accessible and willing to listen to parents.

34. Parents are encouraged to participate in classroom activities.

35. Parents are encouraged to participate in extracurricular activities.

36. Parents are well informed about school activities.

37. School administrators (principal and vice-principals) are accessible to parents.

38. Teachers are available outside of class to assist students.

39. Parents have the opportunity to be involved in helping their student select courses.

40. Teachers at this school contact parents regarding student needs.

41. Parents play an important role in the decision-making process regarding curriculum.

42. Parents play an important role in the decision-making process regarding extra-curricular activities.

Responses to the following questions will be reviewed and used for program planning:

43. What I like about Woodbury High School is:

44. What is the most practical change that could be made to improve Woodbury High School?

45. What grade level is your child? (circle one)   9   10   11   12

Curricular Special Programs

46. Is your child enrolled in:

   A.   Special Education programs   Yes   No

   If yes, does the program provide effective learning opportunities?   Yes   No

   B.   Limited English proficiency   Yes   No

   If yes, does the program provide effective learning opportunities?   Yes   No

   C.   Gifted and Talented programs   Yes   No

   If yes, does the program provide effective learning opportunities?   Yes   No

   D.   Title I (Chapter I) programs   Yes   No

   If yes, does the program provide effective learning opportunities?   Yes   No

   E.   Extracurricular programs   Yes   No

   If yes, what type of activity:

      Sports

      Music

      Drama

      Clubs

      Other: _____

Once you have gathered data through such methods as discussed above, you must use it to form and support your needs statement. The following winning example, which was for five thousand dollars, comes from a successful proposal written collaboratively between the English and English as a Second Language (ESL) departments at a high school.

Sample Needs Statement: English/ESL Computer Lab and After-School Program

Describe the proposed project. Please include a brief description of the needs that will be addressed, the project's objectives, and the activities the grant will support.

Background
Since September 1995 the Woodbury English and English as a Second Language (ESL) departments have created a new English Language computer lab in a small but ideally located room adjacent to the English and ESL offices. In only three months we have established a small but working computer center. Most all of the computers work well for basic computing—e.g., word processing—but will not allow more ambitious projects or instruction. This limitation is significant as most multimedia programs require color monitors and faster processors. We have committed ourselves to building curricular and technological bridges between departments in order to help ESL students acquire the language more quickly and succeed once they enter college prep English classes.

Needs
Our English Language Computer Lab addresses the following needs:

- Students learning to speak a new language need to be immersed in that language and have the opportunity to practice it in as many different media as possible, including but not limited to interactive computer software programs, an option our current program cannot accommodate.

- Students learning to write need to be able to revise their papers in order to become more proficient writers; linked to this is the goal in the new English curriculum for the school district that "students will practice writing as a process."

- Most ESL students do not all have access to technological tools at home; thus the school must provide this access in order to assure equal opportunity to learn about and master these essential tools for their future in order to be marketable in tomorrow's workforce.

- Students must, according to the new district English curriculum, "communicate using various media."

- Students need to collaborate on and produce authentic publications (e.g., Community Resource Directory), as recent findings by the Autodesk Foundation and the Project Based Learning Alliance have found such publications improve student performance and overall academic motivation.

Figure 8.1 shows one way of organizing and presenting your needs so they align with the application's area of focus. This discrepancy model, which contrasts where the program is with where it should be, validates the program's needs assessment as it relates directly to the scoring guide the evaluators will no doubt be using.

Technology-based Teaching and Instructional Practices (Focus Area 1)	
Present Deficits **Where We Are** • Reductionists (students can't do it) • Limited amount of technology integration in a segregated curriculum • No comprehensive and consistent professional development on current, successful strategies for technology intervention and infusion	**Project Benefits** **Where We Want to Be** • Constructivists (students can do it) • Full integration of technology into a student-centered, interdisciplinary curriculum • Cohesive professional development to make positive instructional changes for all students

High Academic Achievement / Standards (Focus Area 2)	
Present Deficits **Where We Are** • Little support for at-risk students once they move to mainstream curriculum • Vague, random, low standards and assessment strategies little use • Technological deprived • Few or not extended learning hours	**Project Benefits** **Where We Want to Be** • Teachers trained to understand and support the at-risk student, and students matched to an adult mentor to monitor progress and avoid learning pitfalls • Defined, ordered, rigorous standards using electronic portfolios • Technologically sophisticated • After school and Saturday learning opportunities to expand, enrich and bridge the instructional gaps

Strengthen Community & Business Support/Career Pathways (Focus Area 3)	
Present Deficits **Where We Are** • Low level of community involvement and understanding of education process (volunteers & business) • Limited marketing and communication skills • Fledgling school to work and business mentoring program	**Project Benefits** **Where We Want to Be** • High level of community involvement in educational process of students (volunteers & business) • High visibility and communication skills in all areas including technology • Fully operational school to work / pathways program capitalizing on community talents and resources

Reforming	Restructuring	Upgrading
• **Instructional Practices** through in-depth, on-site professional development • **Parent Involvement and Skills** through innovative Adult Education based on Epstein's Framework which includes: Parenting, Communicating, Volunteering, Learning at Home, and Working with Community	• **Technology Programs** promotes MASTERY in CORE subjects • **Curriculum and Instruction** from remediation to acceleration • **Extended Learning Opportunities** before/after school and Saturday	• **Technology Training and Usage** to strengthen academic achievement of students, to evaluate student writing with electronic portfolio • **Expanded Community Education Program** in fully functioning Technology Learning Center

FIGURE 8.1 Sample Needs Assessment: Pacific Rim Alliance

Final Thoughts

Successful students, when taking exams, learn quickly what is important, what part of the test merits the most attention. When it comes to writing proposals, the needs section is the gateway. Within this section you must accomplish all of the following in a concise, effective way:

- Identify a crucial need, one recognized as important by those within the community, the institution, and the agency to which you are applying.
- Align that need with the particular grant opportunity and the funder's vision in general.
- Gather or generate the data to support your proposal, taking pains to be sure it is accurate, current, specific, and compelling.
- Build your proposal on the need, creating a sense of urgency while at the same time communicating a sense of hope.
- Convey to your reader that your proposed project solves the problem in a new or more powerful way than others have in the past or are able to in the present and is research-based, offering others a new model to help them solve these same problems.

CHECKPOINT
Answer these questions before moving on.

- Is the answer to what you need a thing? (If yes, re-evaluate.)
- Is your "need" really a "solution," e.g., instead of saying that students need better conflict-resolution strategies (which is a need), did you say that your school needs money to create a peer remediation program (which is a solution)?
- Is your data reliable? Current? Accurate? Is there other data that might better support your argument?
- Did you discuss these needs in the context of past, present, and future efforts on your part or that of your organization?
- Is there ample evidence that you included your stakeholders or clientele in the assessment process?
- Did you double-check your proposal so far, especially the needs statement, against the rubric your readers will use to score your application?
- Do you explain how you determined your needs?
- Are your needs reasonable and appropriate?
- Does your needs statement reflect your desire to meet the needs of all your constituents?

- Does your needs section address the different needs of the community, the clients, and the agency to which you are applying (e.g., does the funding agency seek a model program that can be replicated and used to help others in the same field)?

- Did you criticize others' efforts in an attempt to elevate your own proposal? (If so, revise: funders resent this approach, especially as they might also have funded the program you are criticizing.)

- Did you align your need with the vision of the funder and the specific goals of the grant itself?

- Did you clearly emphasize the benefits of this program beyond the obvious constituents (e.g., yes, the students benefit, but will the community and its businesses also gain in the long run)?

- Do you draw your data from a variety of sources to provide a balanced picture of the scale and types of need outlined?

9

Define and Align Your Goals and Objectives

Love our principle, order our foundation,
progress our goal.
—Auguste Compte

Clarifying Terms: You Say "Objectives" and I Say "Outcomes"

Thanks to trends and reforms, confusion greets the grant seeker when he or she arrives at the goals and objectives section of the proposal application. What some people call objectives others call outcomes; what some call standards others call ESLRs (expected student learning results). And what some educators call goals, others call benchmarks or milestones. Many application guidelines offer what they think are objectives only to learn that they are instead goals or activities. Further confusion awaits the unsuspecting within categories: you find the application referring to performance objectives and instructional objectives, and to not just standards, but performance, content, and delivery standards.

Before we do anything else, then, let's define some of these terms, so that you know what they are and are not, what they do and don't look like.

Goals: Long range and general, goals are what you reach for but cannot necessarily achieve (as in Robert Browning's statement, "A man's reach should exceed his grasp, or what's a heaven for?").

Example: Students at Thurgood Marshall High School will graduate knowing how to read a wide range of challenging material in all subjects.

Objectives: The ends, the outcomes that prove you have arrived. Objectives answer the questions "Who, what, when, under what conditions, and how measured?" They:

- identify the target group that will be involved (*who*)

- describe the product to be produced or the effect to be achieved, or define the service or program to be implemented (*what*)

- state the time frame for completion (*when*)

- outline the means by which the objective will be achieved (*under what conditions*)

- explain the means of assessing achievement (*how measured*)

Example: By May 2000 (*when*), all incoming freshman students identified as "struggling readers" (*who*) (i.e., those who read two or more grade levels below ninth grade as measured by standardized test) will read (*what*) at grade level as measured (*how measured*) by the Gates-McGinitie standardized reading test.

Activities: The means by which you achieve your objectives.

Example: Students in the Reading Workshop will use the following activities to improve their reading ability by May:

- read self-selected books for twenty minutes each day (in class)
- read aloud with the teacher in one-on-one conference for ten minutes three times a week
- keep a daily reading log in which they summarize and reflect in writing on what they read that day, then predict what will happen next and explain their reasoning using examples from the text.

H O T

T I P S

Because agencies use words differently in different contexts, you should always make sure you know exactly what each funder means in their use of a term such as *outcome*. Defining terms is a good thing to do at the bidders' conference or training workshop put on by the funding agency. You can also call the funder and ask for clarification of a term when it is used in the application in a seemingly incorrect or vague way.

Goals Versus Objectives, or Vision Versus Deliverables

A great example of goals is reflected in Carol's vision to create a successful summer enrichment program for all kids K–12 that wanted to attend; not something you do in the course of a single year. Goals are the big picture, your ambitions. Objectives are the deliverable, more measurable steps on the way to realizing goals. Restated in more formal terms, a goal is a general statement that conveys an organization's long-term vision; objectives are what you or your organization expect to achieve by the end of your proposed project. Goals are the building blocks of the program's foundation, since they represent your vision and are—or should be!—directly linked to your project themes, needs, and objectives.

H O T

T I P S

We keep repeating the importance of aligning your themes, needs, goals, objectives, activities, and budget, because any proposal that lacks internal cohesion will appear inadequate alongside a better-organized, more carefully written proposal, even if the ideas are not as good as yours. The grant seeker perceived by the funder as more organizationally capable will be seen as having thought things through more carefully, and will therefore have the competetive edge.

Typically, each major program component—staff development, program development, the client, agency growth—will be paired with a corresponding goal and several measurable objectives. The goals and objectives provide the funder with insight into your expectations, capabilities, ingenuity, and values as they reveal, through your choices and programmatic emphases, the quality of your overall plan of operation. You want to achieve a balance between ambition and realism, all of which communicates to the funder that their money will be well spent if they invest in your proposed product, service, program, or facility.

The following two examples show the difference between a goal statement and an objectives statement. The goal example, taken from a winning elementary school literacy grant application, shows a categorical approach to the statement of goals. Your ability to organize your goals this way will depend, of course, on the application guidelines of your particular funder.

You can find an annotated, complete literacy grant on the CD-ROM.

LEARNING LINKS

Sample Goals: Literacy Grant

ASSESSMENT GOALS

K–2	To refine our assessment tools
Grade 3	To refine and expand our assessment tools
Grades 4 & 5	To develop and implement uniform methods of assessing individual programs and needs

TRAINING GOALS

K–2	To further refine our skills in early literacy practices
Grade 3	To refine existing early literacy practices and learn other techniques that deliver powerful reading instruction to every child
Grades 4 & 5	To acquire techniques in the best literacy practices for students in the upper grades
Others (Parents, Volunteers, and Staff)	To provide our volunteers and parent community with a common language and understanding in supporting literacy acquisition.

MATERIAL GOALS	
K–2	To supplement existing materials and assessment tools
Grade 3	To supplement existing materials and assessment tools
Grades 4 & 5	To acquire materials that support children's varied needs
Others (Parents, Volunteers, and Staff)	To provide additional reference materials for staff, parents, and volunteers

The second example comes from a state health care proposal.

Sample Objectives: Health Care Proposal

By January 2000 (*when*), Kennedy Middle School (*who*), given the resources, time, and training (*under what conditions*), will:

- develop statewide standards for the health and education of young adolescents; and
- create access routes to comprehensive health services and health education in middle school grades as evidenced by communication maps and increased network alliances.

H O T

TIPS

When seeking letters of endorsement from administrators, community leaders, or clients in support of your proposal, be sure that they can refer specifically to those goals and objectives outlined in your proposal, and show how their resources will be committed to the successful implementation of your project. This dramatically increases the credibility of the proposal in the reader's eyes, as those who will help implement it, along with those who will be helped by the proposed program, can publicly and articulately speak in support of its goals and objectives.

Creating Effective Objectives

An objective defines an outcome that supports one of the proposal's focus areas (e.g., safety), needs (e.g., "reduce crime by and against youth in the community"), and goals (e.g., "provide enrichment opportunities for kids"). You are most likely writing objectives if they say things like "to increase," "to produce," or "to service." Goals, on the other hand, would say, "to provide," "to understand," or "to recognize." In *Preparing*

Instructional Objectives, Robert Mager provides the following comparison of phrasing:

WORDS OPEN TO MANY INTERPRETATIONS (GOALS)

- to know
- to understand
- to *really* understand
- to appreciate
- to *fully* appreciate
- to grasp the significance of
- to enjoy
- to believe
- to have faith in
- to internalize

WORDS OPEN TO FEWER INTERPRETATIONS (OBJECTIVES)

- to write
- to read
- to identify
- to sort
- to solve
- to construct
- to build
- to compare
- to contrast
- to smile
- to draw

Mager suggests and warns that objectives such as the following actually undermine your proposal due to their lack of clarity and measurability:

- manifest an increasingly comprehensive understanding
- demonstrate a thorough comprehension

The following questions offer another way to better understand objectives; each questions evokes some aspect of what amounts to a good objective:

- When (will the objective be met)? (*e.g., by January 2001*)
- Who (will participate in or benefit from this program)? (*e.g., 85% of Aspen's senior community over age 60*)

- What (will they do to demonstrate their learning/progress)? (*e.g., will participate in at least two senior support programs or enrichment activities*)
- Under what conditions (will this objective be met)? (*e.g., given the launch of the senior council and its six-month marketing campaign targeted at those over sixty*)
- How (will progress toward this objective be measured)? (*e.g., participation logs, surveys, and random sampling conducted by the XYZ Institute*) (Mager 1984)

Sample Objectives: California Department of Education Title VII Proposal

The best way to assess an objective is to look at one and apply our criteria (the questions "Who, what, when, under what conditions, and how measured?") to it. The following example comes from a California Department of Education (CDE) Title VII Sample Training Proposal and focuses on Limited English Proficiency (LEP) students. The added parentheticals show where and how these questions are answered.

Given new program courses and resource support (*under what conditions*), originally classified LEP pupils (*who*) within five years will meet academic requirements for grade-level promotion in the same proportion and to the same degree as students who are native speakers of English (*what*) as measured by group grade point average (GPA) in academic core courses of language arts, mathematics, science, and social studies (*how*). Annual (*when*) benchmark projections for meeting the objective are:

- First year pupils GPA 1.50 (baseline for LEP students spring 1999)
- Second year GPA 1.75
- Third year GPA 2.0
- Fourth year GPA 2.25 (baseline for English speakers spring 1999)
- Fifth year GPA 2.25 or higher

Here is a second example, taken from the same training sample:

By the project's end (*when*) 80 percent of the identified students (*who*) will increase their primary language proficiency (*what*) as a consequence of new courses (*under what conditions*) as measured by

- an increase of one level per year in the START 9 Achievement Test (*how*)
- an increase of three NCEs annually in reading and language on the APRENDA Test (*how*)
- an increase in writing scores using the district-approved scoring rubric (1–5) (*how*)

Potential funders require measurable outcomes and objectives. Too often proposal writers offer goals as objectives and, as a consequence, your proposal receives low scores from the funder. To determine whether you are on the right path, ask the following questions of your objectives:

- Who is your target audience (e.g., seniors, youth, third-grade students) or client?
- Is your objective too specific, too limited in scope, or does it measure process rather than outcomes (e.g., "by June the department will have attended six workshops")?
- What will a successful proposal (for this specific organization) do?
- Under what conditions will it do this?
- Does the statement have a measurable moment?
- Do you offer evaluation strategies that show what will be accomplished by a stated point in time?
- How well must it be done (see the funder's criteria)?
- When will you be ready to conduct summative evaluation?

Remember, if your objective is too limited (e.g., "staff will participate in six workshops by June"), it is most likely a process objective or an activity. If it is too general (e.g., "we will have a safe community") it is a goal. An objective must describe an expected behavior adjustment.

H O T

T I P S

Review our last example to make sure that you know the five elements (who, what, when, under what conditions, and how measured) of a well-written performance outcome:

By June (*when*) the English department (*who*), after receiving in-service in the use of newly acquired hardware and software (*under what conditions*), will integrate technology more effectively and frequently into the curriculum (*what*) as evidenced by the design and implementation of two instructional units that effectively integrate these new technology tools (computers, Internet, digital cameras, scanners, publication software, etc.) into the unit. Successful implementation will be determined by colleague observation, student surveys, department publications, and unit plans (*how measured*).

Finally, there are a few other characteristics of well-written objectives which, together, can make a difference. Objectives are

- aligned with the themes/areas of focus, needs, goals, scoring rubric, and guidelines used to evaluate your proposal
- written using active verbs and parallel structure (e.g., if presented in a list, each objective begins with a verb)
- reasonable and appropriate
- achievable in a limited amount of time
- written in measurable language (e.g., "at least 80 percent of all participants will achieve a score of three or higher on the state exam")
- specific, detailing the type, amount, frequency
- visually emphasized within the text (e.g., set off by a bullet or number which can be easily aligned to the goals when you list those out)

Goals and Objectives: Additional Considerations

A survey of instructional techniques reveals a variety of styles and approaches, all of which demand that lessons—in this case proposals, which put forth arguments much as a teacher does a lesson—have objectives. These objectives contain other components apart from those discussed above. One of these is the audience to be addressed. What considerations must you make when it comes to stating your objectives to this particular audience (of readers from the community, a corporation, the government, a private foundation)? Another component is the behavior, or what some call the desired performance or outcome. The behavior must be described in precise, active verbs so that the reader knows exactly what is being said; the words *appreciate, enjoy,* and *know* do not say anything concrete or measurable. Certain conditions—equipment, information, skills—might also be necessary to achieving the goals and objectives. In more informal discussions these conditions are sometimes called "the givens," which implies that the asker is able to provide a certain level of support to implement and sustain the funder's investment in the program. Finally, the criteria or degree used to measure an objective's success should be spoken of in measurable terms of how fast, how well, how precisely you expect the individual or program to perform the desired behavior.

Just as a powerful lesson or argument demand a strong statement, a compelling opening to ensure the audience's attention, so too do proposals. As mentioned earlier, your readers look to your vision and goals for proof of your ambition, and to your objectives, methods, and activities for proof of your capacity and creativity. Either way, you must reflect on your proposal as you write it, studying it yourself as the reader would to find and be able to emphasize those moments of heat, those moments of power that all writers try to create and all readers look for.

What you propose—your objectives, methods, activities, programs, and services—must be sustainable; this element must shine through. When Ross Perot sought the presidency, reporters continually asked him what he would do if elected. His telling response was: Everyone knows there's rooms piled high with great ideas that no one ever followed through on, that people piloted and never kept going. Your goals, objectives, methods, and activities for achieving your ends must have built into them the promise that you can and will ensure that your proposed project (e.g., service learning program, computer lab, reading program, Fulbright study, or sabbatical) will last and contribute to the larger community over time, long after the funding period has run out. Think of it this way: most foundations and corporations would like to imagine that their investment is ensuring their own legacy within the community they try to serve. Certainly the Gap Foundation wants positive public attention for its million-dollar contribution to support an elementary school in San Francisco, but it also wants to accomplish more than selling a few more pairs of khakis. It wants the kids at that urban school to get the education they need to be successful in life. Certainly Apple's corporate goals call for increased sales of its computers, which the Roosevelt Elementary School's Apple Technology Grant purchased, but more importantly Apple seeks to improve communities by bringing different groups and generations together through that technology and achieving a goal more noble than a sale. That's what philanthropy is all about.

CHECKPOINT

Answer these questions before moving on.

GOALS

- Did you check your goals against the scoring rubric or the criteria scoring guide your readers are likely to use when evaluating your proposal? Do they flow from your themes and needs statements?

- Did you specifically identify the population that will benefit from the project goals?

- Do the goals truly align with your organization's vision and values?

- Are the goals of this project applicable to and appropriate for a wider audience? (You need ask this only if one of the implied or stated goals of the agency is replicability.)

OBJECTIVES

- Are your objectives aligned with the funder's values and requirements outlined in the application guidelines?

- Do your proposal objectives match up with your project's goals?

- Do your objectives sound like activities? (They should not!)

- Have you clearly defined the client or target audience?

- Does the funder know under what constraints or conditions these outcomes will be achieved and evaluated?

- Do your objectives clearly state the criteria for success and the deadline when they should be met?

- Are the results quantifiable?

10

Describe Your Methods, Activities, Management Plan, and Timeline

*Any enterprise is built by wise planning, becomes
strong through common sense, and profits
wonderfully by keeping abreast of the facts.*
—*Proverbs 24:3–4*

**WORDS
TO KNOW**

activities

landscape

management plan

methods

portrait

Previous chapters have helped you assess your existing conditions and identify what you want to accomplish and why you need to accomplish it. The next chapter, on evaluation, will help you determine the strategies and tools you will use to accomplish it. This chapter helps you decide on and describe the methods, activities, management plans, and timelines that will allow you to address your needs, and establish and work toward your goals and objectives. If your stockbroker says that he will make you a lot of money if you trust him with your ten thousand dollars, he might get your attention, but you won't really be able to trust him until he explains how he is going to accomplish it and why he has chosen that method; and, since it is your hard-earned money, you will expect his plans to make sense. You don't want to hear that he has a nose for the ponies, or that he's just learned how to buy stocks on-line and is excited about the prospect. This analogy reinforces an aspect of grant seeking you can never lose sight of: funders are the real clients and they want good return on their investment, because your success or failure is a measure of their integrity and an expression of their core values.

Many proposal writers run into trouble during this section of the development because of the way the application guideline questions or instructions are worded. Many applications simply ask you to outline your major activities. A typical response might look like this:

- purchase necessary equipment
- hire project staff
- design evaluation plan
- conduct appropriate training
- administer formative evaluations
- implement new curriculum and integrate with technology
- take field trips
- conduct summative evaluation and submit

Such a list might seem to satisfy the application's demands, but it is insufficient. In order to create a powerful, competitive proposal, you must address five separate areas, each one important to your proposal's success:

1. define methods (what your research means, your strategies for achieving outcomes; see p. 85)
2. describe activities (how exactly you will accomplish your project/goal/outcome)
3. establish management plan (who is responsible)
4. present timeline (when exactly you will accomplish your project/goal/outcome)

5. identify evaluation moments/management (when and who will see that your project/objective/outcome is accomplished)

These five components make up a complete and competitive methods and activities section. We will discuss each one separately so as to detail its necessary elements, but remember that they work together to form a collective response to the funder.

Define Your Methods

Always written as a narrative (never a chart), this portion spells out the what and why; put another way, it is the rationale for your approach. This moment provides you an important opportunity to talk to your funder and revisit your site needs, relevant research, challenges and as-sets, as well as your understanding of the problem and the rationale for your solutions. This is your big chance to convince the funder that you have studied what is being done in the wider world, and integrated into your proposed method those "best practices" that will help you achieve your goals and objectives in a way that remains consistent with your in-dividual or organizational vision, needs, goals, and objectives.

H O T

T I P S

Readers and prospective funders want to know that you have done your homework. Your exhaustive investigation into what does and doesn't work, if effectively discussed in your proposal, increases the credibility of you and your ideas and solutions. This is a crucial fac-tor in successful proposals, for even if "evidence of research into other methodologies" is not on the reader's rubric, it is likely to be in his or her mind as an expectation.

The development team faces a difficult decision at this point in the process: should your method be "cutting edge" or "traditional" in its approach? One way to answer this question is to revisit not only the ap-plication guidelines but the funder's annual reports, tax report 990PF, and other available resources to see how the funder presents itself and who it funds. A computer industry expert, for example, has described Microsoft not as a race car but as equivalent to a Lincoln Continental (i.e., a classic, dependable, elite). This analogy illustrates that the com-pany honors performance over potential, rigor over risk, delivery over dazzle. One high school we worked with, a school identifying itself as a "traditional school," was unsuccessful in its million-dollar reform ef-fort primarily because the high-tech corporate funders saw "tradi-tional" as contradicting the very values on which the grant was based. Had the school's grant seekers read through the guidelines more closely to see how the corporate funders described their initiative, they would have realized this and either chosen not to apply or not to identify the organization as "a traditional school."

Another problem some applicants encounter at this stage of development is that the application usually provides an activity form to fill out instead of allowing you to come up with your own format and form. While you must obviously conform to the funder's requirements in this situation, you can work around this obstacle by looking for opportunities that enable you to weave in these five crucial components. If the form leaves no space for a management plan, discuss it in the methods section (briefly, if it is a question you have already addressed). If it omits discussion of a timeline, try to blend that into another answer. Look for other places to address your ideas or philosophical foundations (e.g., methods) so that the reader can gain a more complete picture of what you are trying to do—and why—despite the limitations of the form. Of course such additions should not be conspicuous but should, somehow, grow naturally out of the required categories and questions so that your responses match the application format and scoring rubric.

Describe Your Activities

Most writers are comfortable describing in general terms what they will do, but as the example at the beginning of this chapter shows, most applicants have trouble being as specific as they need to be for this component. Certainly it can be difficult, even impossible, to say, for example, how much training the staff will need in order to accomplish the successful integration of technology into the curriculum, but you need to take at least an educated guess. Below are three alternatives and how they rate.

Poor: We will conduct four training sessions.

Better: We will conduct four training sessions in computer integration.

Best: All site staff will participate in four training sessions in the following areas of technology: word processing and graphic design (conducted by Expert A), using the Internet in research and instruction (conducted by Expert B), creating multimedia presentations (conducted by Expert C), and making effective presentations (conducted by Expert D).

LEARNING LINKS

See Chapter 18 (Workshop 2), "Designing Winning Documents," for more ideas about laying out your activity charts.

Several points warrant consideration when it comes to actually designing an activity chart. Some readers resent having to turn a page sideways to read landscape (e.g., $11'' \times 8.5''$ as opposed to $8.5'' \times 11''$) charts; however, producing an activity chart in landscape format (i.e., so that you have to look at the page lengthwise) allows you to incorporate that much more information in a less dense manner for increased readability. If you're not sure how to format these charts, consult the funder or previous winners to see what is permissible and competitive.

Whichever way you decide is best for you, consider the following example based on the categories common to most applications:

Major Activity	Goal	Person(s) Responsible	Timeline
Field Trip to Zoo	1 & 2	T, A, S, P	March, May

Such a simple format allows readers to see all the information at once, giving them a sense of the whole project and how it ties together. Such an organizational device has the added benefit of forcing the writer(s) to be sure they have all their bases covered. The example above also shows the extent to which your activities and objectives are aligned with the management plan, and how much time is allotted to achieve them. The only confusion you encountered when reading the previous example was "T, A, S, P." "What is TASP?" you wondered. This is why every chart must have a legend, which most readers will expect to find at the bottom of the chart, although where you place it is not important so long as it is clear for the reader to consult. All of these features, to the extent that they address the funder's guidelines and anticipate their needs when reading the document, will further enhance your organizational or individual capability in the eyes of the reader. Organization in any domain inspires confidence in other realms, which may not be directly assessed but are nonetheless always on the reader's and funder's mind.

Identify Your Evaluation Moments/Management

Much of what will be discussed in the next chapter on project evaluation should be reflected in the activity chart so as to show how each activity will not only relate to your project's goals but be evaluated for its effectiveness. Formative evaluations are conducted throughout the project implementation period and these checkpoints along the way should be clearly indicated in the activity chart to further reinforce the notion of accountability. Also included in the timeline should be those points in time by which you will: (1) design the evaluation tools, (2) schedule formative evaluation of assessment tools and progress toward the goals and objectives, and (3) design pre- and post-assessment measures that will be used to develop the summative evaluation report at the completion of the implementation period. A detailed activity chart includes the major formative and summative assessment and evaluation activities to show that your organization has thought this most important proposal section through.

> The organizational chart shown in Figure 10.1 evokes a sense of confidence in evaluators: Everything in the chart conveys competence, organization, and sustainability. These characteristics are just what the evaluating readers will want to see, especially since this was a proposal for a multimillion-dollar project. This chart is designed to explain visually who is involved, at what levels, and in what capacities.

Establish Your Management Plan

Who will monitor or supervise this project, decide about methods, carry out these activities? This answer tends to be either very simple or extremely complicated, the difference often depending on the scale of the proposed project. Understand that the reader will want the project to be managed by someone—or a group—who can bring consistent and quality attention to the task. Thus, identifying the nonprofit director, the board of trustees, or the principal as the supervisor is often a mistake, as they have ample responsibilities in their professional lives and cannot realistically take on the day-to-day administration of such a large project, unless project management is in their job description and is relatively easy to do. Much better, much more competitive, is to say that the project will be managed by a project team, an implementation team, or a site council that represents different interests—e.g., community, students, stakeholders, staff, administrators. Not only will this imply greater stakeholder and network support for your proposal, it will suggest increased accountability at the site level, since the review team exists solely to implement the proposal.

Certainly not all projects will require a management team. A five-thousand–dollar grant to purchase musical equipment for the school band or classrooms does not normally call for high levels of supervision. However, it might make your application more competitive to say that the school site council or the Music Boosters will see that the musical equipment is successfully integrated into the music program or curriculum, and the necessary staff training will be offered and assessed. The funder feels more comfortable and confident if there is a clearly established management process in place; sometimes this will even appear as a question on the application, asking that you:

- define your management plan
- identify key personnel
- outline their qualifications and responsibilities

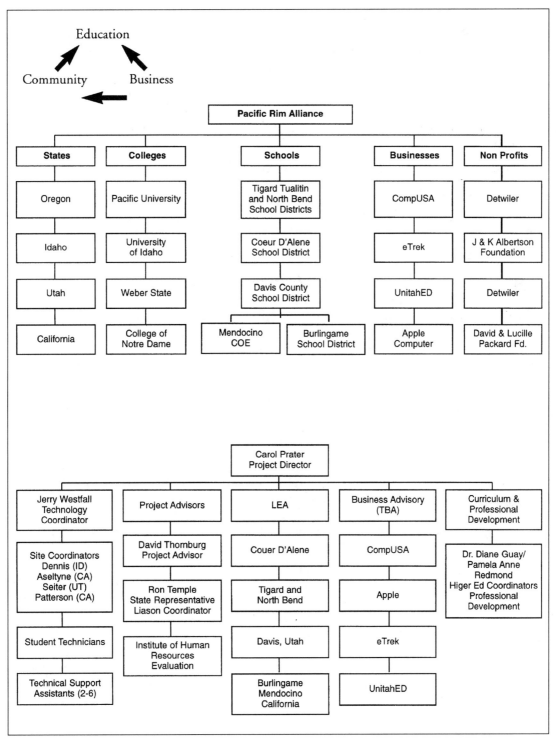

FIGURE 10.1   Sample Organizational Chart: Pacific Rim Alliance

When developing your management plan, you should be aware of several possible complications or obstacles that you need to address ahead of time so that you can respond knowledgeably to the funder's inquiries should they arise later. These complications include such issues as:

- conflicts with union or other organization contracts
- conflicts between proposed responsibilities and the established union contract and job description
- confusion about what participants are actually expected to do versus what they are willing to do once the project begins
- potential implementation difficulties if a part of the project is contingent on other funding sources which may not be secured at the time you submit your application

Present Your Timeline

This portion of the application answers one simple question: when will each major activity begin and end? Timeline increments are usually stated in months, beginning with the first month of the proposal's implementation (as required by the guidelines). There are usually three types of calendar formats and you must know which one your funder requires:

Fiscal year: July 1 to June 30

Academic year: September 1 to August 30

Calendar year: January 1 to December 30

The timeline often starts and ends with the academic year in the case of schools, although this might vary if your proposal called for summer training to begin in July so that staff would be ready for implementation in September. Another tip: If you are proposing a multiyear project, each year, if possible, should have its own timeline (and be clearly identified as such, e.g., Year One). It is much easier to graph the months, as seen in Figure 18.3 in "Designing Winning Documents." The chart in Figure 18.3 helps the reader see which activities are happening concurrently and independently. Again, it is important to be as specific as possible in your timeline, even if you must make an educated guess, since timelines should convey a sense of order, organization, and capability to the reader, participants, and funder.

CHECKPOINT
Answer these questions before moving on.

Go through the following list to determine whether you need to or have already:

- checked the application guidelines' requirements for methods and activities data against your chart design, making sure to follow the prescribed format requirements if defined

- discussed your methods in the context of current research and past experience within the focus areas

- explained your methods and the rationale in sufficient detail, remembering to explain to the reader the benefits of this approach

- stated the rationale for your particular methods and activities (aka, plan of operation)

- stated your activities in the most specific language possible

- presented the activities in a sequence that makes sense and suggests incremental development

- identified a management team (if appropriate) whose primary responsibility is the implementation of this project

- determined whether the methods and activities are consistent with the values of the funder and your own institution

- defined a timeline by months beginning with the first eligible and required month

- anticipated and addressed any potential conflicts, including staff and union issues

- explained how the methods and activities will change if or when the performance and needs of the stakeholders change

- described how these methods and activities will be integrated into the existing program and culture after the grant funding ceases, so as to sustain the program or enhancements and benefits after the funding cycle is completed.

Join "The Tech Trek"

*Technology—
hardware, software,
training
and education*

11

Create Your
Evaluation Plan
and
Assessment Tools

*Make no little plans; they have no
magic to stir men's blood.
—Daniel Hudson Burnham*

If previous chapters have asked you to figure out what your needs are, where you want to go, and how you can best get there, this chapter helps you answer another essential question: How will you know when you have arrived at your desired destination? When it comes to evaluation, however, we must ask other questions such as these:

- If we did not get the outcomes we expected, how did that happen?

- How can we use the formative evaluation information we gathered to improve our future performance and activity selection?

- For what other purposes might we use the evaluation information?

- Do we need outside assistance to evaluate and validate our progress?

Other questions, of a more practical nature, will come up later, but these help to set the stage for the work at hand. What this section of your proposal narrative must accomplish is vital in the long run to your proposal's success, for it is by these plans and tools that the funder—along with you and your other stakeholders—will determine the ultimate success of the project. You must, through your evaluation plan, your assessment strategies, and tools, measure the difference between what you said you would accomplish (your stated objective[s]) and your interim progress and final result (actual outcome[s]). Thus from the beginning of your work on this section, you must consider the integrity of not only your original assessment data, but the means by which the proposal assessment data is gathered and the tools and format through which it is communicated. Think of it this way: you would not give a stockbroker ten thousand dollars to invest if he said little more than, "Hey, really you can trust me! Give me the money and I will do some good things with it and will let you know how it turns out," especially if his evaluation was simply a post card that said, "Your investment is doing just great, don't worry!"

> **WORDS TO KNOW**
>
> assessment
>
> evaluation
>
> formative evaluation
>
> intervention
>
> summative evaluation

Evaluation is so important, and in some cases so complicated, that organizations sometimes hire outside evaluation consultants to oversee this aspect of the design and implementation process.

H O T

TIPS

Types of Evaluation: Formative and Summative

Evaluation must yield a variety of types of information because it nearly always serves multiple purposes. Funders want a careful and insightful accounting of their investment; stakeholders and colleagues often want to see evidence of progress before supporting future projects or continuing current ones. Such data as evaluation yields is used to persuade board members, prospective clients, even voters, of the value certain

products, programs, or projects offer. Their votes, membership, resources, or participation often depends, moreover, on the quality and
integrity of that data, since, as everyone knows, you can "cook the
books" to make anything look good. Ours is a skeptical age, but one
that loves genuine progress and strong evidence of improvement.

H O T

T I P S

Some data may emerge throughout your implementation period
that you had not anticipated, what some call "rich data." You must
always be on the lookout for data to help you improve or better
understand the implications of your proposed project. An example
might be a student who, after participating in a service learning
program, says casually to the program director, "I never planned to
go to college, but after working with these kids I'm thinking of becoming a teacher so I applied." Also, one must look for patterns
within the data: e.g., increased ambition, increased attendance, evidence of improved self-esteem or personal responsibility.

Developing and Using Formative Evaluation Tools

Formative evaluation provides information throughout the project and
is typically used to improve the design or implementation of the proposed project or program. Examples of formative evaluations might include surveys, observations, portfolios, journals, discussions, or
video/audio recordings used during the implementation process. Formative assessments should be used during the developmental stages of
any proposal, and should be seen as an integral part of the actual implementation design meant to constantly improve your organizational capability and capacity by learning from itself. Think of it as the
comments customers write and drop in the suggestion box in the lobby.
The bottom line is to improve the service, the product, the experience.
Taken a step further, formative evaluations are designed to *improve* not
prove performance.

Such evaluation strategies are more common as grant recipients are
held increasingly accountable for not only the money invested by the
funder but also the results promised. Your formative and summative
evaluation strategies and tools also help to determine the quality of certain methods, or types of intervention, as well as the worth of products,
programs, or services.

To collect evaluation data, however, one needs tools or instruments
that answer a few questions:

- Who will be evaluated? (e.g., stakeholders, staff, products, process)

- What are the proposal goals and objectives? (e.g., increase
  participation, improve reading skills, improve ease of use)

- What should be evaluated? (e.g., instructor's success, program's effectiveness, change in behavior, students' performance)

- What data should be collected? (e.g., frequency, amount, speed)

- Who will be responsible for making the evaluation decisions regarding collection, interpretation, dissemination, design, and subsequent revisions of the evaluation plan?

- What tools will yield the most credible information with the greatest efficiency and reliability? (e.g., tests, field notes, databases, video and audio recordings, observations, portfolios, surveys, interviews, focus groups)

- How and when will you obtain the necessary information? (e.g., weekly or daily, at the beginning of the period or at the end, in groups or individually)

- How revisable is your project, your instructional method, your product, the environment in which the program is implemented?

- Why are you evaluating this proposal at this particular time? (e.g., to determine status, to measure progress, to establish routine for subsequent [and more consequential] evaluations, to maintain accountability [of participants, staff, other stakeholders])

Refer to the Sample Data-Gathering Tool developed by parents to identify the needs of the school described in Chapter 8. While this assessment instrument was used to identify needs and thereby give focus to the subsequent report, it could just as easily be used to pre- and post-evaluate the school's success in specific areas identified in the previous report (i.e., as a measure of the progress that had been made toward those objectives or recommendations offered by the accreditation committee).

Such thorough and integrated formative and summative evaluation builds confidence in your organization and project as it shows you are committed to improving, are willing to "ask the hard questions." These reflective questions also have other benefits since they:

- help the project participants maintain or even improve their performance by raising consciousness about their needs and objectives by reminding them what they are supposed to be doing and why.

- raise awareness in other, nonparticipating departments, about what they are doing—or should be doing—and why they should be doing it.

- validate the project's worth by creating special attention, which increases the participants' commitment to making it a success.

- help the funder determine whether to continue—or even expand—funding of the project, creating a sense of momentum that other funders sometimes want to supplement through further investment.

Figure 11.1 illustrates the different roles formative and summative evaluation play in the course of implementing a project. It also emphasizes the systemic nature of such processes and the role analysis plays as projects move from one form of evaluation to another.

Research in various domains—education, business, health care, sports—consistently validates the importance of feedback built into any process. Such design considerations are not only efficient but healthy. As Daniel Goleman writes in *Working with Emotional Intelligence* (1998),

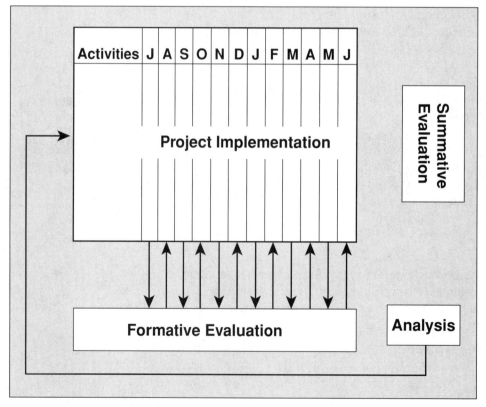

FIGURE 11.1   The Relationship of Project Implementation to Project Evaluation (This model was developed by John Cradler and Ruthmary Cordon-Cradler for their book, *An Educator's Guide for Developing and Funding Educational Technology Solutions.*)

Any organization is "cybernetic," which means being engaged in continuous and overlapping feedback loops, gathering information from within and without and adjusting operations accordingly. Systems theory tells us that in an environment of turbulent change and competition, the entity that can take in information most widely, learn from it most thoroughly, and respond most nimbly, creatively, and flexibly will be the most adaptive. (p. 298)

Goleman goes on to say that such "flexibility," the capacity to be "adaptive," is a sign of great individual and organizational health, for these abilities to respond, change, and improve give them a sense of power, the knowledge that the individual or organization can always become better. Peter Senge, author of *The Fifth Discipline: The Art and Practice of the Learning Organization* (1990), reinforces the importance of feedback and ongoing evaluation in organizations, writing "There are also 'virtuous cycles'—processes that reinforce in desired directions. . . . In business we know that 'momentum is everything,' in building confidence in a new product or within a fledgling organization" (p. 83).

Few books better demonstrate the power of using assessment data to improve performance than Mike Schmoker's *Results: The Key to Continuous School Improvement* (1996). In his chapter titled "Performance Data," Schmoker writes, "They introduced many interventions, including a system in which students had to demonstrate competency in writing, reading, and mathematics before graduating to the next level. Students had to move up before moving on. . . . The system enables students to know how they are performing, which helps them focus on continually improving" (p. 29). Schmoker used such data not only to improve reading performance for students across his district but to receive and increase fiscal investment in his programs, which the government was pleased to do given the evidence (and obvious integrity) of his evaluation strategies, collection tools, and assessment data regarding student performance.

Anticipating the subsequent discussion of summative evaluation, we can offer no better example than Schmoker's book itself, which offers his concluding evaluation and summative proof of what his program accomplished over several years, as compared to the interim measures provided by formative evaluations of progress from one semester or year to the next.

H O T

T I P S

Sample Formative Evaluation Plans

The evaluation plan shown in Figure 11.2 comes from a California Department of Education (CDE) Title VII training proposal, several portions of which have been examined elsewhere in this book. Not only is the information succinct and valuable, the format itself helps to emphasize the clarity of the organization's process, something that cannot help but impress a reader who will find it that much easier to grasp the CDE's point.

Evaluation of Project Objectives

OBJECTIVE	EVALUATION PROCEDURE	TIMELINE/PERSONNEL
1.1 LEP Student L1 Reading Performance	Administer Prueba de Lectores (standardized, norm-referenced examination) and miscue analysis in Spanish	Annually in May Classroom Teachers
1.2 LEP Student Gains in English Proficiency	Administer SOLOM (Student Oral Language Observation Matrix), district writing sample, and miscue analysis.	Quarterly in September, November, February, and May Classroom Teachers
1.3 Overall LEP Academic Performance	Compile semester GPAs for each grade level cohort of participants	Each semester Project Evaluator
2.1 Teacher Spanish Proficiency	Administer TOLOM (Teacher Oral Language Observation Matrix) during lesson observations of teachers participating in Spanish language development courses.	June of each year Resource Teacher
2.2 Teacher Proficiency in L1 and SDAIE Classroom Practices	Administer TAP (Teacher Proficiency Assessment) to teachers-in-training during classroom observations.	Once each semester Project Coordinator and Project Evaluator
3.1 Parent English Proficiency	Administer Oral Language Observation Matrix during lesson observation of parents participating in ESL courses	Twice during each 8 week course Class Instructor
3.2 Parent L1 Literacy	Evaluate parent-developed L1 books using district-developed literacy inventory	Once for each of five "best" books as selected by parents Resource Teacher

All analyses will provide individual and group results and will show gains in (1) reaching "proficient" or "satisfactory" level and (2) closing gap between target students and English only peers, where appropriate. Source: California Department of Education January 1997.

FIGURE 11.2   Sample Evaluation Plan

Project SITE (Science Integrates Technology Effectively)

The following example was part of a winning federal grant that allowed several different school districts to integrate science and human services through a collaboration with the outside organizations. It is formatted differently than the previously shown plan, though a careful examination of the writing reveals a tight organization within the paragraph.

Process Evaluation: The products of the project will include: (1) science skills scope and sequence with a cross-index matrix, (2) criterion-referenced measures, (3) teacher's resource guide, and (4) an implementation and training guide, which will be evaluated for "face" validity by at least twenty teachers. The feedback will provide, in part, the basis for program revision. An evaluation form will be designed for face-validity evaluation. Upon implementation, teachers will evaluate all aspects of the training session as well as completing a criterion checklist to indicate their perceptions of the changes in student performance.

Product Evaluation: A pre-post comparison group design will provide student impact data which will determine the effects of combining computer-based instruction on student performance. The assessment of student performance will be based on: (1) criterion-referenced measures of science skills, (2) normed measures of science skills and related critical thinking skills. The evaluation design will separately show the effects of (1) teacher-based instruction, (2) computer-based instruction, (3) teacher-based combined with computer-based instruction, and (4) an absence of specific instruction in critical-thinking skills (control groups). This design would include students from grades 3 to 6 enrolled in four elementary schools in two districts located within South San Francisco Unified School District and the Burlingame School District. A final case study of the project that is suitable for widespread distribution and possible utilization of individual schools, school districts, and educational policy makers.

These two examples illustrate nearly all the principles outlined in this chapter so far. They both:

- structure the evaluation and yield data that can be used for multiple purposes to improve the programs, refine their methods and activities, assess the programs' effectiveness, and hold the stakeholders accountable
- show for each objective the following:
  - who will be responsible for implementing and monitoring evaluation activities
  - what strategies and collection tool(s) will be used
  - what assessment data will be collected (and by what method)
  - when the assessment will be conducted
  - how the data will be analyzed and interpreted

- how the results will be compiled and the outcomes reported
- how the results will be used to improve the project during the period for which the program receives funding
- explain the responsibilities of the evaluator, staff members, and stakeholders who will conduct and participate in the evaluations
- identify how they will measure progress toward meeting national or state standards as described in a governmental or research document (i.e., Goals 2000 and Title 1 state-level plan).
- explain how they will compare one group (e.g., Limited English Proficiency (LEP) participants and non-LEP students) in specific areas such as:
  - school retention
  - academic achievement
  - gain in English-language development
  - native language proficiency (where appropriate)
- explain how they will measure and report program results such as:
  - appropriateness of the curriculum as it relates to grade-level and course requirements
  - program management
  - staff development, including language instruction
- identify and explain how they will report on program content indicators that describe the relationship of the funded activities to the overall program and other federal, state, or local programs

Review of the Formative Evaluation Process

The following model comes from John and Ruthmary Cradler's *Educator's Guide for Developing and Funding Educational Technology Solutions* (1994). The Cradlers, who have written grants of every size, for every purpose, in just about every state, describe the evaluation planning process this way:

1. Define project component outcome indicators.
   - curriculum component
   - learning resources management
   - staff development component
   - other components
2. Identify target participants.
   - students (clients)
   - staff (or volunteers)
   - others (stakeholders, support network)

3. Identify data sources.
   - qualitative
   - quantitative
4. Determine when to collect data.
   - pre-post
   - interim
   - post only
5. Define support and implementation indicators.
   - planning and monitoring
   - implementation
   - curriculum alignment
   - staff development resources
   - learning/technology resources
   - constraints and support factors
6. Manage the evaluation.
   - collect data
   - score data
   - analyze data and information
7. Report results and analysis.
8. Use the findings to suggest project (and process) changes.
9. Begin the formative evaluation process again at the appropriate time in order to maintain accountability and continually improve results.

Remember throughout the evaluation process that your answers (and thus your data) can only be as clear as your assessment strategies, tools, and questions allow. It is always a good habit to try out your evaluation tools on a few participants for feedback before actually using the tools to see if they provide the feedback you require. Watch carefully for confusion in their responses. If you continually have to explain what a question means, revise it or drop it. Avoid ambiguous or negative language.

HOT
TIPS

Designing and Conducting Summative Evaluations

Though it has been alluded to throughout the last section of the chapter, summative evaluation is different from formative evaluation in several important ways. Instead of being ongoing, it takes place at the end of the implementation funding cycle. It usually concentrates on the product, clients, program improvement, or services instead of the process: regardless of what methods and activities you used, did you achieve your objectives and predicted outcomes? Have services improved? Products been developed? Facilities renovated? Obviously if the answer is yes, the next question is: How well did you accomplish that? Have you solved the problem? Addressed the proposal needs? Adopted better methods? Raised standards?

You might begin your summative evaluation—which, by the way, can use data from all the other measurements and methods discussed under formative evaluation—by reviewing your stated objectives. At the end of the funding cycle, you will, for example, be expected to present your summative results to the funder, the governing board, the community, or even at a conference where people have come to learn from you how to accomplish these same results in their own towns or organizations. Considered from another perspective, you might use the summative findings to do any of the following: persuade, inform, educate, inspire, or, of course, secure subsequent funding for continuation or expansion of your project.

CHECKPOINT
Twenty-six tips for program evaluation

Instead of offering a set of evaluative questions as we have in previous chapters, we conclude here with a set of twenty-six tips for program evaluation planning that come from John and Ruthmary Cradler's book (1994).

1. Use data sources that already exist in the school, such as attendance records, grades, student behavior reports, local district tests, school-level tests.

2. Carefully analyze and define the outcomes as they could be observed and select assessments that match.

3. If selecting tests, review the items to determine if they reflect the subject matter being emphasized by the intervention.

4. Use more than one measure. Often tests are not sensitive enough to measure impact of an intervention, so use "process" measures such as teacher observations and perceptions of student changes toward the expected outcomes.

5. Use teacher ratings of the impact of the intervention on student grades and behavior ratings as a way to measure changes in academic performance. In this case the teacher relies on his/her own accumulation of experience to serve as norms, criteria standards, or reference points from which to judge levels of student performance.

6. Highly structured technology projects with high levels of time allocated for sequentially computer-introduced subject matter lend themselves to the use of pre-/post-standardized or criterion-referenced tests.

7. Staff development components and outcomes should be measured in terms of the level of use and impact on students of the skill and knowledge acquired by the teacher in the staff development.

8. It is critical that all student interventions occur for a long enough period of time each day for the students to acquire the skills or knowledge. For example, an intervention that occurs for five to ten minutes each day may not show an improvement.

9. Assessment includes changes in teacher behaviors and/or attitude or levels of use of the project intervention such as a type of technology. Make sure to select instruments and design the evaluation to include staff outcomes.

10. Make sure that the assessment instrument is appropriate for the age and type of student (example: handicapped students vs. mainstreamed students).

11. Surveys should be short and easy to complete in less than fifteen minutes.

12. Avoid the use of open-ended surveys unless staff are available to review, aggregate, and analyze the information.

13. Interviews should not exceed thirty minutes and should include the same questions or prompts across all interviews.

14. When using norm-referenced tests, make certain that the norms are up to date.

15. On achievement tests, use only the subtests that relate to your project objectives and activities.

16. When comparing the pre-/post-test results, compare the number of correct answers rather than the percentile or grade-level ranking.

17. Schedule your pre- and post-testing to occur as close to the beginning and ending of the intervention as possible.

18. Utilize only the scores from the tests of students who actually participated in the intervention.

19. Try to locate district-developed tests. These are usually more closely aligned to the curriculum that the technology is supporting.

20. Inspect the test items to make sure that they coincide with the intervention.

21. Make sure the district didn't switch forms of the same test during the intervention period. For example, did it switch from CTBS Form UV to CTBS Form IV? On the new version the students will

score one to two years lower because of the change in test items and norms, not necessarily because of the curriculum.

22. Try to avoid using the California Assessment Program (CAP) results. These do not give individual scores and so are unreliable for evaluation purposes. These should only be considered in a schoolwide project that utilizes a Computer-Assisted Instruction (CAI) lab model serving over 60 percent of the students.

23. Individual achievement tests are recommended for projects that utilize small-group instruction with intensive use of curriculum-based software or video courseware.

24. Assessments should not be so cumbersome as to significantly decrease instructional time.

25. From the teachers' perspective, it is teacher-developed tests that accompany curricular materials, which figure most heavily in instructional planning.

26. When there is staff development and training in testing, teachers are found to be more positive about the quality and utility of tests, and test preparation.

12

Develop and Justify the Budget

Money, if you pardon the expression, is like manure: it is useless until you spread it around.
—Dolly Levi in Hello Dolly

Everyone pays special attention to the budget section of a proposal. You suddenly have to account very precisely for what you will do with the funder's money if it is awarded to you. Budget allocations also reveal your real values: Are you buying expertise? Learning? Material goods? Time? People?

Many important questions surface immediately upon entering into this section. Luckily, most funders provide specific spreadsheet forms to guide your work in this section. Funders do this so that all their concerns are addressed. It is critical that you adhere to these forms and fill them in exactly as directed in the guidelines. Any digression from the funder's expectations could be fatal to your proposal's chances. Depending on who reads your proposal, you should remember that some—the "numbers people"—see this as the most important section and subject it to a level of scrutiny that far exceeds that given to other sections. Some readers jump straight to this section the way some newspaper readers skip straight to the sports page or the comics. To these readers, errors here mean that you are incapable of competently implementing a project.

Typical Budget Categories

**H O T
TIPS**

We have chosen to focus our examples in this chapter on education, since that is our primary area of expertise. Each field has its own special categories, though some, like "Personnel," are universal. Be sure to follow the categories and format described in your application packet when creating the budget. If you are unsure about acceptable allocations, call the funding agency and ask for clarification.

Most educational grant budgets follow a standard setup, detailed as follows.

• *Salaries and Wages.* These rates are derived mainly from employer salary schedules. When the grant development team knows which individuals will staff a project, those individuals' actual salary rates (adjusted for cost-of-living increase) should serve as the basis for calculations. If the grant development team does not know who will staff the project, the rule of thumb is to use the highest certified salary schedule and the highest classified salary schedules of compensation. Even so, it is preferable to overstate than to understate salaries, since staff who have not yet been identified may actually be at the top of the salary schedules. Sometimes, instead of using yearly salary rates, it is more appropriate to use hourly rates, which may rest on hourly schedules or be prorated from yearly salaries. In the first case, the development team distinguishes between instructional and noninstructional time. Faculty should receive the instructional rate for actually teaching or counseling in a project and the noninstructional rate for functions like planning, designing material, and the like. The prorated approach should be used to cover regular certificated employees who will be released from their regular duties to staff a grant project. In developing the salary line, the budget designer will rely heavily on the various schedules available in the business office of your nonprofit, public agency, school district, or county office of education.

• *Employee Benefits.* A rule of thumb is 21 percent of personnel salaries for benefits (e.g., administrators, teachers, and counseling and guidance staff) and 34 percent for classified employees (e.g., instructional paraprofessionals, secretaries, clerks, data analysts, etc.).

• *Travel.* This line might include airfare, ground transportation, lodging, and meals. For shorter automobile trips, the rate for in-town meetings is twenty-five cents per mile while the rate for out-of-town mileage is twenty-two cents per mile. (Of course, over time these figures will change; you should always ask the funding agency up front what the rate is.)

• *Equipment (aka Capital Outlay).* When equipment is included in the proposal, the developer should get quotes from reliable vendors. It is important to involve potential vendors in the development of the proposal equipment budget. If the proposal calls for large quantities, vendor discounts may be possible. The time that it takes for the bid process to be implemented causes delays in equipment procurement. This should be taken into consideration when developing implementation activities time frame. Most funding agencies want detailed specification for computer equipment and clear explanations about how such equipment will be used in the proposed project.

• *Materials and Supplies.* In determining these items, the development team might imagine the operation of the project and all those things that stakeholders and students will need to participate in it. This would include computer software, manuals, books, videotapes, and so on.

Other Budgeting Considerations

In addition to the items listed above, you might need to include or discuss several other pieces of information in your budget.

• budget narrative and justification
• fringe benefits
• fiscal manager

- consultants
- other funding sources
- in-kind contributions
- administrative costs (aka "indirects costs")
- tax status

Sample Budget Narrative: Government Technology Grant

The following sample narrative comes from a federal technology grant worth $10 million. This is the first year's budget narrative; you can see the detailed version of the same budget in Chapter 18 (Workshop 2), "Designing Winning Documents."

Budget Narrative
Basis for Estimating Costs: Year One

A. Direct Costs

1.1 Salaries (Professional & Clerical)   The basis for estimating the costs of professional salaries and clerical support is the current acceptable practice based on the average salary schedule for the seven Alliance sites where the "Virtual Conference Centers" will exist. Key Project Personnel have been contacted and their estimated project time and per diem rate has been noted. We expect to have many visitors to the Pacific Rim Alliance (PRA) sites as well as many pre-service and in-service training sessions for staff and community at each PRA model site. This would require additional technology support stipends for teachers and clerical assistance. Unique to this project will be the use of students from the PRA high schools to be employed as Project Student Interns, handling as much as possible the day to day operations shadowing their adult counterpart.

1.2 Employee Benefits   The basis for estimating the costs of employee benefits is the current acceptable practice in the Burlingame School District. Retirement, Social Security, Medicare, Unemployment, Workers Compensation, and where applicable Health/Welfare Benefits are included in this estimate. Employee benefits are directly related to the costs outlined in section 1. Salaries and are calculated at a rate of 15% of gross salaries.

1.3 Employee Travel   The basis for estimating the costs of employee travel is the current acceptable practice in Burlingame School District. Mileage is computed using the standard IRS rate of $0.315 per mile.

Due to the nature of the Pacific Rim Consortium (covering four western states), travel will be a necessary cost item. Evaluators will be required to travel over the life of the grant. Leadership personnel will be required to travel to Washington, D.C. (2 trips), Regional Meetings (2 trips), and major conferences to ensure that the components of The Pacific Rim Alliance: Schools

Without Boarders are successful. Technology Coordinators and Virtual Conference Center Directors will need to meet with Project directors to establish initial direction of the program.

1.4 Equipment The seven "Virtual Conference Centers" (VCC) will all submit a budget allowing them to move their site to the next phase of implementation (approximately $80,000 per year per site). We have included funding in the first year to standardize the computer equipment for teachers at each of the PRA sites to be able to test and implement the Internet backbone, technology-based curriculum, and electronic portfolio assessment components of the Pacific Rim Alliance (PRA). Each Virtual Conference Center within the PRA sites will be offered assistance in helping them publicize their projects. The hope is that each of the seven PRA Virtual Conference Center locations will have a solid understanding of marketing, fund-raising, networking, and development and will be able to attract additional resources, "clone" new model sites in their region, and become self-sustaining as project funding diminishes.

Members of the Consortium will be contributing much of the equipment/hardware needed at their site to ensure that the goals of the project are met.

1.5 Materials and Supplies The basis for estimating the costs of materials and supplies is past practice and experience with similar projects and grants. Burlingame Schools, CA (LEA) asked several vendors to supply cost estimates to determine our projected expenses. The major cost items for software and supplies relate to the proposed activities in the areas of Professional Development, Virtual Conference Center Expansion, Development, Marketing, Evaluation, and Networking.

Members of the Consortium will be contributing many supplies and materials needed at their site to ensure that the goals of the project are met. Each of the key Project personnel (Westfall, Prater, Temple, Seiter, Aseltyne, Guay) will have compatible hardware (laptop, scanner, printer, copier, etc.) to help information flow and the project be fluid in organizational design and to help market the program to other schools and universities in the PRA states.

1.6 Consulting and Contracts The basis for estimating the costs of consulting and contracts is past practice and experience with similar projects and grants.

The major contractors: CompUSA, eTREK; Project Evaluators; Consultants to assist Center's Project Directors with fund-raising and development expertise; Disney to assist in marketing project products and services; Westfall to design and implement our virtual professional development network; and university personnel to analyze and revise current teacher-training practices.

1.7 Other The basis for estimating the costs of materials and supplies is past practice and experience with similar projects and grants. The estimates that have been developed are reasonable and reflect acceptable values for services rendered.

B. Indirect Costs

The basis for estimating the indirect rate is past practice and experience with similar projects and grants. The indirect cost rate for Burlingame School District, Burlingame, CA is currently estimated at 7%.

Sample Budget Table: Literacy Grant

Figure 12.1 shows a portion of the budget for an elementary school literacy grant.

Chapter 18 (Workshop 2), "Designing Winning Documents," offers further guidance in the formatting of your budget. That workshop also includes several other examples of budgets to give you some helpful ideas.

    The entire grant excerpted in Figure 12.1 is included on the CD-ROM.

"The single most important activity for building the knowledge required for eventual success in reading is reading aloud to children."

Becoming A Nation of Readers, The Reports of the Commission on Reading

Part 4 - Proposed Budget Year One:

Training

1. Literacy Training Coach for Lincoln School
Consultant/Reading specialist, Ellen Haas
Seven month Contract @ $ 1000 per month=$ 7000 $ 7000

2. Release time for Lincoln staff to observe and
support the integration of a balanced Literacy Framework.
16 staff @ 3 days each = 48 days @ $100 per day= $ 4800 $ 4800

3. Staff stipends for development of Literacy Assessment Rubrics
(9 staff @ $100 materials fee = $ 900)
(4 staff trainers @ $1000 stipend = $4000 to prepare and present) $ 4900

4. Early Literacy Training Library for staff, parents and volunteers $ 3000

5. Creation of the *How to Read to Your Child* video $ 2500

6. Registration fees for West Coast Literacy Conference/LA $ 2500

7. Registration fees for Reading Association Conference $ 1500

Materials, Equipment and Technology

8. Classroom library augmentation from the proposed list
Ten Gr. K - 2 classrooms @ $ 350 each = $ 3500
Six Gr. 3 - 5 classrooms @ $ 600 each = $ 3600 $ 7100

9. Purchase leveled books/software to fill gaps in
materials needed to fully implement guided reading
for K - 5 classroom libraries and computers
Eight K - 2 classrooms @ $ 200 each = $ 1600
Eight 3 - 5 classrooms @ $ 1000 each = $ 8000 $ 9600

Assessment

10. Staff stipends for development of Literacy Assessment Rubrics
Nine staff @ $100 materials fee = $ 900
Four staff trainers @ $1000 stipend = $4000 to prepare and present $ 4900

11. Purchase Developmental Reading Assessment kits (K - 5)
16 kits @ $ 100 each = $ 1600 $ 1600

Total Requested Year One $49400

FIGURE 12.1 Sample Budget Overview

Analysis: Characteristics of an Effective Budget

Using the preceding examples to illustrate, let us summarize what a good budget will accomplish. An effective budget will:

- present numbers that add up *perfectly*
- align its categories with those provided in the funding guidelines
- avoid any costs that are not consistent with the funder's core values or that are not covered by the terms of the grant
- be broken down into clear percentages to show where the money is allocated
- be formatted for easy reading, ideally under headings that use the same categories as the guidelines
- be coded appropriately (especially important if receiving funding from government agencies)
- indicate all in-kind or other contributions (e.g., matching funds) from others, including your own organization
- identify people by their function/role, not their name (e.g., "Project Manager" not Colleen McNally)

CHECKPOINT
Answer these questions before moving on.

- Did you organize costs in a helpful and logical format for easy reading?
- Did you include a detailed budget and justify expenditures somewhere in the narrative?
- Does your budget ask only for what you/your organization need(s)?
- Are all figures based on realistic and current prices for goods and services?
- Did you use the budget worksheet, forms, or guidelines provided in the application packet?
- Have you checked to be sure that all costs are consistent with stated needs, goals, objectives, methods, and activities as well as the values of the funder to which you are applying?
- Did you include all indirect costs?
- Does your budget add up correctly?
- Did you list all in-kind contributions of staff, materials, facilities, or labor?
- Have you identified any long-term or future funding sources?

Sports, recreation, and physical fitness

13

Write the Abstract, Overview, or Summary

Things are always at their best in their beginning.
—Blaise Pascal

Perhaps nothing better captures the purpose and role of the abstract than people's reason for reading the *TV Guide*: "How do I know whether I want to watch a show unless I know what it's about?" Sometimes called the executive summary, project summary, or overview, the abstract greets the reader and offers a synopsis of the entire proposal. It is essential to your proposal's success for, aside from your cover letter (if required or accepted), it provides your reader a glimpse into the entire proposal. It is the store window through which the reader takes in all you offer; it is the basis from which they form their earliest opinion of your ideas and your ability to accomplish them.

Elements of an Effective Abstract

A good abstract will include information in these five categories:

1. *Problem:* a brief statement of the problem or need your agency has recognized and is prepared to address.

2. *Organization and Its Expertise:* a brief statement of the name, history, purpose, and activities of your agency and its capacity to implement the proposed project.

3. *Solution:* a short description of the project, including what will take place and how many people will benefit from the program, how and where it will operate, for how long, and who will staff it (one or two paragraphs, preferably with bullets if space allows).

4. *Funding Requirements:* an explanation of the amount of grant money required for the project and what your plans are for funding it in the future.

5. *Funder's Requirements:* information mandated by funder's guidelines to appear in abstract.

Keep in mind the following as you look at examples of other abstracts and prepare to write your own.

- The abstract is usually read first.
- Its title (e.g., "Project T.E.C.H. [Teaching Everyone Creates Hope]) can help to quickly establish your proposal's place in the mind of the reader.
- The abstract frames the entire proposal.
- Some readers will only read this part of your proposal; if you lose their interest here, it is hard to win it back.
- Nearly all funding agencies require abstracts.

Sample Abstract: Beginning Teacher Grant

Project LETTS (Learning Enhanced Through Teacher Support) is a joint proposal that addresses the issue of new-teacher induction. Seven elementary (K–8) districts (Bayshore, Belmont, Brisbane, Burlingame, Menlo Park, Millbrae, San Bruno Park) in San Mateo County have joined together in a collaborative effort to determine needs of the new teacher and plan an effective program to meet these needs. The districts have worked in consultation with the San Mateo County Office of Education (SMCOE), San Francisco State University (SFSU), and Far West Laboratory.

The seven communities are all located on the Peninsula, approximately ten to twenty-five miles south of San Francisco. Their size and ethnic makeup vary greatly but their mission to effectively support new teachers is identical (please see Element 5: Attachment A & B for District-Community descriptions). Burlingame School District will serve as the Local Educational Agency (LEA) for the project and employ the project director. All participating districts as well as the SMCOE will provide in-kind support to the project. The Project Steering Committee, made up of representatives from sponsoring agencies, will ensure that the project meets the needs of the local districts, new teachers, and the Walter S. Johnson Foundation.

Forty to fifty percent of all new teachers leave the profession by the end of the seventh year. WHY?

As the seven districts, SMCOE, SFSU, and Far West Labs began to research and design their new-teacher induction program, it was clear that the topic was multifaceted and complex. The field of new-teacher induction is in its infancy, "the final word" is clearly premature. With that in mind, this proposal was created to serve a dual purpose, to:

- stimulate new thinking and action, as we locally develop, implement, and refine a pedagogical assessment program for new teachers in the collaborative
- retain and support promising new teachers who might get discouraged and otherwise abandon the profession. It is the result of local needs assessments as well as needs identified by a review of existing literature.

The major goals of Project LETTS are to:

- establish an interagency collaborative network to make the best use of resources
- provide small-district collaboration with a structured, supportive, replicable model for entry in the teaching profession
- conceive, implement, and evaluate formative and summative assessment tools. The Peninsula Collaborative is seeking a grant to begin July 1990 and continue through June of 1993

Research validates the fact that new teachers feel extremely isolated. Most feel they simply "survive" their initial years. Their skills and assignments vary greatly, as do their needs. To ensure the individual needs of the twenty-eight new teachers who are eligible for the project will be addressed, an Individual Learning Plan (ILP) will be developed by each new teacher in concert with his/her support team. The ILP will include areas selected from a project-developed "New Teacher Skills Assessment Tool." The professional development "menu" will contain five strands:

1. instructional planning and student achievement
2. classroom/time management
3. cultural/linguistic diversity
4. curriculum content and pedagogy
5. professionalism

It reflects the "California Standards for Competence and Performance" and areas in which new teachers traditionally have needed support.

The project funding level is $59,257 for 1990–1991, at $2,116 per new teacher. The funding for years two and three would be determined when the number of new teachers interested in participating in the project is determined. The budget breakdown for WSJ Foundation funds in year one is:

- 13%   Teacher released time
- 33%   Teacher-adviser stipends
- 26%   Project staff salaries and benefits
- 7%   Trainers
- 6%   Conferences

The balance (15%) is for other expenses as outlined in the detailed budget (Element 3).

The small-district collaborative effort; the individualized mapping approach of new-teacher skills, using refined resources from other New Teacher Projects; and the efficient use of existing resources throughout the nine agencies are distinctive and special features of Project LETTS.

When Should You Write Your Abstract?

The lists and example above provide the necessary guidance to write a winning abstract. The tricky part is knowing when to write your abstract: at the end of your development process. We did not, for example, write the introduction to this book until we had written everything else. We needed to have some sense of what we had created before we knew what "unique features" or other useful information the book and CD would offer. It also serves as a helpful summative evaluation of your proposal helping you to answer the question, "Do I have everything covered?" The abstract should serve as a means of checking your work.

Once you have written it, you should show it to as many stakeholders as you can to get their feedback. Have a variety of people read it for specific reasons: for spelling, grammar, words that might be confusing or insulting. As my friend's father said to his son and his son's friend before they drove across the country, "Make sure you keep all your eyes on the road!" You cannot have too many people read and respond to your abstract.

H O T

T I P S

> **Y**ou might want to consider hiring a consultant to polish up your abstract or asking someone like Carol (who has read hundreds of grants) to critique it as if they were a reader.

This marks the end, for most application guidelines, of the actual proposal. Though you may have supplemental documents—e.g., resumes, profiles, data—to gather and include in your appendix, you have completed your argument, you have stated your case. Now all that remains is to prepare and submit it in the most competitive way possible.

14

Assemble the Necessary Attachments and Appendices

If you are not distinct, you will become extinct.
—*Tom Peters,* The Circle of Innovation

Your proposal's appendix will include all those stray documents that the funder either requires or allows you to submit. These might include letters of support, charts, graphs, or support documents such as a glossary; the purpose of all these attachments is to support the reader and complete your overall application packet. Always make a list of what the funder requires and will permit; some specifically call for an itemized appendix in the guidelines and specify what it should include (and in what order), while others limit what can be included or do not permit an appendix with supplemental material to be included at all. If you are not sure whether you can include something—e.g., photographs, computer disks, a videotape, letters of support—call the funder and ask.

Most applications request support material in the appendix, examples of which include:

- staff resumes
- project job descriptions
- letters of support or commitment
- stakeholder profile: this might include evidence of previous success
- test data/statistical data
- charts/graphs
- fiscal audit of nonprofit, school, or public agency
- list of support network, coalition, "vertical or horizontal slice" involved in this proposed project
- bibliography/references
- glossary
- footnotes/endnotes

In addition to these common attachments, there are others that funders will, depending on the nature of the grant, request. These might include an organization's:

- IRS determination letter and ID number
- DUNS number (Dun and Bradstreet number)
- overall operating budget for the previous year
- brochures, annual reports, or newsletters
- strategic plan and needs assessment for the applicant's organization

Each attachment included in the appendix should be clearly labeled using the terms provided in the guidelines so that the reader knows exactly what they are looking at. The above lists include a wide range of possible documents to include; which ones you ultimately use depends on the scale of your proposal. For a thousand-dollar grant to fund a visit to a local museum for a day, one will not need all these support documents; a regional hospital project such as the Centenarian Project in Hayward, California, which works with all the centenarians in the county, would likely need to document all those who will participate in and implement the proposed program. Such documentation only helps to further establish your network and organizational capability as it shows the funders and readers how conscientious you are.

CHECKPOINT

Answer these questions before moving on.

- Are appendices allowed or encouraged?
- Is there a specified table of contents or required/suggested order, or length?
- Is all the data in the appendices aligned with the narrative and plan of operation?

H O T

T I P S

> **M**any times crucial information arrives late in the writing process (e.g., consultant stipends, training components, network support, job descriptions). It is important to your credibility that the data in the narrative be properly aligned with the appendices.

- Are any of the job descriptions in conflict with the union contracts or funding agency guidelines?
- Are any of the consultants or trainers in conflict with union contracts or funding agency guidelines?
- If there is no limit to the contents of the appendices, have you ordered your contents from most important to least important?
- Have you labeled them according to guidelines or the traditional A, B, C identification system?
- Have you included the most current organizational data possible? (Note: Old data is often worse than no data.)
- Are all the graphs and charts required readable, and have you offered captions to lead the reader to the appropriate place or conclusion?
- Are all the attachments that require signatures signed and in the correct presentation order?

15

Revise, Refine, Complete, and Submit Your Application

*Genius is one percent inspiration and
ninety-nine percent perspiration.*
—Albert Einstein

Approximately 50 percent of all accidents happen within five miles of home. Researchers have found that people lose focus, begin to relax as they get closer to the journey's end. They believe the hardest part of the adventure is behind them; and of course this is true, unless they get careless. So it goes with the final stretch of preparing the application packet. You have the actual proposal written; everything now is a matter of getting it safely to the agency.

This means taking care of the following matters:

- checking what you have against what the guidelines require
- assembling the appendix and making sure all appendix materials align with the proposal narrative
- making final changes to the document
- printing the final draft: paper, ink, binding, and signatures
- making copies of your proposal
- writing a cover letter
- mailing or otherwise delivering your proposal

Discuss Future Funding

Many philanthropists are reluctant to fund projects that are of interest to the nonprofit or schools only if outside funding is provided. To separate opportunistic proposals from proposals that reflect a true commitment, the funder asks for evidence that the project will be continued beyond the funded period. This is especially important for getting "seed money," which is special funding to support initiating a new program with the intent that it will become part of the regular program. This section of the proposal can be sensitive. Proposal writers are sometimes tempted to promise more than their nonprofit organizations, public agencies, or school districts are willing to commit.

Sustainability and dissemination of aspects of the project can be built into the proposal narrative without committing the organization to future costs. This can be accomplished in the following ways:

- Use project funds to train staff and volunteers to provide training, a skill that the organization can continue to use beyond the funded period.
- Produce instructional materials or products that clients or stakeholders will continue to use within the regular program, beyond the proposal's funding cycle.
- Use project funds to test new strategies and services that can, if proven successful, replace strategies or services now in use and model that program as a visitation site for other organizations.
- Use project funds to train staff and volunteers to do their jobs in different ways, ways that can be continued beyond funding, without further training.

WORDS TO KNOW

cover letter

dissemination

philanthropist

seed money

sustainability

Plan for Dissemination

To some funding agencies, dissemination means distributing or publishing information about the project; to other funders it means getting other nonprofits or school districts to adopt or adapt your project. Dissemination is especially important if the project will test an innovative strategy or otherwise develop new information that could improve the quality of facilities, services, or programs. Dissemination strategies for proposals may include:

- publishing and distributing a project newsletter
- contributing articles to professional journals
- reporting to professional conferences and meetings
- developing materials for the media about the project
- conducting workshops to train others on how to implement or adopt the project
- producing a kit of instructional materials and software for potential adapters/adopters

Check Your Application Against Agency Requirements

Despite the absolute importance of this item, a point that cannot be made often enough, there is little to say aside from the fact that you have to do it again and again. Somehow, for all the times you read the guidelines and the scoring rubric, there is always that stray detail that seems to have appeared out of nowhere. For instance, one time we were working with a school on its National Blue Ribbon Award application, and thought we were done. The team made the final edits, printed out the proposed narrative, and went off to copy it only to find out at the last moment that, due to the National Paperwork Reduction Act, all but one of the required four copies had to be submitted double-sided. The crisis avoided (or so they thought), they ordered their copies to be made accordingly. Hours later, having picked up the copies, they rushed across town to the district office, where the proposal was due by five o'clock, only to realize, en route, that none of the copies had been made double-sided. They pulled off the freeway, found another copy store, and got the necessary copies made, arriving at the district office only ten minutes before it closed.

Examples of unusual requirements you might not think about include:

- color of ink you can use to sign the final application forms and letters (we suggest blue, unless black is required)

- binding (usually one staple or a two-hole clasp on the top, unless otherwise directed; proposals are alway bound but rarely have covers)
- color or type of paper (good quality white paper, standard size, 20 lb.; depending on funder, recycled paper might also be used)
- size of margins and font (usually one-inch margins on all sides, unless otherwise stated)
- use of headers (e.g., always include in the header the project name, contact phone, and page number on each page unless the funder prohibits it or requires something different)
- page requirements (some guidelines allot a certain number per section; *do not* exceed any limits)

Write Your Cover Letter

H O T

TIPS

Consider having two or more people write cover letters independently. Then compare them and choose from each those elements you like best to create the final cover letter. See pages 124–125 for a sample cover letter.

Your cover letter greets the reader and quickly establishes several important points. It:

- introduces your organization
- establishes a relationship between the reader and the organization
- explains how the proposal that follows will further the funder's mission and reflect its vision and values

Effective cover letters have several other characteristics you should keep in mind when writing yours. They are:

- addressed to the funder's contact person identified in the application packet (make the necessary effort to find this out!)
- formatted as required or, in the absence of such directions, as a formal business letter
- written in a concise, succinct style that (usually) does not exceed two pages
- printed on quality paper bearing the letterhead of the individual or institution that is applying

They also include the following information:

- name and all necessary information of your organization's contact person(s)
- assurance of support from all appropriate stakeholders
- expression of willingness to meet in person to answer any questions about your proposed project

Sample Cover Letter: Professional Development Grant

The sample cover letter included here illustrates the points just outlined:

October 15, 1997

Carol Ann Prater
Burlingame School District
Burlingame, CA 94010

Francis Woods, Program Officer
The ABC Foundation
111 Winner's Circle
Mountain View, CA 94025

Dear Ms. Wood:

Enclosed is Project LETTS (Learning Enhanced Through Teacher Support). Seven elementary (K–8) districts (Bayshore, Belmont, Brisbane, Burlingame, Menlo Park, Millbrae, San Bruno Park) in San Mateo County have joined together in a collaborative effort to determine needs of the new teacher and plan an effective program to meet these needs. The districts are collaborating with the San Mateo County Office of Education (SMCOE), San Francisco State University (SFSU), and Far West Laboratory. The seven communities are all located on the Peninsula, approximately ten to twenty-five miles south of San Francisco. Their size and ethnic makeup vary greatly but their mission to effectively support new teachers is identical.

The field of new-teacher induction is in its infancy; "the final word" is clearly premature. With that in mind, this joint proposal was created to serve a dual purpose, to: (1) stimulate new thinking and action, as we locally develop, implement, and refine a pedagogical assessment program for new teachers in the collaborative; (2) retain and support promising new teachers who might get discouraged and otherwise abandon the profession. From our perspective the proposal matches the ABC Foundation guidelines and criteria for grant applications. The Peninsula Collaborative will provide a visible model for other small districts to follow in developing cost-effective ways to deal with new-teacher induction. It will provide a model curriculum and instructional program as well as materials that can be replicated by other districts. The assessment tools that will be locally developed will aid our districts in future planning and program development.

The issue that is of paramount concern to many school districts in our nation is the severe shortage of qualified teachers. More than 50 percent of the present teaching staff in San Mateo County will be retiring in the next five years. We hope Project LETTS will encourage good new teachers to continue teaching and will promote the use of experienced teachers as resources for their peers.

If you would like any further information or if you have any questions that may require an immediate answer, please call me.

I want to thank you for considering our grant proposal. The ongoing support and concern of the ABC Foundation regarding the education of our youth is exemplary and greatly appreciated.

Sincerely,

Carol Ann Prater
Special Project Coordinator

Make Final Changes

Now is your last chance to find the grammatical, informational, and semantic errors that might undermine all the efforts you've made so far. By this point you should have consulted the guidelines many times and found those discrepancies. We have included the GrantSAT scoring guide on the CD to help you walk through your entire proposal one last time. If the agency to which you are applying provides its own rubric or checklist, be sure to use that one in addition to ours, as ours addresses not only content but format, process, and product components. You can find our other scoring rubric in Chapter 18 (Workshop 2), "Designing Winning Documents." If you are working as part of a team, it is ideal to work through the scoring rubric together in case there are questions.

Print the Final Draft: Paper, Ink, Binding, and Signatures

Presentation is everything. Your proposal's appearance communicates as much as any set of clothes you wear. The challenge is to match the feel and format of your application with the spirit of the agency. Corporate and foundation annual reports, according to Lisa Chadderdon in *Fast Company* magazine (May 1999, p. 44), have begun to transform themselves into "branding vehicles and statements of strategy." The point is not to be reckless or innovative just to be different, but rather to use the documents you create to communicate what you represent and are trying to achieve. Chadderdon sites examples of annual reports for the company Network General that resemble a Boy Scout guide, one for

Adaptec that looks like a children's book, and another for a biotech company that utilized only one piece of paper. Chadderdon quotes Bill Cahan, president of a top design firm, who says that his firm tries to "look and listen for the hidden kernel of an idea that will tell a company's story—and tell it in a way that will engage people" (ibid).

The important point to remember is that the proposal's layout (of your application packet) should meet the reader's and funder's needs and expectations. If, for example, you are seeking funding from an organization known for its support of innovative ideas, let a creative spirit shine through in your document. One major reform proposal we wrote included multimedia presentations of student work, a video we created in collaboration with students to introduce our vision to the funders, and an interactive assessment tool we proposed to develop further as part of the project if it were funded. Because the nature of the funding opportunity emphasized thinking differently, this made sense; were we applying to a more conservative agency, we would have taken an entirely different approach.

As with all other stages of this process, the place to begin designing your final document is in the application, for funders often include very specific ideas about how they want the documents to look. Here are a few suggestions to help you finish your application.

LEARNING LINKS

You can find other ideas and further discussion about formatting in Chapter 18 (Workshop 2), "Designing Winning Documents."

- Use a laser printer if at all possible.
- Use a high-quality typewriter to enter data on any forms or assurances that must be filled out. Before typing, however, make copies of the blank form(s) in case you make mistakes and so that you can practice spacing of the typed answers.
- Sign the original forms in blue ink (unless otherwise directed) so that it won't get mixed up with the photocopies.
- Print your document quality stock (at least 20 lb.) white paper.
- Adhere to any application guidelines for binding the document. In the absence of any instructions, staple it in the upper left corner and attach no cover.

Get the Necessary Signatures

We warned you early on that you should not have embarked on this journey without the explicit endorsement of any administrators, board members, or other parties to whom you must ultimately answer. So we will assume that you are not seeking signatures from people who do not know what you are proposing. We have seen people bring an application before the board for final authorization only to find the proposal rejected the night before it was to be mailed because board members opposed the initiative. To review one last time, you should check whether you need signatures from the following:

- school superintendent, public agency managers, union officials, or nonprofit executive directors
- finance office
- trustees, committees, governing boards, superintendents
- government or local agencies
- site directors

Some people suggest having the different signatories provide original signatures, even to the required copies. We have also found it useful—i.e., it makes a powerful impact on readers—to have all the key players sign on a signatures page at the beginning of the document if space allows. This dramatic visual element further reinforces the commitment of all stakeholders to the proposed idea.

When making copies, first take care of the immediate commitment: How many copies does the funding agency require you to submit? Are there any special instructions about copying (e.g., double-sided)? Next, think ahead to other stakeholders: Do you need copies for board members, administrators, other alliances? You will want to make copies to keep on file and others to distribute for further review or use by another development team. You will want to keep a clean copy on hand in case someone asks to see the proposal and, of course, back up all documents on disk for future use.

Submit Your Proposal Package

More often than not when people finish such endeavors as you have just completed, when the last page comes out of the printer, it is, to quote Shakespeare, "so late we may call it early." There remains only the question of delivery. Before we talk about how to send it, you must double-check *where* to send it. While the addresses of local foundations might be obvious, other proposals might need to go somewhere not so obvious: a regional office, a state department (that would then submit it to a federal competitive grant process), or a corporate headquarters located on the other side of the country. If the guidelines are not clear about where, or to whom, or even how to submit it, call the funder and inquire. Be aware, however, that in the days just prior to submission, phone lines are often tied up and the funding agency's staff is often inaccessible.

Now that we have the *where* and *who* question out of the way, let's concentrate on the *how*: no one wants to get rejected because they came across the finish line a day late. The following list provides the key points about mailing or personally delivering your proposal:

- Most applications are received by mail, though on rare occasions they may be submitted electronically. *Never* send your application by e-mail unless it is clearly permitted. Always request a receipt.

- Submissions deadlines are *strictly* observed by federal and state authorities. Even FedEx next-day service is only acceptable if the package is sent two days prior to the actual due date.

- No supplemental or revised information from applicants is normally accepted after the filing date; nor will most agencies accept supplemental or revised information after an application has been submitted.

- It is important to know if the proposal must be *received* or *postmarked* on or before the submission date. It is also valuable to know if you can hand-deliver the proposal and if the address for hand delivery is different from the mailing address.

- It is important to have a street address for next-day delivery when you are using a commercial carrier. Only the United States Postal Service (USPS) delivers next day to a P.O. box—and depending on where you're shipping from, next-day delivery won't be an option for many cities. Rule of thumb: check out your options ahead of time to avoid a crisis (or a tragedy).

- It is important to have an address for hand delivery or delivery by courier service. You must also know the hours the funder accepts deliveries.

- Proof of mailing will be necessary. The acceptable options include:

  - a legibly dated USPS postmark

  - a legible mail receipt with the date of mailing stamped by the USPS

  - a dated shipping label, invoice, or receipt from a commercial carrier

  - any other proof of mailing acceptable to the funder

- The following proofs of mailing are usually not acceptable:

  - a private metered postmark (e.g., an organization's own meter)

  - a mail receipt that is not dated and stamped by the USPS

- Applications submitted to most federal agencies in a timely manner will receive a grant application receipt acknowledgment. If this does not arrive within two weeks, you should call the program officer at the Federal Application Control Center at (202) 708-8493 or the number listed in the application guidelines.

- Any federal, state, or private funder that does not issue a submission receipt should allow you to enclose a receipt card (e.g., a self-addressed stamped postcard acknowledging that the funding agency has received your proposal). They will sign it and return by mail. Our best advice: *always* send your proposal by certified mail (with return receipt requested) or by a commercial shipper that requires a signature from the receiving party.

- Typically, multiple copies of the application must be submitted. Funding agencies encourage applicants to send all copies together in one package to ensure a proposal does not get logged in twice and consequently read and scored by two teams of readers.

Final Words

That's it! Congratulations! You're ready to send it off.

Now the wrap-up process begins. Take a moment to catch your breath before moving into the next phase—cleanup, interviews, implementation, visitations, appeals, public relations, marketing—which we will talk about in the next chapter.

16

Wrapping Up: What to Do After You Submit

All's well that ends well.
—*Shakespeare*

Returning from the post office, where you happily sent off your proposal to the readers, you find a group of people sitting around the same table at which you first met some weeks before. The table, probably even the room, is awash in papers and computer disks, most of which are not labeled or are affixed with Post-its containing scrawled notes and identifiers. The people around the table, as well as some carrying on their lives elsewhere, have contributed remarkable intelligence, energy, and time to see the proposal birthed. Now they need recognition, thanks, evidence of appreciation. You might need a final boost from these people in the weeks ahead if the funder requests an interview or site visitation; moreover, if in the future you choose to revise the proposal to meet the requirements of other funding agencies, you want this wonderful development team ready and willing to work together again. This chapter is designed to help you prepare for these different wrap-up events.

**WORDS
TO KNOW**

organizational
capacity

systemic

wrap-up event

Clean Up, Organize, File Away

Regardless of the size of your proposal, you have generated an impressive amount of information and text that you do not want to lose. Future proposals, potential interviews, and subsequent projects might call for much of the same information. Thus you need to take the extra time to sort through it all, label it properly, and store it somewhere so that you can easily find it later on. A quick system for sorting through would require that you:

- decide what system will work best for you: file cabinets, zip disks, storage crates (that can accommodate hanging files), binders; within this storage system, determine the essential "buckets" (see Chapter 5) into which you can sort everything: e.g., research, other application packets, sample proposals and other data, drafts and support documents

- use this same system on your computer: e.g., folders with the same names, housing the same documents

- sort the different drafts of the proposal into piles, and save those that contain valuable ideas that did not make it into the final draft

- label all drafts and notes clearly across the top, making sure to include version number, dates, or titles—whatever will help you to know what the item is when you look at it down the line

- write down any helpful information that was useful to you and that you do not want to have to search for again: e.g., Web sites, organizations, books, people

Prepare for Visitations and Interviews

L E A R N I N G   L I N K S

See Chapter 21 (Workshop 5), "Giving Dynamic Presentations," for tips on preparing for a visitation or interview.

With most review processes, you will be informed if a visitation is part of the evaluation plan. However, even if you are told to expect a visit, you may not be informed about when or why someone will come. People going through a potentially large award process can suddenly find themselves talking to a representative from the organization who notifies them that a visitation has been scheduled for the following day. Sometimes a representative visits to clarify information on your application. This is especially common with respect to planning grants: the funder wants to be sure the institution or community at large supports the proposed project.

If a representative(s) is to visit—or in anticipation of such a visit—you should have the following in place:

- a contact person and representative interview team
- an informed population (everyone the team might possibly encounter during the course of their visit should know and be able to answer questions about the project)
- an elite team whose knowledge of the project and skills will enable them to impress visitors
- copies of the completed proposal to all key players—e.g., signatories, administrators, or those who wrote letters of commitment—in the event that they receive a follow-up phone call from the funding agency wanting clarification
- designated meeting place to host visitors
- copies of your proposal on hand in case questions arise

If a site visit is requested, it is important to inform others of the stakes and to alert them about what will happen. You might even go so far as to call the funding agency and ask if there is something specific the representatives will want to know more about or see so that you can be prepared to meet their concerns and expectations.

Recognize the Proposal Development Team

Whether it is an individual or a group consisting of fifty stakeholders from all domains, appreciation is crucial to the mission's success—regardless of your proposal's final outcome. As mentioned above, you may well need—or hope—to call on these people again to help you. After all, you have established relationships, figured out how to work with one another, and accomplished something together.

No one wants to work without appreciation, especially on projects like the one you have just finished, which probably required long hours over and above normal working hours. Nor should recognition come only from the team or its leader; it should also come from the directors, administrators, superintendents, or boards that asked you to write the proposal. This might mean being honored before the board of trustees, at a staff meeting, in the organization's newsletter, or at a special dinner hosted by the administration. Of course, not all people in administrative positions think about these matters. Some like to think that they already recognized you by asking you to use your talents to create this project. In such instances, it is then appropriate for the proposal development leader to approach the administration and let them know what needs to happen, perhaps reminding them that such fine people will not be there to ask tomorrow if they are not appreciated today. Such a show of gratitude might, ideally, even include the families of those people who put in the extra hours; hours inevitably taken from time otherwise spent with their loved ones.

If you're short on ideas when it comes to recognizing people, check out *1001 Ways to Reward Employees*, by Kenneth Blanchard.

H O T

T I P S

In addition to the proposal development team, you will need to thank others who helped you during various stages of the process. These might include:

- funders (for help they provided)
- politicians (who may have offered assistance at a certain crucial point)
- local businesses (who may have provided materials, food, help)
- foundations (who might have provided support money to sustain the team)
- others, including clients or community members, who might have offered feedback or undertaken miscellaneous helpful tasks (e.g., editing, researching, running errands, cleaning up, making copies)

Finally, it is a wise investment of goodwill for the development team or its leader to write a short note of thanks to the administrators, site councils, trustees, or other vital stakeholders to congratulate them for their vision, their support, their commitment to the process. Very often they, too, feel unappreciated by the community or clients whose needs they are trying to better address through such proposed changes. Your recognition of their commitment and courage will help to cement the goodwill between you and help you all to work more effectively together in the future.

Prepare to Implement, Inquire, and Resubmit

Until the "We wish to thank you for applying" letter arrives, you must assume that you will win. It is essential that you and your organization keep in mind the proposal as you develop your schedules, agendas, and programs. Often educational grant notifications arrive during the summer, when many schools and support organizations are shorthanded or busy planning, forcing your organization to create a Plan A and Plan B depending on the outcomes of the proposal. Such considerations are very complicated, but you should consider how your decisions might look in the eyes of the funder: if you do nothing to prepare for the possible implementation of your ideas—regardless of whether you get the grant—the funder will sense a lack of commitment. Also, it is best to approach such projects as you proposed systemically, which demonstrates your commitment to the process you are hoping the funder will support.

You must anticipate and address certain possible problems that might arise due to any delay in notification. Most of these potential obstacles have to do with contractual issues that involve:

- consultants' schedules and how they handle the cancellation of commitments
- employee constraints related to the amount, duration, and dates of training programs, and staff development days
- facilities needed to implement your project, which may or may not be accessible
- equipment or other materials that need to be ordered to begin preparing for or implementing the project

Market Your Vision and Your Success

You must continually sell your ideas to the community and clients you serve. As we have said throughout this book, your proposal by its nature represents change and challenges your clients and the community around you to think and work differently. A solid foundation is essential to the long-term success of your plans. Consider the following avenues for promoting your project and its larger goals:

- newsletters
- Web site

- media coverage: radio, television, and newspapers
- community forums
- informational postings in the organization's office
- informational brochures
- bumper stickers, street banners, store signs
- a large sign in front of your institution stating progress with stakeholders' money

Marketing also includes inviting the key players and essential stakeholders to social events so that they feel a part of the organization you are asking them to support. While we have emphasized throughout the importance of establishing individual or organizational capacity to accomplish what you say you will, the same goes for your community: now that you have won the bond election, received the reform grant, been awarded the federal grant for technology, you must convince (and keep convincing) the stakeholders that you can accomplish your aim. Marketing your success in winning the grant also means marketing your efforts throughout the implementation process in order to demonstrate to both the community and the funding agency the outcomes of your project. Such sustained communication with the different stakeholders can translate into crucial support for further investment or new directions as the project unfolds.

If you win, you need to move quickly to announce this great news. First, you need to contact the funders—by phone and a letter—to thank them. Emphasize your excitement about working with them in the coming months, treating them as a partner in your project. Returning to some of the items mentioned above, you need to then turn your attention to announcing to the community and your organization that you won. From the five-hundred-dollar grant to help create a classroom library for a first-grade teacher to the multimillion-dollar grant that builds a new theater, community playground, or staff development institute, grants provide hope and cause for serious celebration. Such celebration not only provides requisite fun but also creates the goodwill and sense of community necessary to successfully accomplish the proposed project.

If you are not successful, there are several things you can do, each of them important for different reasons. Immediately upon hearing you were not awarded the grant, you should begin one or more of the following processes:

- Find out who did win—and why; you can even call winners and ask for a copy of their proposal or discuss with them those sections of your proposal that received low scores.
- Review scoring rubrics and reader comments.

- Interview readers, if possible, to gain key information about how to improve your proposal.
- Call or write the funding agency to inquire about the reasons your proposal was rejected if no scoring sheet was returned to you.
- Hire a consultant to help you improve your application for subsequent grant awards if you do not know how to improve it.
- Take pieces of the application that are extremely competitive and position those for smaller or more narrowly focused—e.g., technology—guidelines.
- Revise and resubmit your application elsewhere, taking advantage of the additional information gained from the previous funding agency review.

Final Words

In the end, no one who embarks on this journey loses. The individual teacher who strives for the National Endowment for the Humanities in- stitute, the Fulbright scholarship, or the sabbatical gains a wealth of in- sight into their own strengths and professional needs, all of which can be adapted for other, increasingly exciting opportunities. The depart- ment or group that endeavors to improve its capacity to teach, help, or provide for its community wins through the improved relationships, the professional dialogue that has been opened up, the commitment to im- prove that has been unleashed within themselves. And the institution that sets out to expand its mission, goals, or facilities succeeds where others cannot because it engages in the process of reflecting and revising itself to meet the ever changing demands of the modern world. If you follow your own instincts, develop what Tom Peters calls "Wow Pro- jects," you are assured of eventually finding someone, some agency, some foundation that will say, "Yours is a great idea, I'll grant you that," and will be happy to give you the money you need to do the things you propose.

We have included three different grants in their entirety on the CD-ROM so that you can look at some complete grants as you pre- pare yours.

17

WORKSHOP 1
Writing with
Power

Writing proposals often brings with it the challenge of working under incredible pressure at a task that is not easy or comfortable for any of us. This is, after all, "real" writing, meaning writing that counts, that is, quite literally, for the money. As a writer, you need to give yourself permission to begin, to tell yourself you are not writing *the actual, final* proposal. Who knows, maybe you are; worry about that later. Just find a way to get going on it before your brain gives you a million reasons not to.

Getting Started

See yourself as a writer; take yourself seriously.

Anyone who sits down to make a genuine effort at writing is a writer. John Steinbeck's wife had to correct all his spelling and grammar mistakes; just remember that being a writer is about getting the winning ideas down.

Know the questions your proposal needs to answer.

The application itself offers most of the guidance you need to write the proposal. Using that rubric and application guidelines as checklists, try to create sets of question for yourself to get started. Here are some generic but typical examples:

- Our department wants to _____.
- We want to do this because _____.
- If we get _____ we will be able to _____.
- This _____ is crucial to our progress because it will allow us to

  _____.

- Our past efforts complement this next phase in several important ways. (List and explain these past efforts.)

You probably won't use these exact sentences—they lack any real voice—but they can help you get started. You can revise for voice and tone later.

Stop, think, make notes.

Instead of jumping straight to the keyboard, spend some time reading over the application guidelines, making a mess of clusters, outlines, notes—whatever works for you. We know we are ready to write when we begin to hear the language of the proposal coming to us. Consider one of these forms (we call them tricks) to help you refine your thinking before you begin drafting; each one asks you to sum up what it is you are trying to say in your proposal.

- postcard proposal (you get three-by-five inches to sum up your proposition)
- Dear Mom (explain it to your mother—or whoever)
- business card proposal (you get the space of a typical business card to spell out your proposition)

Be clear about the purpose of the writing.

Pay attention to the verbs the application guidelines use: if it says "discuss," that is different from "examine" or "outline." If you remain unclear as to what, exactly, the funding agency is asking you to do, consider calling a representative there to ask.

Addressing the Needs of Your Audience

Organize your information for the greatest effect.

In short, the beginning and end—of the sentence, a paragraph, a list, a section, the proposal—offer the most obvious points of emphasis. If your argument depends on the cumulative force of increasingly powerful examples, make sure these are organized from least to most important. On the other hand, if you are not sure how much time your readers will give to a section, be sure to get the crucial piece right up front, especially if you think they will come to the proposal with a prejudice. In other words, anticipate and meet head on those likely questions about your eligibility, credibility, or capacity. Shorter paragraphs will allow you to organize your ideas into smaller pieces, each one getting the benefit of a paragraph's emphasis.

Establish and maintain the appropriate voice.

When you think of voice, think of attitude. If you sound arrogant, you might put your readers off. Make yourself sound perfect and they will wonder why you need to make the changes your proposal outlines. Sound too humble and they will doubt you have the confidence necessary to win in the big leagues. To help you determine the best voice for this proposal, ask yourself the following questions:

- Who will read this?
- What will be the reader's most pressing concerns?
- What will make him or her reject a proposal?
- What will make him or her take me seriously?
- What assumptions can I make based on the reader's position (e.g., as a principal, or a business person, or a parent)?

Voice also involves the way you convey your information to the reader. While many proposals restrict your writing by forcing you to adhere to a prescribed format, there are ways to make the proposal more personal. Consider the following opening paragraph of a federal Blue Ribbon School award proposal in which we presented the proposal as a portfolio of the school's achievements. Note how we go on to use student quotes to provide the piece with a more intimate voice, to "give voice" to the students by letting them speak on behalf of their school:

Dear Reader:

New Haven Elementary School, located in New Haven, Connecticut, invites you to learn more about our school through this portfolio of achievements we have assembled with the help of students, faculty, and members of the surrounding community. This success is the result of years of hard work that dates back to 1959 when the school first opened to serve students in New Haven Unified School District, the largest school district in the state. New Haven Elementary is itself a showcase of some of New Haven's best students, since this magnet school for talented children draws from all over the city. Despite this relationship with the greater New Haven area, the neighborhoods surrounding New Haven have always been an integral part of the school's community. Local professional experts in the areas of science and business, art and technology, contribute to the school's program in ways that make New Haven an example for all other schools.

Student Focus and Support. New Haven Elementary's students are its greatest achievement. As Brian Chiu, a fourth grader at New Haven, said, "Because the teachers think we're bright, we are." The school's faculty, which consists of twenty-five teachers and hundreds of committed volunteers, inspires such confidence in its students as a result of their constant investment in their own teaching. Reform programs such as the New Haven's Schools of Tomorrow and participation in ongoing institutes with universities foster professional exchange that yields greater learning. The different strategies and methods teachers learn through such research and training enable them to focus on students' individual needs and support their learning through the most appropriate instructional methods while simultaneously using those materials adopted by the New Haven Unified School District. Whether it is through such in-house programs as the Wee Deliver student-run mail service, or the Reading Club, which pairs older students with younger students to help them improve their reading, New Haven offers every student a path to success and the means to achieve that success. When students do achieve their goals, they can look forward to schoolwide recognition at the monthly assembly, where they are awarded honors for improvement, contributions to the school community, or other achievements. Asked what she liked about New Haven Elementary, fifth grader Brynna White said, "The teachers here at New Haven never give up and they teach us not to give up also."

Another essential aspect of voice is its uniqueness: You don't want to blend in, although you don't want to stand out in some distracting way, either. Writing the proposal as a dialogue between two second graders arguing about how bad the playground equipment is might amuse the readers, but it won't win you the money to buy a new set of monkey bars. Consider this opening to a major technology grant, which brought in over $100,000 for an elementary school by helping readers see what the proposed community would look like:

Three months after receiving the equipment, students in Mrs. Connor's third-grade class huddle around the computers, waiting to check their e-mail: it is the morning ritual, one they all enjoy. The mail would be coming from their "senior friends" at a nearby retirement home where a computer was also connected to the school's network. The seniors, many of whom have trouble sleeping at night, will often write the children letters in the wee hours; their relationship with the children at Bayside, combined with their new computer skills, invests them with a sense of purpose some have not felt in some time. Teachers at Bayside, including Mrs. O'Connor, get to school a little earlier to get the system up so it's ready when the kids arrive at eight. They have no trouble doing this because John Gage, the district's technology coordinator, provided several workshops on maintaining their hardware and using the software within the context of the curriculum.

Three months later, and six months into the project, the students at Bayside Elementary have learned to create, edit, and maintain their school's Web site. To this site they regularly add a range of literacy projects reflecting the variety of work and celebrating the accomplishments of the school's students. Their senior friends visit the site regularly, making comments on how nice their work is, posting these comments to them on e-mail. Early links to such local environmental sites as the Bayside Preserve allow the students to take "virtual field trips" which their senior friends can also take; these trips allow them to share their observations through writing and the drawings the students make of the different habitats.

John Gage and other on-site mentors have, by this time, finished training all members of the staff and all students in a peer-tutoring program. Fourth and fifth graders, after demonstrating mastery, teach the students in the lower grades how to use the Internet by visiting the Web site of their favorite television show *Kratt's Creatures*, and letting them develop their computer skills through the different activities the Kratt's site offers them. John Chin, a third grader with severe hearing difficulties, tells his senior friend, Mr. Hill, about the site; the next morning John has an e-mail from Mr. Hill telling him about the time when he traveled in Africa as a young man and saw his first real lion. Everyone is jealous and wants to read John's e-mail. Mr. Hill also mentions that he, too, wears a hearing aid and tells John that he likes being able to turn it off when he doesn't want to listen to people. John thinks this is funny and shows it to his other deaf friends at school.

Obviously, your voice will depend on your audience. An NEH or Fulbright application will likely be read by academic professors who take scholarship very seriously. They want to know not only why you want to study modern poetry but what you will contribute to the seminar. Thus your voice must be one of authority and intellect, as in this excerpt from a winning NEH summer institute application essay:

This seminar offers me, through its themes and format, great nourishment as both a writer and a teacher. My own writing has often grown out of my work with students and helped me to be something of a mentor to aspiring writers. This work with students, particularly young poets, is my blessing, one that yields a steady stream of pride in the words they write and the poets they read. When I find myself facing the skepticism of students who wonder what role poetry plays in our lives, I often think of Seamus Heaney's remarks in his essay "The Government of the Tongue," in which he writes that "no lyric ever stopped a tank." And yet, he goes on, "in the rift between what is going to happen and whatever we would wish to happen, poetry holds attention for a space, functions not as distraction but as pure concentration, a focus where our power to concentrate is concentrated back on ourselves." It is that "pure concentration" found in such masters as William Carlos Williams and John Berryman that I hope to spend my summer thinking about.

Write first for yourself, then for the reader.

This is very useful advice because it gives us permission to write what Donald Murray calls a "discovery draft" (Murray 1996, 18). This was also Ernest Hemingway's advice. (Hemingway's other famous piece of writing advice was that "every writer should develop a high-powered bullshit detector," but I think that statement is better directed at the *readers* of grants.) Once you get a draft down on paper, you can begin to go through it and ask yourself whether this or that accords with the potential funder's expectations, whether this is the best tone, if this is the most effective order in which to present your ideas. This is also the point at which you can return to the grant application and check to see that you are answering the questions it asks.

Think in bullets.

Though addressed elsewhere in this book, it's worth emphasizing the importance of structure and format in any writing task. You are writing to be read—and read quickly—by people whose minds are rapidly turning to Jell-O as they pore over all the different proposals. This section of the book models what I mean by "thinking in bullets": the main ideas are quickly discernible and can be glanced in a minute. If you want to read beyond the bullet, there is text to help clarify the idea.

Bullets or similar devices force you to clarify your ideas into short phrases and organize them. If you have time, it can be very useful to go through your draft and organize it into an outline if you are not already writing from one. This reverse approach to outlining can force you to crawl deeper into the structure of your emerging document to find—or realize the absence of—the organization. Such organization of the crucial ideas is essential to your proposal's success: these are the ideas the readers will be looking for. You might find it additionally helpful to revisit the application guidelines before rereading your own text to remind yourself what you need to emphasize. You could even go so far, if you have not already done so, as to create two parallel outlines, one from the application and the second from your current draft. If you do this, try to match everything up to see where you need to concentrate your efforts in the next draft.

Ask and answer the Essential Questions.

The Essential Questions—who, why, where, when, what, how, and so what?—help you develop your text by fleshing out the obvious details: Where is the school? Who is involved? How did the program begin? They also help you to go into greater depth in your writing by considering such questions as these while you write:

- What needs will this proposal meet?
- How will it meet them?
- What are the greatest obstacles to your proposed project's success?
- How will you overcome them?
- Why do you think this will work?
- How do you know?
- Why is this important?
- How is this different from—or similar to—what has been done in the past?

In addition to asking yourself these and other such questions as you write, you need to anticipate the obvious questions the readers will ask. During a school accreditation committee meeting recently, for example, people at my school wanted to write down statements like "A faculty senate was eventually dismissed as a viable solution to the previous problems," and "The developmental reading program was recently discontinued." Their initial inclination was to offer the visiting committee no explanation as to why these decisions were made. It was inevitable that the site visitation committee would ask us to explain these two events, if for no other reason than these two subjects were specifically mentioned in our previous accreditation report; we realized it was in our best interests to explain. Successful writers, like chess players, always anticipate the moves of the other and try to provide readers the answers they need to help them keep reading easily and quickly.

Establishing Helpful Habits

If you find yourself getting writer's block, go to the section in Chapter 22 (Workshop 6), "Making Room for Creativity," on getting unstuck. There you will find helpful strategies to get you writing—or thinking—again.

LEARNING LINKS

Write first; edit later.

You can only juggle so many balls at once when writing. Ironing out the grammatical errors is the least of your concerns at this point. No one ever won a million dollars or the chance to spend the summer studying modern poetry because they had no grammatical errors. Certainly these details matter—tremendously so!—but they are best addressed later on when the writer can bring the full measure of his or her attention to bear on that one aspect of the writing.

Stop only when you know what you will say next.

If I stop now, I know exactly what to say when I sit back down tomorrow. If, however, I finish this chapter and go to bed satisfied with my work for the day, I may well wake up to find I have no idea what to do next or how to begin. Sometimes writers who follow this advice stop midsentence so that they can easily pick up where they left off the next day.

Set deadlines for yourself.

We should add "realistic deadlines," but too often proposals demand unrealistic amounts of work. Example: the week during which we wrote this chapter, Jim's son's principal called to ask on Wednesday if he could try his hand at a large literacy grant for the whole school. When he asked when it was due, she said sheepishly, "Friday." That's about as realistic as getting his son to do all his homework as soon as he walks in the door.

Revising and Editing for Correctness and Fluency

Use proven techniques to help you find your errors.

The most important technique is to have as many people read and proofread your proposal as time allows. Aside from that, however, these methods will help you:

- Read aloud.
- Read for one type of error at a time.
- Have others read it.

If time allows, use revision techniques to improve your proposal.

- *So what?*: Simply read back through your document and ask yourself this question whenever possible (e.g., when you wrote, "Our program ensures that all graduates will have mastered the basic digital literacies"). It will force you to explain the importance of certain ideas that you may have thought were obvious but might not be.

- *Essential Questions:* Reread your proposal, stopping wherever necessary to ask the obvious questions such as "Who did that?" or "When did that program begin?" or "How many kids did that benefit?"

- *Revision:* After having put the proposal down for a day—or whatever you can spare to create some distance—return and reread with fresh sensibilities. Look for inconsistencies in tone, voice, references, ideas. Look for places where evidence can be provided to further support or clarify what you propose. This is the time to ask the hard questions such as "Does this make sense?" or "What are the questions I am not asking myself—but should be?"

- *Hire a professional proposal writer:* This is one of the many different points in the process when you should consider, if the stakes are high enough to warrant the expense, bringing in a professional who, with their wisdom, can see the flaws you cannot. The simple tweaking of a few sentences could mean the difference between winning and losing.

Writing for Style and Effect

Obey the essential principles of good writing.

In their wonderful book *The Write Way*, Richard Lederer and Richard Dowis (1995) argue that the five most important characteristics of good writing are that it be:

- clear
- correct
- concise
- complete
- considerate

We're hard-pressed to come up with a more succinct list. Consider the following proposal, which is included in its entirety and which, by the way, was awarded the money requested within one day.

> Our freshman Honors English program collaborates with the World History classes to provide a more integrated study of cultures through the use of literature from those countries (and writers from those countries who now live in the U.S.). Specifically, we study in great detail India, China, and South Africa. While the students read major novels from these countries, they lack access to a wider range of voices. Two years ago I was able to purchase one class set of the anthology *World Writers Today*, an excellent, comprehensive anthology that includes poetry, speeches, essays, and stories from major writers around the world. The anthology has a rich offering of authors from those

cultures we study and other stories from different cultures that would complement our studies as well. The problem we face is that the class sizes have grown and we now have two teachers dividing the teaching assignment. Thus books we might otherwise read go unused because we cannot afford more, a loss to our course and, more importantly, to the students. The money from this grant would allow us to purchase an additional thirty books, thereby enabling us to use the books for the current and next semester. When used before, the book proved valuable; the students found the readings by such writers as Nadine Gordimer and Maxine Hung Kingston helped them better understand not only the countries they studied but the people from those countries who often now sit beside them in class here in Burlingame, California.

Keep Lederer and Dowis's five characteristics in mind as you read through the following summary of important aspects of writing:

• *Avoid the passive sentence structure.* Example: "Students were taught to use a variety of computer programs." This sentence ignores the crucial fact that corporate mentors from Oracle came into the class to provide this instruction, a point no savvy proposal writer would want to leave out. Better to write: "Technology experts from the local Oracle headquarters provided direct instruction in how to create and use databases so students could better organize their data as they collected it."

• *Cut the fat.* Taking the time to make your sentences more concise saves space, which can be crucial in proposals that limit you to a certain number of pages per section; it can also make them more powerful. Often the "fat" is caused by the use of passive sentence structures. Example: "In the area of technology, one thing about which we are particularly proud is our program through which students were taught to use a variety of computer programs by local experts who were brought in through a corporate mentoring program." Another way we often clutter up our sentences is with unnecessary words: e.g.,"another aspect of our program about which we are particularly proud and very satisfied." *Proud* and *very satisfied* are redundant; better to write, "We are very proud of our program."

• *Use precise language.* This will ensure that your reader knows what you are talking about and communicates that *you* know what you are talking about. Such language as "Our faculty hopes to expand its use of technology throughout the disciplines" is well intentioned but too general. Better to say, "Our English Department plans to integrate the use of on-line resources and multimedia presentation skills into its curriculum."

• *Vary your sentences to emphasize ideas and enhance your style.* If every sentence dances to the same beat, soon the reader loses interest and you lose the ability to emphasize one idea over another, since everything begins to sound the same. More importantly, each example provides a slightly different emphasis, something you always want to consider when writing. Consider the merits of each of the following examples:

- Because Internet skills are crucial to students' future success, our English Department intends to expand its use of technology to include on-line research techniques.

- On-line research techniques, which all students will be expected to possess in the future, are central to the English Department's plans to expand the use of technology.

- The English Department intends to expand its use of technology so as to give all students those skills, such as conducting on-line research, that they will need in the future.

• *Use modifiers to save space and add power to your sentences.* While there are a number of different types of modifiers, the most immediately useful ones are:

APPOSITIVES

- *Weak*: Del Dayo Elementary School is located in a beautiful neighborhood. Del Dayo is attended by a socially and culturally diverse student population.

- *Improved by use of appositive*: Del Dayo Elementary School, *a school consisting of a socially and culturally diverse student population*, is located in a beautiful neighborhood.

ADJECTIVE CLAUSES

- *Weak*: The Wee Deliver program is a very successful program. This program is successful because it involves all students in some way. This involvement develops such skills as independence and responsibility in all our students.

- *Improved by use of adjective clauses*: The Wee Deliver program, *which involves nearly all students and develops in them independence and responsibility*, is very successful.

SUBORDINATING PHRASES

- *Weak*: I must admit that I have no formal knowledge of poetry. I am sure I can find some way to make a contribution to your summer institute. Being an art teacher provides me with some insight into how artists represent their ideas using symbolic language.

- *Improved by use of subordinate phrase*: Being an art teacher and lacking any formal knowledge of poetry, I realize I am at a disadvantage; *however*, my insights into how artists represent their ideas in other, more visual, media will help me to make a meaningful contribution to your summer institute.

- *Make all lists and series parallel.* Nearly all proposals will include lists, sometimes many of them. Be sure to check that all such lists follow the same grammatical form; in most cases this means either that they all begin with a verb (e.g., *expand* the use of technology, *train* all teachers in its use, *integrate* the use of technology into all disciplines . . .) or a noun (e.g., "We request the following in order to achieve the goals outlined herein: *high interest reading books* in all classrooms, *dictionaries* for each student, and *anthologies* that contain more contemporary reading selections").

- *Avoid jargon.* For practical reasons, your proposal might be read by people who do not know what "ESLRs" or "delivery standards" are. Certainly you can, and sometimes need to use such language; however, if you must, be sure to clarify such terms. However, the writing will always be better—i.e., more compelling, more concise, more colorful—if you use natural language.

- *Think twice before you break the rules.* Everyone loves to catch experts making mistakes, especially people who suffered at the hands of a teacher who corrected their every error. While there are many sources to back you up if you break the following "rules," it is better when writing a proposal not to distract the reader with such matters. Therefore, whenever possible:

- Do not end a sentence with a preposition.
- Do not split your infinitives.
- Do not begin a sentence with *and* or *but*.

- *Find out what the reader prefers when it comes to gender references.* Traditionally we referred to a generic person using the masculine (e.g., "Any student entering his project in this competition must realize that he will be judged"). In the past decade, it has become increasingly common for publications to require the use of non-gender-specific language (e.g., "Students entering their projects in the competition must realize that they will be judged according to the same standards used to judge their peers across the nation").

- *Use strong, active verbs.* Active verbs are words that describe an action you can see or feel. Consider the difference between these two sentences:

- *Weak*: Our school *is* one of only a few schools to use these instructional techniques schoolwide.

- *Strong*: Our school *integrates* these instructional techniques throughout its curriculum, making it one of the few schools in the state . . .

- *Weak*: Students *are able to communicate* using a variety of media by the time they graduate from our school.

- *Strong*: Students *graduate* from our school having mastered a variety of media which allow them to communicate their ideas more effectively.

• **Use transitions.**   Transitional words—e.g., *however, because, although, certainly, thus, since*—make your writing flow and help your ideas link up better by establishing a relationship between them. Transitions appear between sentences and paragraphs. The proposal included above for *World Writers Today* anthologies contains a number of examples. Without transitions, your writing becomes choppy, fragmented; it loses its ability to convey the ideas effectively.

Final Words

When you get right down to it this book is about the importance of writing. Good ideas get lost in weak language. Proposals get dismissed quickly if they cannot engage—or if they offend. Writing is a public act, one to which people bring an often exacting scrutiny. How able are you to create a powerful program if, for example, you cannot create a document free of errors? This chapter strives to help you make your words and sentences as strong as the ideas they contain. There comes a time, however, no matter how many times you revise, reread, and refine, when you must abandon your creation and send your proposal off where it will be judged according to the standards, criteria, and prejudice of the different readers it encounters along the way.

18

WORKSHOP 2
Designing
Winning
Documents

Good design brings absolute attention to data.

—Edward Tufte

Appearances cannot be deceiving: they must sell and communicate your ideas, your passion, your capacity to do what you propose. Depending on the size and requirements of the proposal, you may have to achieve this in one page; of course, if you seek a million-dollar grant, you might have to accomplish all the funder asks in forty pages, organizing the information in a way that keeps your reader from getting lost and missing your point. Our emphasis within this chapter is on making every element—from your fonts and margins to your tables and diagrams—communicate your ideas with power, efficiency, and style.

Let us begin with a couple of quick examples drawn from our own experience to help you better understand what we mean when we refer to appearances, visual explanations, or graphic elements.

• It's 4:30 on a Thursday after a long day of teaching. We've been asked to help read a bunch of one-page proposals for a technology grant.

We're tired, but willing to be interested in teachers' ideas if they engage us. Most of them look like they were written in thirty minutes: Geneva font, three-quarter-inch margins, all text (i.e., no bullets, graphs, tables), photocopied. The winner: Palatino font, bullets, one-and-a-quarter-inch margins, an embedded table that allows us to see in a flash what they want, why they want it, how much it costs. In addition, they printed it on a heavy stock quality paper using a laser printer. Each bullet, paragraph, and table appears in the order outlined in the guidelines. Finally, as this was a technology grant they sought, every detail of their application conveys their skill with the tools they said they knew how to use.

• A group of teachers from an elementary school is rushing to finish their school's National Blue Ribbon application. The application can be no longer than twenty-nine pages, single spaced. Instead of offering pages of text describing what they do in each curricular area, the school uses the government application's guidelines to create a table which is cross-referenced with the scoring rubric the reader is using. This allows the teachers to organize their information effectively and economically within one page so the readers can, at a glance, see what the school offers. Moreover, this impressive display of complicated information enhances the credibility of this faculty, further distinguishing them in the eyes of the readers.

The visual elements of any document should accomplish several important ends. They should help the reader by making the information more interesting and clear. Certainly in this era of desktop publishing, we bring to each document a set of expectations that would have been unimaginable even ten years ago. As Robert Bringhurst writes in his classic book *The Elements of Typographic Style*, the proper elements on the page, a balance between typographic and visual information, can achieve "some earned or unearned interest that gives its living energy to the page" (p. 17). The intelligent use of these different textual elements can accomplish a variety of important goals, any of which might make the difference between winning and losing the money you seek. They can:

• clarify ideas

• emphasize important information

• reveal crucial relationships between programs and ideas

Considered together, these different elements create a unified effect that should be appropriate to their intended audience. If, for example, you are writing to members of the business community, you want to appear conservative, a safe investment to them, one that will represent their businesses in ways that they will be proud to recognize. Others, however, want to see something different, something new; in which case your application offers the first opportunity to set yourselves apart from the others. On one grant we used the talents of an art teacher to add images to our application, which we offered as a portfolio of our dreams. In this way, even the form in which you submit the application—e.g., scrapbook, portfolio, annual report—contributes to the appearance and, ultimately, the outcome.

Questions to Ask Before You Begin

A few questions asked at the beginning of any project can help save time and avoid disappointment later on:

- What do the guidelines say regarding the text (e.g., font size, margins, line spacing, headers and footers, number of pages, pictures)?
- What information is most important?
- How can I best communicate the essential information (e.g., table, photograph, diagram, multimedia, a story, bulleted list)?
- Is my idea—e.g., use of photographs—permitted?
- Who is my audience?
- What special needs might the reader have that my text can anticipate and meet?

   This last point is crucial. Almost all proposals are read by a group of people brought together for a day or two. They are intelligent, committed people who can easily spot competence and know what excellence looks like. They will read tons of text, some of which will make their eyes hurt, some of which will simply confuse them.

The Page: Form, Function, and Format

The visual elements of the page engage the reader's senses by interrupting the flat plane of the page, the redundant field of words. It also builds in the reader's mind (i.e., the judge) that you think in multiple dimensions, something that can only further convince them that you are able to accomplish what you propose.

   Everything about the format of the document, from the fonts you use to the visual display of information, should help them make reading your document a pleasure; the last thing you want is to make your reader curse you as they read your single-spaced ten-point font application whose Nobel Prize–worthy ideas the reader is too aggravated to notice. Because documents are read by different people for different reasons in different ways, you want your proposal to function on several levels. This means using such organizational devices as headers and subheaders so a foundation's director can, as with a resume, scan through and see if the application is going to hit the main ideas.

H O T

T I P S

Headers and subheaders can, if aligned with the application's scoring rubric, make reading your proposal very easy by allowing readers to concentrate on *what* you are proposing. Such formatting also shows your proposal is anchored in the funder's expectations and organized to meet these demands.

Choose Fonts Carefully

Fonts give voice to the document. If too small, too narrow, or poorly chosen, the font can not only make a document difficult to read but also undermine its message. Carefully written words deserve a typeface that will evoke their spirit. Figure 18.1 provides guidance in the most crucial areas common to all written documents. These recommendations derive from readability research as well as the long-standing tradition of typography. If time allows, it is best to do the actual formatting—i.e., choosing the fonts and such features as bullets—after you have actually finished the document; this allows you to concentrate on one domain at a time.

Visual Explanations

The most common devices you will use include:

- timelines
- maps
- webs
- charts
- graphs
- diagrams
- photographs
- multimedia displays
- drawings
- reader's rubric
- site visitation score sheet

Images and other graphic options offer you a second language that, if you use it correctly, can convey more information, with greater

Do Use	**Do Not Use**
• a serif font (e.g., Palatino or Baskerville) for the body text of any document	• **bold** unless you have a good reason; to emphasize, use *italics* instead
• sansserif fonts (Helvetica) for headers	• fonts like Times Roman unless you must
• nice margins for white space; this makes it easier to read and looks nicer	• a font smaller than 12 unless you cannot otherwise fit in what you must
• an indent no larger than one em (i.e., no more than three spaces) in your paragraphs	• more than one space after punctuation
• left-justified margins to improve readability	• <u>underline</u> as this interferes with reading
• sansserif fonts in diagrams, tables, charts	• any fonts that would otherwise distract the reader
• the same font for the header text as the body text	• clip art to spice up your text
• real or "smart" quotation marks and apostrophes	• footnotes; better to use sidebars so the information is near the reference
• spacing if possible; single spacing is too crowded (always check guidelines!)	• colored inks unless they serve a specific purpose (e.g., in a chart)
• the best printer and paper you can so the final product looks perfect	• more than two fonts on a single page
• the same fonts in the same way throughout the document (i.e., consistent use of same font for body, headers, subheaders, etc.)	• different fonts and formats if writing in a group: standardize right off and submit all documents in this agreed-upon format

FIGURE 18.1   **Font and Format Guidelines**

rhetorical effect, in less space. Though we cannot include an example of video on these pages, we do want to recognize its potential value as a medium through which you can, if allowed, make a strong impression on the readers, particularly if it is student-produced and the proposal is for a grant related to technology. Visual explanations have the power to create a central metaphor that can, if used effectively, provide a sense of unity to your proposal (e.g., by showing relationships, evoking particular details of the community or program, positioning the entire package as a portfolio). Figures 18.2–18.5 provide examples of documents that help the reader visually navigate through the information.

Figure 18.2 is a sample page from a multimillion-dollar budget from a proposal. Note how categories are clearly delineated and aligned with those required by the application. The format achieves clarity through order and formatting.

1. Salaries for Project Manager, Coordinators, and Advisors					
Name	Salary	FTE %	Grant	In-Kind	Total Invested
Carol Prater	80,000	.75	60,000		60,000
Jerry Westfall	60,000	0.5	30,000	15,000	45,000
David Seiter	60,000	0.5	30,000	15,000	45,000
Ron Temple	60,000	0.25	15,000	15,000	30,000
Dennis Aseltyne	60,000	0.25	15,000	15,000	30,000
7 site Secretaries@	20,000 each	0.25	35,000	20,000	55,000
Dr. Guay/P. Redmond	80,000	0.25	20,000	15,000	35,000
		Total	205,000	95,000	300,000
7 Site Directors	50,000 each	0.25	105,000	65,000	170,000
7 Site Technicians	40,000	0.5	140,000		140,000
		Total	245,000	65,000	310,000

2. Employee Benefits		
Employee Benefits (15%)	67,500	67,500

3. Travel		
Conference Meetings	10,000	10,000
Washington, DC	5,000	5,000
Regions Meetings (auto,air)	7,000	7,000
Total	22,000	22,000

4. Consultant/Contracts					
Consultants	Days	Per/Diem	Grant	In-Kind	Total Invested
Dr. David Thornburg	12	1,000	6,000	6,000	12,000
CompUSA	12	1,000	6,000	6,000	12,000
Sonoma Evaluation	40	1,500	40,000	20,000	60,000
eTREK	24	1,000	12,000	12,000	24,000
UintahED (CD/Portfolio Production			25,000	40,000	65,000
Website Productions			15,000	15,000	30,000
		Total	104,000	99,000	203,000

5. Equipment				
	Qty	Grant	In-Kind	Total Invested
Laptop Computers	7	22,500		22,500
Computers 10 - per site @ 7 sites	70	40,000	100,000	140,000
Scanners 2 per site @ $200	14	2,800		2,800
Color Laser Jet Printers - 1 per site @ $3000	7	21,000		21,000
Xerox Machine @ $3000	2	6,000		6,000
Virtual Conference Centers	7	175,000	180,000	355,000
Multimedia Presentation Hardware -$3,000 per site	7	21,000	2,000	23,000
College of Notre Dame Computer Lab	1	40,000	15,000	55,000
	Total	328,300	297,000	625,300

FIGURE 18.2   Sample Budget Illustration: Pacific Rim Alliance

6. Materials and Supplies

	Qty	Grant	In-Kind	Total Invested
Instructional Supplies - $6000 @	7	42,000	42,000	84,000
CDROM/Video Materials - $5000 @	7	35,000	3,000	38,000
Office Supplies - $2000 @	7	14,000	14,000	28,000
Software - $6000 @	7	42,000	4,000	46,000
Books/subscriptions - $1000 @	7	7,000		7,000
	Total	140,000	63,000	203,000

7. Other

	Qty	Grant	In-Kind	Total Invested
Meeting Facilities as needed		6,000	6,000	12,000
Printing		3,500	6,000	9,500
AV Rental Equipment		2,000	4,500	6,500
Mileage		4,000	2,000	6,000
Telephone		3,000	3,000	6,000
Postage		4,000	1,000	5,000
Field Trips/Buses		10,000	5,000	15,000
Release Time @ $100 per day70 days(10 per site)		7,000	7,000	14,000
35 Teachers Prep Time 20 days @$250/day			175,000	175,000
35 Teacher stipends10 days @$250/day		87,500		87,500
	Total	127,000	209,500	336,500

Summation

	Grant	In-Kind	Total
1. Salaries	450,000	160,000	610,000
2. Benefits	67,500		67,500
3. Travel	22,000		22,000
4. Consultants/Contracts	104,000	99,000	203,000
5. Equipment	328,300	297,000	625,300
6. Materials/Supplies	140,000	63,000	203,000
7. Other	127,000	209,500	336,500
Sub-total 1,238,800		828,500	2,067,300
Indirect Cost (7%)86,716			86,716
Total 1,325,516		828,500	2,154,016

FIGURE 18.2   *continued*

Figure 18.3 shows a timeline Carol created for an ambitious proposal that demanded a high level of organization across time and agencies. The timeline visually explains the information, which has been broken into steps in the columns by month. This chart achieves a high level of organization, which simultaneously conveys competence to the evaluator.

Figure 18.4 illustrates another way of organizing and presenting information for a timeline. This example differs from Figure 18.3 in form but not function: there is less information to convey and thus the bulleted structure is adequate.

Year 1: Preservice, Planning and Material Development	A	S	O	N	D	J	F	M	A	M	J	J
Select PRA Project Coordinator	•											
Set-up organization/management system for program	•											
Assign completion dates for first year training and tasks	•											
Establish Challenge training topics	•											
Schedule first-year training and consultants		•										
Hire technology facilitator and paraprofessionals		•										
Implement training activities			•									
Plan, Develop, organize cross-age tutoring program			•									
Organize and plan parent education committee			•									
Plan, Develop, organize, order materials for TECH Center			•									
Establish Portfolio Guidelines		•										
Restructure Staff Development curriculum			•									
Research and order material for Enrichment Program			•									
Order technology equipment and software				•								
Set-up Enrichment Classes					•							
Begin staff technology training							•					
Set-up model site visitations and conference attendance			•									
Begin community education activities							•					
Do formative/process evaluations				•								
Begin cross-age tutoring on limited basis							•					
Establish interdisciplinary teacher teams; begin curricular software review & planning				•								
Plan for Open Houses for year 2								•				
Meet with evaluator to establish evaluation system; gather baseline data				•	•	•	•					
Set-up staff development (Recycle & Refurbish classes) for Year 2									•	•		
Year 2: Beginning Implementation	A	S	O	N	D	J	F	M	A	M	J	J
Review, assign completion dates for year 2 training & tasks	•											
Hold Open Houses for incoming parents, students, sites	•											
Order computers and supplies	•											
Implement interdisciplinary thematic instruction		•										
Schedule year 2 training and consultants		•										
Begin computer maintenance and instruction program; order materials per needs		•										
Produce PRA newsletter		•	•	•	•	•	•	•	•	•	•	•
Begin Electronic Portfolios planning (after school hours for enrichment)		•										
Begin Saturday tech classes for teachers / community			•									
Activate Computer Lab Norm referenced software		•										
Train staff and students on use of electronic portfolio			•	•	•							
Institute use of electronic portfolios							•					
Initiate comprehensive community education program			•									
Data collection; evaluation of new curriculum, assessments					•							
On-going program evaluation; 2nd year report to fed. gov't.		•	•	•	•	•	•	•	•	•		

FIGURE 18.3   **Sample Project Timeline (Chart): Pacific Rim Alliance**

Year 3: Ongoing implementation of programs:
• schedule third-year training and consultants / bring on new sites • continue refinement of instructional materials and assessment • purchase additional equipment and supplies for Tech Learning Labs • ongoing development of Staff, Students in Electronic Assessment / Refurbish • ongoing data collection, curriculum and assessment evaluation • redevelopment/corrections/adjustments in program implementation based on student outcomes and program evaluation
Year 4: Full project implementation:
• ongoing and follow-up training • continue refinement of instructional materials and assessment • purchase additional equipment and supplies for Tech Learning Lab • ongoing development of Enrichment Center • ongoing data collection, curriculum and assessment evaluation • redevelopment/corrections/adjustments in program implementation based on student outcomes and program evaluation
Year 5: Review, refinement, sustainability and dissemination:
• full implementation of the PRAs program • ongoing assessment, refinement, redirection of program • final program evaluation • project dissemination • future plans

FIGURE 18.4   Sample Project Timeline (Narrative): Pacific Rim Alliance

Figure 18.5 is an assessment tool we created for our evaluators. When they opened up the proposal packet they found this tool, which we designed to help them find their way to the information we knew their scoring rubric would require. They found this device impressive and useful.

Final Words

Remember what you already know: appearance counts. Everything says more than it seems: fonts, format, images—these all contribute to or detract from the effect of your message depending on how you use them. All these details are meant to achieve greater rhetorical effect and help readers navigate their way through the information easily so that they can find what they need. Like a customer whose every need has been considered and anticipated, the reader who encounters a document formatted for easy reading will feel a gratitude and measure of confidence in your ability that can only increase the likelihood of your winning the funding you seek.

Challenge Assessment Tools

Challenge 2000 Principles	Portfolio Guidelines	Page
Silicon Valley students will be the most sought after in the world for skills, knowledge, citizenship	• Vision for making progress towards the Challenge 2000 Principles • Plan to improve student performance, and to insure continuous improvement of performance	#1 7–9
Demonstrated, measurable progress toward world-class standards in core subjects—focus on literacy, critical thinking, communication skills	• A demonstrated focus on all students	# 8
Demonstrated ability to recognize ethical issues and act appropriately	• Substantial demonstration of a "vertical slice" team	# 42–43 55
Ability to function in a multicultural environment and work as a team member	• A clear vision of how the emphasis on one or more core subjects will infuse substantial systemic improvements throughout our schools	#1–2 9, 18
Demonstrate the ability to use information sources and technology effectively	• Plan for coordinating the improvement process between schools	# 8 41
Schools will be exciting, effective learning environments where teachers are coaches and facilitators and students are self-directed learners	• Partners participated in portfolio development	# 1 vi viii
System-wide commitment to continuous improvement; measurable outcomes and accountability for results	• Assessment of the current work of the Renaissance Team, how the Team will move to the next stage, and how the Team schools will sustain their efforts over time (including beyond the scope of this partnership)	# 51–53
Teachers will have their performance rewarded and are supported and valued by community as professionals	• A variety of measures will be used to assess student performance at every grade level	#16–17 33, 51
Demonstrated, measurable partnership with all members and levels of the slice	• A demonstrated commitment of human and financial resources from the schools • The name of the Renaissance Team Leader with address, fax, and phone number • A list of the Renaissance Leadership Team members with their affiliation/background and their phone numbers	#1–2 11,19,27, 35

This information is to help you find specific information in the Challenge 2000 portfolio.

FIGURE 18.5 Sample Reader Assessment Tool

19

WORKSHOP 3
Organizing for
Success

When it comes to organizing, a scene from *I Love Lucy* in which Lucy and Ethel are working on an assembly line at a candy factory comes to mind: They get off to a good enough start, but soon the work speeds up and because they don't know how to cope with the rising demands, they begin stuffing the chocolate candies in their mouths, apron pockets, and dresses in a desperate attempt to keep up. Certainly not all proposals are this demanding; however, for those that require us to manage a complex array of schedules, abilities, deadlines, resources, and needs, we need to get organized before we start if we are to succeed. In his book *Eiger Dreams: Ventures Among Men and Mountains*, writer Jon Krakauer (1997) regularly describes mountain climbers who set out without having anticipated their needs and thus find themselves, often at critical moments, unable to continue their ascent. Proposals are mountains we set out to climb, but can only do so if we have marshaled the proper skills and resources.

Most proposals, regardless of their size, involve organizing the following components:

- time
- resources
- talent
- the process
- information

There are different stages throughout the process of putting together a proposal, each with its own organizational demands. It is best to think of your organizational demands as divided up into several different domains:

- long term (e.g., the entire project in all its pieces)
- short term (e.g., pieces or stages of the entire project)
- situational (e.g., meeting, brainstorming, writing, producing)

Organizing Information

From the moment you begin reading the proposal application you begin taking notes, taking in information you will use later to make your application competitive. Some people have minds that work in neat linear ways; others, however, work more associatively, their minds spawning ideas about one part of the proposal while they read about or work on another part. Thus you need a way to sort through and use your notes in different ways at different times throughout the process.

Note Taking

There are many ways of taking notes, but the one we have found most efficient is commonly known as the Cornell system. In short, this system requires that you draw two lines down the length of the page, dividing it into thirds. This is the note-taking system we used throughout the writing of this book, for example, which is little more than a proposal for one way to write proposals. The left margin then provides a space to make notes of all different types. You can, for example, skim back through what you've noted and write "Goals" next to those sections that somehow relate to the goals section of your proposal. Or you might write focus questions—e.g., "Why should you get the opportunity over all the others, especially since you received it once before?" It is in the margins of our messy, fertile notes that the connections begin to take place, where the ideas begin to weave themselves into something more than they can accomplish on their own.

Additional Considerations

- If we know we will want to make different sets of notes in the margins as we move through different stages of the project, we will sometimes make extra copies of our notes before we begin making marginal annotations.

- Always clearly identify the date and time and page number across the top of your notes. Once you get under way, all paper just becomes scribbles and blank marks on white paper, little of which can distinguish itself from the other dozens or even hundreds of pages.

• You have to decide for yourself whether you can take notes the way you need to on a computer and still listen and move around as needed. We have never found note taking on a computer to be efficient—we always want to make marginal notes; sometimes the setting won't tolerate your clacking away on a keyboard; you don't always have access to an outlet—you get the picture. The good ol' paper (eight and a half by eleven, so you can put it in a binder) method works fine for us, allowing us to make different kinds of notes in places where we know to look for them. Bottom line: whatever works for you. Some people swear by index cards; others like the security of a tape recorder. Most proposals don't give us extra time to go back and transcribe or even play back tapes, however. You have to be able to work well on the run.

Organizing Ideas

During the heated phase of brainstorming it is essential that no ideas get away. Furthermore, it is important for people to be able to see what they are thinking about by getting the ideas in front of them. This gives them something to react to, allows the facilitator—different from the secretary—to interact with the text the group or individual is creating. When we sat around discussing the Apple grant, for example, we mentioned that we happened to be working on a home page and wondered if that might not offer us a starting place to organize our ideas or even get us thinking metaphorically. Thus we wrote down "Home" on the sheet, and kept brainstorming associations, all of which began to coalesce when we hit on the idea of "Our Town," which would later become a virtual community consisting of senior citizens and elementary school students at the nearby school. (See Chapter 22, Workshop 6, "Making Room for Creativity," for more on actually generating ideas.) Our point here is that you need to be able to catch those ideas and organize them in ways that will keep the flow of thinking at its peak.

There is no one right approach, and how you do this work largely depends on whether the proposal is being written by one person or a team or a coalition. A coalition, for example, could include as many as one hundred people from all domains of the school community. In such cases it is better to use an overhead so that everyone can participate effectively. Smaller groups can use butcher paper or newsprint, making sure they write in large enough letters so that the entire group can read it. Finally, if you are working on your own, you can use whatever means appeals to you most. For example, we like to use the outlining feature in such software programs as Inspiration or ClarisWorks, because these programs allow you to revise and manipulate information independently in ways that would be impossible with a larger group.

Additional Considerations

• Have different colored markers (for butcher paper and overhead transparencies) to help you distinguish where one idea leaves off and another begins. If you can, provide some visual indicator—e.g., alternating color text or bullets with extra space between ideas—to signal these divisions between ideas.

• Throw away nothing, even if you transcribe it into the computer.

• Have the secretary go through and write up the notes from the overheads or butcher paper—if you have time. Otherwise, photocopy the transparencies as they are for the group, and keep the butcher paper up on the walls where people can add to it as they wish. One writer we know tapes up pages of poetry or fiction he is currently working on right next to his bathroom mirror so that while he shaves or brushes his teeth he can watch the text and test out other ideas against what he already has.

Managing Information

When you start spreading out your information, your applications, your data, and your resources in different places, it gets hard to manage the info; after all, if you cannot find it, you cannot use it. The following tips will help you avoid such disasters as deleting files that contain your latest version of the proposal that *was* going to win your school district a million dollars.

• *Stay digital whenever possible.* Large proposals written in pieces by different people will be much easier to manage if everyone is working on computers. This means, if possible, sending drafts of documents to the primary writers via e-mail instead of by fax so they can plug that digital text into the master document and thereby save time.

• *Establish protocols immediately.* You can lose information by not being able to access it due to cross-platform or software incompatibilities. Carol once spent an entire Saturday during a crucial period for a National Blue Ribbon Award application typing up thirty pages because she couldn't open the document they sent her. Thus in your initial setup meeting, decide on a word processing program, the platform (Windows or Macintosh), and the version of the program itself (e.g., Word 98). If you need to buy it for everyone, it's worth it for the headaches you will avoid later. This is especially crucial if you plan to feed it into some larger document that will be created by someone else later on. If this is the case, find out what they're using and make that your "industry standard."

• *Label everything.* Every document, draft, or page of notes should be clearly identified according to the section, version, author (if working in teams), and pages. This is an example of a label as it would appear atop a page of a school's WASC report: "WASC Report/Home Group/Vision Section/Berryman/4/23/99 @ 12:25 P.M./page 4." And when the next version is created, you do not replace the earlier version, but save it, instead, as "Vision Section 4/24/99 @ 4:13 P.M."

• *Centralize your operation.* This applies to the individual writing a proposal as well as to the large coalition. All proposals need a center where people can gather to exchange information, get new information, update their own assignments, revise the master To Do list, check the timeline, get supplies. There is no best way here, just the way that works best for you. On large projects, for example, Jim's home office usually becomes the center of operations since, as the writer, all information must flow toward him. Carol, on the other hand, as the strategic planner, might be the omnipresent voice coming to people over the phone or the fax, or in the meeting letting people know what they need to get to Jim. Jim can then, in turn, let Carol know what he needs from the others, and in this way a complementary system evolves.

• *Use the Bucket System.* This method offers the most useful system of organizing the different parts of the proposal. To summarize what we discuss at length in Chapter 5, you create a file system (preferably in a portable crate with hanging file folders) whose folders match the sections of the grant for which you are applying. In addition, you have a folder for samples written by others, and useful background information on the program, the grant making agency, the idea. Thus your buckets should consist of the following file folders:

- one for each section of the application (e.g., "Budget," "Goals and Objectives," etc.)
- background info on the program, company, etc.
- samples of past winners and losers
- notes, miscellaneous
- originals

Managing the Project

Groups seeking one million dollars and individuals hoping to spend a summer in a National Endowment for the Humanities institute need to organize the project so they get it done right, on time, and well. Most people lose because they lack some essential information or did not follow a crucial rule (e.g., "proposal must be double-sided in accordance with the National Paperwork Reduction Act"). The following will help you in this area:

- Use the application to create a master To Do list which includes, when possible, when tasks must be completed and who will do them.
- Create a master timeline that clearly describes what needs to be done by when—and by whom.
- Create a master Needs sheet to which people can add resources (e.g., "Need last WASC report") and materials (e.g., software, supplies).
- Create and update as needed the master Contact sheet that includes the following information about everyone involved:
  - name
  - address
  - phones: at home, work, office, cellular, fax, pager
  - e-mail/URL
  - contact person (if a company)
  - best time to find them at different places
  - their role

Organizing People

Another essential resource that must be carefully organized is talent. Not everyone can do everything, especially if you're involved with a massive project. Even individuals, however, need to look to others to help them on certain aspects of the project. Don't waste the talent and energy of the artist in your group on work that is not "theirs." Keep them in the wings, ready to come in when you need the art work. This will ensure that everyone works at peak efficiency and maximum satisfaction.

Organizing for Your Readers

The final product—your proposal—must help the reader find the essential information in a logical, efficient manner. The end result of all your efforts to organize information, ideas, time, and talent must be a text that is designed to help readers and persuade them of your idea's credibility and your capacity to deliver what you promise. Consider the benefits of different forms and how each functions to organize information; ask yourself if one of these, or some variation, would make for a compelling proposal:

- scrapbook
- yearbook
- anthology

- portfolio
- Web site
- pamphlet
- resume
- letter

Final Words

In his memoir about coaching the Chicago Bulls, Phil Jackson (1996) writes about managing chaos. Chaos is what makes writing proposals so difficult and so exciting, for we are writing them, developing the programs that need the funding, while we are doing our "real" jobs full time. We are trying to find time between classes and meetings to read or write the next section that is due to the team that afternoon. Organization—of time, talent, and demands—will help keep the logistical concerns under control so that everyone can concentrate on the real game: producing the winning proposal.

20

WORKSHOP 4
Running Effective
Meetings

Working intelligently means working effectively and efficiently, and running great meetings. Some meetings need to be little more than courtside conferences, quick time-outs to help you regain your focus. Other meetings might take place over the phone, in public libraries where community members have come to hear your proposal, or in corporate offices where you must be well-prepared if your vision is to win their investment and confidence.

Whether you are working on your own or as part of a large coalition, you will use meetings to:

- plan
- gather information
- create
- evaluate
- follow up
- implement
- present

Because each meeting has a unique purpose and ranges in length, it helps to prepare yourself before even scheduling the meeting. Try asking yourself the following questions, ideally taking time to write down your responses if you have the time:

- Who is our audience at this meeting?
- How will we make decisions?
- Who will handle _____?
- How will we handle _____?
- What compensation—time, money, materials, recognition—can we offer those who participate?
- What do we need to leave this meeting having accomplished?
- What do we need to have ready—i.e., materials, handouts, etc.—to accomplish that?
- What will people need to be able to work well at this meeting?
- What objections or concerns should we expect to encounter at this meeting?
- Why are we having this meeting?
- What is the best time to meet?
- Who needs to be at this meeting?
- Who will facilitate this meeting?
- Who might have special—e.g., emotional, physical, other—needs at this meeting? (And how can we meet those needs so that they can be a productive participant at this meeting?)
- What worked well at the last meeting—and why?
- What did *not* work well at the last meeting—and why?
- What do we need to do to ensure that all ideas get heard and all feel needed?
- Who does this meeting belong to?
- What are the questions this meeting is trying to answer?
- What roles can the different people at the meeting play to help it succeed?

Which of these questions we ask will depend on who we are meeting. In the course of a project you or your team might meet with any of the following:

- community leaders
- parents
- administrators
- students
- faculty
- local businesspeople
- corporate leaders

- politicians
- foundation representatives
- special interest groups
- consultants
- higher education liaisons
- funding agency representatives

Each comes to the meeting with different needs that the following questions—here written from the perspective of those you must convince—can help you anticipate and prepare for:

- How is their proposal consistent with our organization's core beliefs and vision?
- How are they demonstrating their ability to achieve what they propose?
- How have they addressed our earlier questions or concerns about their proposal?
- How does their work add to the larger field of work in this area?
- Why do they want to do this?
- What is the likelihood of its long-term success?
- How prepared are they as evidenced by their agenda, materials, and presentation?
- Why did they want to meet with me today?
- How committed does the rest of their team/organization/school/ community appear to be?

Setting Rules and Clarifying Expectations

Not everyone who participates in a meeting feels safe or even welcome. The new teacher might be just as excited to have been asked as she is terrified that she must work in a group with the principal, whom she fears will not be impressed with her contributions. Because we never know where an idea might lead us, because everyone involved is a crucial member of the team, they must know they will be heard. Deborah Tannen, in *Talking from 9 to 5: Women and Men in the Workplace: Language, Sex, and Power* (1994), devotes an entire chapter to the struggle many women face in getting their ideas heard in meetings. One way to ensure that everyone is heard is to provide an opportunity for everyone to speak about a particular idea before moving on.

Designing an Effective Agenda

Successful meetings have one primary question they are trying to answer or one subject to address (e.g., the need to expand and improve the use of technology through the curriculum, the purpose of the proposed senior center, the reason the English Department should be sent to a particular convention). While this does not preclude discussing other items as part of your opening business, the agenda should clearly offer one primary focus.

Think of a meeting as an essay: all good essays have a clear subject and all subsequent paragraphs work to keep that focus while also developing that one idea. It thus becomes clear when you are drifting from your purpose if the agenda clearly states the proscribed focus. More importantly, a focused, compelling essay stirs us awake, kindles our own intelligence and creativity. Meetings must at all costs inspire confidence in the vision, enthusiasm for the project, and trust in the ability of the team to accomplish its goal of a successful proposal.

While some meetings might seem to wander, their purpose may be to dream in all directions. Such concept or planning meetings are crucial, but no less structured around a single agenda item: to brainstorm a range of possible options to solve the problem at hand. Unnecessary, enervating meetings could be avoided if you:

- Send around a project update that briefly outlines who is doing what and reminds everyone of the next deadline, clearly identifying what each person or team is expected to bring to that meeting.

- Check in with team members when you see them to maintain an informal sense of how everyone's doing.

- Call key members to encourage and update or evaluate the project's status.

- Agree among the members of the team that each shall update a project status sheet in some centralized location so that everyone can check in at their convenience to see what needs to be done by the next meeting.

The First Meeting: Things to Accomplish

In *Working with Emotional Intelligence*, Daniel Goleman (1998) describes a study done by Bell Labs that identified "five simple secrets of success": rapport, empathy, persuasion, cooperation, and consensus building (p. 229). Leading the teams through a series of exercises that helped them to establish a strong rapport with each other independent of the work they would eventually do as a team, Burt Swersey, a professor at Rensselaer Polytechnic Institute, found the teams to be among the most dynamic, innovative, and ambitious he had ever seen.

We don't often have time to spend developing such rapport when putting together a proposal, but the lesson is clear: such factors matter because they affect performance and the quality of the work. Thus when holding that first meeting—and in subsequent interactions—invest the extra time in nurturing these crucial capacities. Also, keep these factors in mind when choosing members of a team; we all know how much fun and how exciting it can be to work with the right people, especially on such an important project as the one you've chosen to undertake.

One way to get—and keep—people talking is to create a team directory that contains all the essential information for reaching everyone on the team. This directory should include the following information for everyone on the team and the funding agency to which you are applying:

- name
- division/department/site
- address
- phone numbers: office, home, fax, mobile, other
- e-mail
- Web site (URL)
- where they are at different times of day/best time or place to reach them
- their role(s) on the team
- additional information

The first meeting is crucial as it will define the process, establish the goals, create the rapport, and inspire the confidence necessary to carry you and your team through the process.

What to Do: Different Roles

As you leave your first meeting, everyone should clearly understand their role in the process and have established what they are willing to do. Most experts identify the following roles as crucial to any effective meeting:

- facilitator
- timekeeper
- recorder
- group member

While each of these is necessary, we include here a few other roles to consider assigning to those in your group:

- coach
- strategic planner

- outsider (or novice)
- pillar
- expert
- supply/logistics person
- technology person
- details person
- artist

Where Should You Meet?

If the meeting involves the funding agency, you go wherever they ask you to and get there whenever they tell you to. If, however, you are meeting with your team, other considerations come into play:

- Do you need special equipment or space to do your work?
- If you will meet for a long period of time, do you have what you need to work happily (e.g., food, rest rooms, drinks)?
- Is this a place where people can actually work efficiently—or is it full of distractions?
- Is this environment energizing—or depressing?
- Is it easy for everyone to get to?
- Does it meet your working needs: e.g., walls to tack up (and leave) brainstorm notes, photocopy machines, fax machines, reference library, phones, computers, big tables?

Where you meet is of vital importance, though it's not always under your control. You also have to know your own style and match the environment to that. Some people find it very helpful to gather at a person's house where they can order pizza and drink Coke into the night as they assemble their portion of the school accreditation report, while others need the forced sterility of the district office to keep them focused.

When You Should Meet

If the meeting is with representatives of the granting agency, you meet whenever they say; you accommodate yourself to their needs since they are, in this relationship, the customer. Otherwise, you schedule your meetings at those times when people are available and alert. Many of us are not at our best between 3:00 P.M. and 5:00 P.M.; thus it can be much more effective to schedule earlier in the day or after the late-afternoon lull. Also, if you are working as a team, it is important that everyone continue to feel vital to the enterprise; thus you must schedule time accordingly so that they can attend.

Make sure you have plenty of food and drink to keep your meetings social and healthy. This means not just doughnuts but bagels, not just fruit but candy bars, not just coffee but juices. Good snacks keep the mind alert and the body happy. They also show you care about the people who give up their time to meet.

If your meeting bogs down and needs to get unstuck, consult Chapter 22 (Workshop 6), "Making Room for Creativity," for ideas to help you jumpstart your meeting.

How to End a Meeting

At the end of each meeting, certain procedures are important to follow as they can save you time and avoid trouble later:

- Agree on what to report out.
- Sum up and clarify what was accomplished or agreed on.
- Sum up and clarify what people agreed to do next or have ready for the next meeting.
- Clarify what they should expect in the near future (e.g., "I will type up the note and copy it for you by tomorrow").
- Update the master To Do list.
- Update the master Contact/Info list.
- Thank people.

The Secret of Successful Meetings: Great Teams

In this era of rapid technology, where one of the most widely read magazines is called *Fast Company*, meetings have begun to be reinvented, their purpose and structure reevaluated. "Hot groups," for example, are one of the most powerful forces within many of the leading companies. Described as a group of elite, innovative people who are totally passionate about a task, hot groups (Lipman-Blumen and Leavitt 1999) gather around an idea or a problem and don't have meetings so much as sessions which are led by the most appropriate person—e.g., a member with certain expertise. It was through such groups that many of our best technology products were invented.

We—the authors—also constitute a team: two people working in collaboration to write a book, or, on other occasions, to write a proposal. If the proposal is big enough, we assess the demands of the project and decide how big our team needs to be and what talents we need represented on that team. One essential characteristic of successful teams is what Daniel Goleman (1998) and others have come to call "emotional intelligence" (EQ). In his book *Working with Emotional Intelligence*, Goleman offers a useful example while discussing how a venture capital firm in Silicon Valley evaluates the proposals it receives: "A team thinks it's selling us on the technology and the product or service, but actually we're thinking about *them*—the team members. We want to understand who they are, how they will work together."

Any group of professionals in a field like yours has the collective intelligence to come up with great ideas; fewer possess the necessary capacity to achieve and sustain over time what it is they propose to do. Thus your ability to establish your or your team's capacity to work together may make the difference between getting funded and getting thanked for applying. You need to remember at all times that the agency to which you are applying is the customer, the one who is looking for a sound investment, not a risk. To return to the venture capital company for a moment, they receive twenty-five hundred proposals a year, about *twenty-five* of which they ultimately invest their money and confidence in.

Thus, when assembling a team you should consider the following questions:

- How able are they to work successfully with others?
- Are they capable of managing their own needs and getting their work done?
- What, besides their expertise in a particular area, do they offer the group?
- Are their own views and philosophies consistent with or at least complementary to those of the group and the project at hand?
- What specific expertise does this particular project demand?
- How many people are necessary to accomplish this?
- How will this team work best?

This last question is crucial, since most teams work under unforgiving timelines and in the midst of many other demands to create these proposals. We have learned, after many false starts and dead ends at late hours, that we work best if we stay in our separate domains—i.e., home offices—and work by fax and phone. Working in the same space, we easily get distracted by our working styles and mutual enthusiasm. Thus by constantly evaluating your work, reflecting on the process by which you and your colleagues are working, you become a more responsive, intelligent group. More to the point, you become a *team*, for prior to such sensitivity and cohesion, you are merely a group of people working near each other. The moment you become a team is when you realize what the others need, what you need; you feel you can communicate—should communicate—your need for a rest or your colleague's obvious need to go home and sleep. Moreover, you feel the energy of belonging to something larger than yourself, to which you contribute a vital piece. You begin to feel that you are working together to accomplish something noble and excellent that you could not necessarily do on your own but which has deep meaning to you and your community.

21

WORKSHOP 5
Giving Dynamic
Presentations

Presentations are often crucial to your final outcome. We give them in a variety of circumstances, usually at some critical phase in the proposal process such as when:

- we seek participation and support from essential stakeholders (e.g., faculty at large, parents, community members)

- we must report our team's information to the larger group

- we receive a site visit from the grant maker as part of the final stages of the process

- the grant maker asks us to prepare a short presentation for a meeting with representatives from the foundation

- we are asked to present our proposal to the school board

In most cases your presentation will not be longer than twenty minutes. Nor should it be. The people you are working with are all overextended, probably coming in to hear your presentation late in the afternoon or early in the evening. They are tired. Thus you need to get your essential points across clearly and quickly, while simultaneously entertaining the audience members, drawing them in, winning them over so that by the time you finish your presentation you are all a group of friends sitting around talking about how great the idea is.

Focus Questions to Help You Prepare

The following questions will help you get started:

- What are we trying to achieve in this presentation?
- What do we want listeners to walk out feeling, thinking, having learned?
- Who is our audience?
- What is the most effective means of presenting this information?
- What questions and concerns is the audience likely to have?
- How can we best address those concerns?
- What are the three main points we want to emphasize?
- How can we engage listeners and, through such participation, help them better understand the ideas (without dragging out the presentation)?

Rules to Guide You

Don't you hate it when you are on time and the presenter starts late? They seem unorganized, something you never want to convey to people who are there to decide the fate of your proposal. Everything about your presentation should communicate professionalism, integrity, capacity, competence. Therefore you should always be sure to do the following:

- Begin on time.
- Have extra copies of all handouts.
- Query your audience for their questions up front so that you can be sure to address them.
- Clarify your identity and role so that they know who they are listening to. (You might be a familiar teacher, but remember that today you are, for example, the "WASC Committee Chair" or the "Project Manager.")

Tools to Consider

Your tools will depend on the size of your presentation. Handouts might be adequate, unless it is a large audience or you need to add a little power to convey your professionalism. While we love technology, we have seen too many people with state-of-the-art laptops go down in flames as their systems crash before an audience. We have learned to always have a backup plan if a presentation calls for me to use a computer to make my presentation. Even overheads develop problems during presentations. The moral of the story is to always be prepared, ideally with handouts that will ensure that the audience has something to help them better understand your proposal.

Depending on the size of your audience, the following tools will help you present information:

- overhead transparencies, different colored pens, and an overhead projector
- white or dry board (with different colored pens)
- flip chart (with different colored pens and tape)
- computer presentation system

Structure of a Presentation

People want to know what you are going to talk about so that they know how to listen, what to expect. Therefore the most logical structure to any presentation is simply to

- state what you plan to say (intro)
- say it (body)
- repeat what you said (summary)

If they—parents, faculty, funder—requested the presentation, call ahead of time to find out what exactly they want to hear more about so that you can target your presentation. If you cannot do this, try at least to figure out what questions they are likely to ask. This proved to be a tremendous help as Jim sat in the lobby waiting for his sabbatical interview; they asked nearly every question he predicted. To assure them that you will address their questions, consider starting out with lines such as:

- "There are two questions we need to answer when we talk about this subject."
- "The three most important ideas to address today are . . . "
- "I realize you're on a tight schedule, so let me get right to the most important point, then I would be happy to answer any questions you have."

This last example illustrates a very important point that you must never forget: you are trying to bring these people on board, to get them on your team. Your primary goal is most likely to establish or further develop a rapport with them to enhance the relationship and, through this relationship, your credibility. Thus you must try to involve them in the conversation, making it interactive, participatory, whenever possible. This has the added benefit of keeping them active and interested. They need to know that you care what they think and are willing to listen to them. This is, after all, a crucial moment in your proposal: You might be making a big presentation to the faculty to gain their approval; you might be seeking the school board's permission to proceed; you might be making your final pitch for five thousand dollars to a team sent over by the foundation.

Looks Count

You have to pay if you want to play. If you are asking someone to pay for you to spend a semester pursuing graduate studies, or to create a new computer lab, you need to impress them in every detail. This means your presentation must be polished: professional dress, laser-printed documents (with color if appropriate) on quality paper, flawlessly proofread.

Special Considerations

Audiences have different needs. Parents and community members, for example, may need help understanding the terms and ideas in your proposal. Corporate or philanthropic foundations might have promotional considerations you need to address. Faculty members may not have even been aware that you were pursuing this opportunity; thus you face a potentially hostile audience. Because each audience and presentation is unique, it is hard to offer specific suggestions; we can, however, suggest that you step back from your presentation while planning it, and ask yourself or your team if you need to anticipate any special needs in these areas to ensure your presentation's success:

- background knowledge (e.g., professional terms they don't know or earlier projects on which this project is built)

- emotions (e.g., anger, frustration, resentment because they weren't involved in the decision to pursue the opportunity or participate in the process)

- politics (e.g., parental agendas that might undermine reforms)

- special needs (e.g., if anyone on the panel or audience needs special accommodations such as a translator)

Evaluation

You cannot know whether a presentation was successful—i.e., achieved its goals—unless you reflect or ask. Evaluation can take place after the presentation in the form of debriefing with colleagues (e.g., "Do you think they understood?" or "How should we follow up tomorrow?"), or through a more informal Q & A session with the audience. This latter option offers people the chance to be sure they leave with all their questions answered; it has the added benefit of giving the impression that you are prepared and capable, not hiding anything. Other possible means of evaluating your presentation include:

- giving the audience a formally prepared survey to assess their opinion on specific issues, or allowing them a less public means of asking other questions
- providing them index cards on which they can write down questions anonymously for you to answer or follow up on later
- making contact with them within a reasonable time after the presentation—e.g., by phone—to ask if they have any other questions and to thank them for attending
- brainstorming (with your colleagues) possible responses to questions you anticipate down the road as a consequence of your presentation (e.g., "How can we explain that even though the school's foundation raises $40,000 a year, it is not available to us for this project?")

Final Words

Think of a presentation as a celebration of what you are ready to do. Bring to it an atmosphere of achievement and enthusiasm that conveys your readiness to work with your audience to accomplish—together!—what you are attempting. If it's possible, warm the atmosphere up with food and drinks to help everyone settle in and be a bit more social. This has the added benefit of letting them talk and have a cup of coffee while you finish setting up or distributing your handouts. Make them feel special: tell them a story they will want to be a part of, a dream they will want to help make come true.

22

WORKSHOP 6
Making Room
for Creativity

Every step of the proposal process requires creativity because we constantly face problems we must solve. Creativity, often misunderstood as artistic talent, is the critical element in any winning proposition, for what is a proposal if not a means of solving a problem in a new and effective way? We must be innovative in managing our resources, presenting our ideas, and proposing our solutions. This chapter offers you a variety of strategies to do the following:

- generate compelling ideas
- present your ideas in dynamic ways
- get unstuck when you run out of ideas

Being innovative does not mean being reckless. It gives you permission to dream, to think "outside the lines," but your solutions must make sense to those who are deciding whether you get money, a sabbatical, or accreditation. In *Built to Last*, Collins and Porras (1994) found the most innovative and successful corporations intentionally allowed their employees room to dream, time to pursue their "accidents" to see what they might yield (e.g., Post-its). IBM found that its repairmen in the field spent significant amounts of time gathered at regional parts stations sitting around drinking coffee; only after studying them more closely did they learn that this time yielded abundant solutions to difficult problems they encountered in the field. But what singled out the "gold medal" companies in their study was that all dreaming grew out of deeply held beliefs and values that provided sound foundations.

Before we get down to the practical, think about the most crucial problem you face any time you submit a proposal: distinguishing your ideas, yourself, your capacity, or your organization from all the others applying. Consider the thoughts of one man who heads the admissions office of a major university. His school receives twenty thousand applications out of which it can only accept four thousand. When it comes to reviewing these applications, his team works according to a three-bucket rubric: the student's essay advances the candidate, does nothing, or undermines their chances. He is grateful for those essays that engage him in interesting ways without being silly or reckless. You must continually ask yourself how you can separate your proposal from the others.

Generating Ideas

Regardless of the size or purpose of your project, you will face that moment when you sit down to brainstorm possible responses to the proposal application. When brainstorming, there are a few simple rules:

- Write down everything. (Put another way: reject nothing.)
- Get it all down so you and everyone else can see the thinking as you brainstorm.
- Avoid either/or thinking so that you can make room for new directions.
- Gather the most diverse group—even if just for this stage—so as to increase the range of perspectives.
- *Never put down anyone's ideas.*
- Keep these brainstorms up or available throughout the process.

The creative process goes through its own seasons, each of which plays a vital role. Often we think we have dried up, for example, only to realize later that was the calm before the storm of ideas. Sometimes it's wisest—if you have the time!—to trust the silence, to listen to it for signs that the ideas are about to come. In general, creativity goes through one or more of the following stages at one time or another:

- preparation
- frustration
- incubation
- gathering
- developing
- dreaming
- testing

Focus Questions to Get You Started

Throughout these different stages it helps to have questions to guide your thinking. The most crucial question to ask at any stage of the process is "What are the questions we should ask at this stage of the process?" The right question, asked at the right time, can unlock the entire project and put you in the winner's circle. Consider the following questions and use them the way people use kindling to get larger fires started:

- What is the question your proposal is trying to answer?
- What is the problem your proposal is trying to solve?
- What is the question you need to ask—or the conversation you need to have—but are reluctant to allow?
- What is everyone else doing and how can you either do that better or differently in a meaningful way?
- How does this proposal build on and relate to what you've done in the past?
- What would you say if you *did* know the answer to the question?
- What is the obvious question we are not asking?
- What are we trying to accomplish?
- What do we need to do to accomplish this?
- How will this grant/opportunity help us to accomplish that?

Tools and Tricks for Thinking

At each stage of the process we need different strategies to help us dig deeper into the compost pile of our ideas, ways to help us go beyond the obvious. Tools offer helpful ways to play around with ideas, manipulating them to see what they look like in different configurations, from other perspectives.

Use the following tools to help spur your thinking:

- index cards
- stickers (of different sizes, shapes, colors)
- butcher paper
- Post-its (of different sizes, shapes, colors)
- transparencies
- computer outlining programs
- graphic organizers
- pictures
- scrapbooks

- yearbooks
- metaphors/similes
- Web page design
- clusters (also known as webs)

People who get paid to be creative for a living play and laugh constantly. It releases stress, makes the work fun, and frees up other parts of the brain so you can access deeper ideas. We find this part of the process is often the most exciting and satisfying: If you come up with a good enough idea, it stokes everyone's fires, getting them to feel part of a larger vision which they want to see fulfilled. Thus, while you are creating your idea maps, shuffling the deck of index cards, brainstorming possible metaphors, consider using some of the following techniques to get you thinking even deeper or in new directions altogether:

- Look for patterns and connections (e.g., by sorting them into categories or connecting elements of a cluster).
- Search for moments of heat (aka Wow! moments) in your pile of ideas.
- Free associate, risking embarrassment and laughing in the process.
- Think about your ideas from different perspectives (e.g., parent, student, funder).
- Bring in outsiders and listen to what they say about your ideas.
- Think outside your own domain: how would a musician, scientist, or graphic artist think about this problem?
- Role play.
- Change the form and change the function: what if you presented your idea as a portfolio or a story?
- Ask what/who do I want the reader of this proposal to be when they begin reading this document?
- Provide time for exploratory talk (i.e., time to wonder "what if?").

What to Do If You Get Stuck

Mark Twain referred to this experience as having a "dry tank," suggesting that writers simply wait until it can refill itself. Most people writing a proposal don't have that leisure: they cannot call the National Science Foundation and say they just aren't feeling inspired but hope to have something to submit within a month. It's due Friday. No exceptions.

Here is a grab bag of ideas to help "refill your tank" in a pinch. If one doesn't work, try another.

- Read *Jump Start Your Brain*, by Doug Hall.
- Ask the obvious questions: who, where, why, how, so, when, and so what?

- Work in different configurations to cross-germinate: rotate groups, change sizes, jigsaw.
- Talk talk talk talk—with different people, about different aspects, in different ways, at different times (e.g., focus groups, design teams, writing team, hot groups).
- Use metaphors to prime the pump: This is like _____ because _____.
- Think in headlines. Somewhere along the way we began to do this, usually coming up with terrible ones, but the idea works well the other way, too: School Announces Program to _____!
- Brainstorm titles/names for your program.
- Surround yourself with relevent materials. Our bookcases during the writing of this book are choked with texts on all sorts of subjects; we just thumb and handle them sometimes in the hope that they will say something to us.
- Read the world. Read through different magazines and newspapers, looking for anything that might unstick your mind or make you think a new thought—this is reading to think. We also like brochures from stores like Noah's Bagels or Starbucks: they have amazing designs and include ideas for services and other things. Go to the library and rummage the magazine section, or type a relevant word into Yahoo and see what the search brings up. This last method has proven particularly helpful to us, often bringing up things we never would have considered related. Also, in Netscape you can hit a little button called "What's Related" which will gather things from the Net it thinks are somehow related to your request.
- Call up your mother (or a six-year-old, or your spouse) and explain what you are trying to do and ask her what she thinks.
- Return to what was done and failed in the past and ask if it is not time to reevaluate its viability in light of new discoveries and conditions.
- Rewrite an entire section without looking at anything you've written before. Some writers even throw away chapters of their novel to force themselves to recreate what they had in hopes that it will be better than the previous version.
- Work in a different media: e.g., draw your idea, or think about it as a song or painting or commercial.
- Change environments.

The proposal should be directly linked to a meaningful problem you *and* the agency are both committed to solving. During the course of the process, the proposal must be a problem you (and your team) inhabit until you complete it. Only when you are surrounded by the problem you are trying to solve can you achieve maximum creativity.

Writers sometimes describe a story as a dream the writer creates and offers to the reader without any holes to let in the light of the world outside the book. Your proposal must achieve the same end: you are offering a fully developed, thoroughly imagined dream of what should/could be, and you must anticipate and patch up any distracting light that might leak in; read it as your reader would and ask others to do the same.

Check yourself. Remember that the primary reason many proposals are rejected is that they miss the mark—i.e., do not address the application—so you must check your creative ideas after you come up with them to see that they clearly match what is being asked. Sometimes it is a simple matter of just reframing the idea or its terms to better reflect the application guidelines; but sometimes an idea we love is just not appropriate.

23

WORKSHOP 7
Managing the
Change Process:
Planning,
Implementing,
Sustaining

Proposing Change: Beginning the Dance

This entire book is about change in one way or another. To propose something is to imply it is not adequate as it is, that the proposed change can, somehow, in some way, remedy or improve the status quo. Herein lies the fundamental anxiety about our work: there is no arrival. In the age of rapid results, the era of constant change, we are driven by the ideal of constant revision of purpose. Furthermore, many educators are left to hunt down their own funding to support the changes society or the government or the community or industry demand; it is this competition for educational wealth and this drive to improve that brings you to this book.

In some ways, however, getting the grant you seek is only a part of the process, some would even say the easiest part. So you got your million dollars, your schoolwide Internet connections, your new computer lab. The question now is, can you actually accomplish what you proposed? The first grant we ever sought together called for systemic K–14 innovative reform; if we received the grant, we would receive one million dollars to implement the program. Like many educators, we were thrown into the situation by administrators who asked us to attend an informational meeting.

As we moved through the process, we realized that our team had been working in total isolation, dreaming a new world to which we had neglected to invite everyone else. This lack of communication is common under such circumstances: once we had been "invited" to write the proposal, we all disappeared into a district office, emerging only to teach our classes. Suddenly the possibility of a site visit arose. Had the visitation team arrived that afternoon and asked the faculty about their wonderful vision for twenty-first century schools as outlined in the recent proposal, no one would have known what they were talking about—not even the principal who told us to write the proposal in the first place.

While it might seem strange to admit this in a book about writing winning grants, we were very relieved to learn we were not chosen. There was no permission to move ahead, no commitment to the project. So began our lessons about change, difficult but crucial lessons during which we realized that proposals inevitably seek to change more than the obvious ailment. They must grow out of the culture, be a credible expression of the organization's vision.

Types of Change

Some proposals seek to change one aspect of an organization; others seek the complete overhaul of the existing framework. Any serious proposal, however, attempts to change most of the following, often simultaneously:

- policy
- practice
- programs
- organizational structures
- culture
- beliefs
- values
- attitudes
- perceptions
- process
- product

This list alone, along with the word *change*, could supply Dilbert's creator Scott Adams with enough material for a year's worth of cartoons. Educators, like people in the business world, are constantly hearing about the new initiative, the new vision, the new plan. As Larry Cuban and David Tyack (1995) point out in *Tinkering Toward Utopia*, those demanding such reforms are often outsiders—politicians, university professors, businesspeople—who seek immediate results they can use in the next election or their study. We bring this up, in part, to emphasize the importance of understanding why people are asking you to change. What is their motivation?

Communicating Your Vision

Communication is crucial to any successful change process. Our experience with the million-dollar proposal taught us this difficult lesson. From the beginning, it is essential for any coalition or leader to decide—and reevaluate throughout—the following:

- Who are the essential stakeholders with whom I must regularly communicate?

- What do they need to know?

- What is the best means of communicating this information to them?

- How frequently do they need to be updated?

- Why do they need to be in the communications loop?

In *Leading Change* (1996), John Kotter identifies three patterns of ineffective communication, all of which are common:

- The leadership coalition holds a few meetings to inform the organization, following these up with a few memos reminding everyone that there is a New Way in place.

- The primary leader (e.g., principal) speaks often to the members of the organization, but the managers (e.g., assistant principals) remain silent on the subject, thereby sabotaging the leader's message.

- The leadership coalition invests considerable time and effort in various communications—newsletters, speeches, memos—but key leaders within the employee community publicly undermine the proposal through their actions.

If the proposed change is not part of a larger vision, one that grows out of the organization's culture, it cannot succeed. In *Built to Last: Successful Habits of Visionary Companies*, Collins and Porras (1994) emphasize the centrality of "core ideology" in all "visionary" companies: "Like the fundamental ideals of a great nation, church, school, or any other enduring institution, core ideology in a visionary company is a set of basic precepts that plant a fixed stake in the ground: 'This is who we are; this is what we stand for; this is what we're all about'" (p. 54). Others fail to effectively launch change efforts because they cannot communicate them quickly and effectively enough; in such cases, it is imperative that you retreat and refine your vision down to a simple, memorable message.

One school, for example, embarked upon an ambitious program of learning reforms, beginning with a meeting where the ESLRs (expected student learning results) were debuted—all forty-seven of them. By the tenth bullet people began to get up for more coffee, grade papers, talk to their neighbors. In the wake of this initial failure, the leadership team revised the ESLRs down to five succinct statements, each of which grew out of the faculty's suggestions, each of which met with enthusiastic acceptance because they were helpful—and clear.

The Challenge of Changing

Think of your own struggles to change. How many times have you started an exercise program, even joined a gym, as part of a resolution to get in shape, only to find yourself months later wondering when you stopped. How many times have you sworn, in the wake of some delicious home-cooked meal, to make time in your routine for such rituals despite your busy schedule; then months later, as you are paying the pizza delivery man, you remember something about promising not to do this anymore. Asking ourselves—or others—to change demands courage and commitment. It is easy to begin; everything new excites us. As many scientists observe, however, any force immediately encounters an opposite force that inhibits it. In *The Dance of Change: The Challenges to Sustaining Momentum in Learning Organizations*, Peter Senge (1999) and his colleagues identify ten challenges common to all change initiatives. The first four, they argue, arise at the outset, with the invitation to change:

- "We don't have time for this stuff!" (the challenge of control over time)

- "We have no help!" (the challenge of inadequate coaching, guidance, and support)

- "This stuff isn't relevant!" (the challenge of relevance)

- "They're not walking the talk!" (the challenge of management clarity and consistency)

Once the process has begun, mostly through what Senge calls "pilot teams" of pioneering members of the community, other challenges arise:

- "This stuff is _____" (the challenge of fear and anxiety)
- "This stuff isn't working!" (the challenge of negative assessment of progress)
- "We have the right way!"/"They don't understand us!" (the challenge of isolation and arrogance)

If the initiatives gain momentum and achieve a measure of acceptance within the community or the organization, other challenges arise:

- "Who's in charge of this stuff?" (the challenge of prevailing governance structure)
- "We keep reinventing the wheel!" (the challenge of diffusion or transferring knowledge across organizational boundaries)

In addition to the previous challenges, several others arise with increasing frequency as the rate of change increases:

- lack of necessary skills or capacity to do what they are asked
- absence of crucial knowledge
- lack of trust or faith (in the idea, the motives, the leaders)

Solutions to Consider

In his book *Leading Change*, Harvard professor John Kotter (1996) proposes that these challenges can be effectively addressed by:

- establishing a sense of urgency
- creating a guiding coalition
- developing a vision and strategy
- communicating the change vision
- empowering broad-based action
- generating short-term wins
- consolidating gains and producing more change
- anchoring new approaches in the culture

Kotter, like Senge, emphasizes the need to sustain this transformation process. In the diagram outlining Kotter's eight steps, an arrow links step eight to step one, signaling that the process must continually begin again, establishing a new sense of urgency in order to achieve still better performance.

Focus Questions to Help You Plan

At this point, it might be helpful to ask yourself some of the following focus questions to help you anticipate the challenges you may encounter along the way:

- What are we trying to do or change?

- Why do we want to change it?

- What outcome do we seek?

- What obstacles—internal and external—should we expect to encounter?

- How might we bypass such challenges?

- How will others perceive this proposed change: i.e., as profound or simple, deep or superficial?

- Who is most likely to feel most threatened by the proposed change?

- Why might they feel so threatened?

- What can we do to address their concerns and get them on board?

- Who can we look to as our pilot group to help us get started?

- What kind of change are we proposing? (e.g., behavioral, cultural, structural)

- Who are the natural leaders within the organizational community whose support we must get up front?

- What is the "problem" our proposal seeks to solve?

- Who is part of the problem? Who is part of the solution?

We are, ultimately, creatures of comfort; we settle into routines easily and quickly. Some teachers thrive on change, finding it energizing. English teacher Jennifer Abrams, after teaching successfully for some years, decided she "needed to get scared again," and applied for a Fulbright scholarship; then, upon returning, she accepted a district leadership position in technology. She craved the challenge these new opportunities gave her. Others resist such invitations to change, seeing them as criticisms of their own teaching methods or the institution's values. Still others stand their pedagogical or ideological ground, reminding the ambitious technology director, for example, that Thomas Alva Edison proclaimed that "the motion picture is destined to revolutionize our educational system and that in a few years it will supplant largely, if not entirely, the use of textbooks" (Cuban and Tyack 1995, 111).

People who resist change do so for some good reasons sometimes. Schools are flooded with administrators who pass through every couple of years, leaving in their wake a portfolio of initiatives they were eager to include on their resumes. Thus anyone proposing to change the culture or practices of a program or organization should stop and assess their organization. They should do so honestly, asking themselves what they are capable of achieving given their existing resources, one of which is the willingness to inquire into current practices with an eye toward improving them.

Senge and his colleagues at MIT emphasize the importance of the following strategies when beginning any serious change process:

- developing learning capabilities
- identifying and establishing "pilot groups"
- causing a fundamental shift in thinking
- recognizing the different types and roles of leaders
- "reinforcing growth processes"
- developing tangible activities
- starting small, growing steadily
- specifying intended results and useful tools (as opposed to a detailed plan)
- realizing that initial commitment is almost always limited to a few people
- fixing the crisis first, if you are in a crisis
- walking the talk, especially the recognized leaders

Final Words

The word *propose* means "to put forth for consideration," to "make known one's intentions"; in other words, to suggest changes to what currently exists. *Change* itself, if traced back to its alleged Celtic roots, means to exchange, to trade this method for that, this value for that. It can be a volatile process depending on the catalyst. In the face of intense and mounting criticism, some people allow themselves to imagine that they can change the current order by willing it; this is the equivalent of believing your flowers will grow by telling them to, especially if you yell at them. Change in education is particularly complicated due to the dynamic nature of the institution and the whims of public opinion.

In the end, everyone who studies change agrees that it takes time: Change is, they remind us, a living process, one that must be carefully begun, thoughtfully sustained. Unfortunately this is not always possible: Too often schools resemble an evening news show with five different clocks, each one measuring a different set of expectations. The process clock ticks on slowly, patiently; meanwhile, the political or community clock is spinning like a Twister dial, signaling the immediate need for evidence of change.

This chapter cannot possibly offer all that you need to know, or tell you how to successfully implement your own proposals for reform. It can establish the importance of "the dance of change" in the hope that you or your organization will spend as much time dreaming of all the ways you will change things as you will spend thinking of how to sustain those changes. Without such reflection, without such envisionment, you will find your initial commitment deteriorating like a hastily arranged wedding to someone you did not really know. You will find everyone leaving the church before you have even finished your vows.

APPENDIX A
Works Cited

Beck, Isabel L., ed. *Questioning the Author: An Approach for Enhancing Student Engagement with Text*. Newark, Del: International Reading Association, 1997.

Bringhurst, Robert. *The Elements of Typographic Style*. 2d ed. Point Roberts, Wash.: Hartley and Marks, 1996.

Cameron, Julia. *The Right to Write: An Invitation into the Writing Life*. New York: Putnam, 1999.

Chadderdon, Lisa. "Annual Reports." *Fast Company*, May 1999, p. 44.

Collins, James C. and Jerry I. Porras. *Built to Last: Successful Habits of Visionary Companies*. New York: HarperBusiness, 1994.

Cradler, John, and Ruthmary Cordon-Cradler. *Educator's Guide for Developing and Funding Educational Technology Solutions*. 3d ed. Self-published, 1994.

Cuban, Larry, and David Tyack. *Tinkering Toward Utopia: A Century of Public School Reform*. Cambridge Mass.: Harvard University Press, 1995.

Dowis, Richard, and Richard Lederer. *The Write Way: The S.P.E.L.L. Guide to Real-Life Writing (Society for the Preservation of English Language and Literature)*. New York: Pocket Books, 1995.

Goleman, Daniel. *Working with Emotional Intelligence*. New York: Bantam Books, 1998.

Hall, Doug, with David Wecker. *Jump Start Your Brain*. New York: Warner Books, 1995.

Heaney, Seamus. *The Government of the Tongue: Selected Prose, 1978–1987*. New York: Noonday Press, 1990.

Imperial County Office of Education. "Desert Without Borders."

Jackson, Phil. *Sacred Hoops: Spiritual Lessons of a Hardwood Warrior*. New York: Hyperion, 1996.

Kiritz, Norton. *Grantsmanship Center News*. Undated.

Kotter, John P. *Leading Change*. Boston: Harvard Business School Press, 1996.

Krakauer, Jon. *Eiger Dreams: Ventures Among Men and Mountains*. New York: Anchor, 1997.

Lipman-Blumen, Jean, and Harold J. Leavitt. *Hot Groups: Seeding Them, Feeding Them, and Using Them to Ignite Your Organization*. New York: Oxford University Press, 1999.

Mager, Robert F. *Preparing Instructional Objectives*. Atlanta, GA: Lake Publishing Company, 1984.

McNeill, Patricia, and Jane C. Geever. *The Foundation Center's Guide to Proposal Writing*. 2d ed. New York: The Foundation Center, 1999.

Murray, Donald. *Crafting a Life in Essay, Story, Poem*. Portsmouth, NH: Heinemann, 1996.

"Better to Give." *Education Week*, May 5, 1999, p. 5.

Parker, Roger C., and Patrick Berry. *Looking Good in Print*. 4th ed. Scottsdale, AZ: Coriolis Group, 1998.

Peters, Tom. "The Wow Project." *Fast Company*, May 1999, pp. 140–148.

Schmoker, Mike. *Results: The Key to Continuous School Improvement*. Alexandria, VA: Association for Supervision and Curriculum Development, 1996.

Senge, Peter. *The Fifth Discipline: The Art and Practice of the Learning Organization*. New York: Currency/Doubleday, 1990.

Senge Peter, et al. *The Dance of Change: The Challenges of Sustaining Momentum in Learning Organizations*. New York: Currency/Doubleday, 1999.

Somerville, Bill. "Proposal Writing Kit: Tips and Techniques." Unpublished article.

Tannen, Deborah. *Talking from 9 to 5: Women and Men in the Workplace: Language, Sex, and Power*. New York: Avon, 1994.

Tufte, Edward R. *Visual Explanations: Images and Quantities, Evidence and Narrative*. Cheshire, Conn.: Graphics Press, 1996.

APPENDIX B
Glossary of
Useful Terms

(The following glossary was created by John and Ruthmary Cordon-Cradler; it reflects years of knowledge and experience. We have added a few words of our own to it, but the credit is theirs. Not every term included in this glossary appears in our text.)

Abstract: summary of a proposal, usually limited to one page and usually the first page of the narrative. *See* Executive summary.

Acronyms: a word formed from the initial letters of a name, such as WAC for Women's Army Corps, or by combining initial letters or parts of a series of words, such as radar for radio detecting and ranging.

Activities: any process or procedure intended to stimulate learning through actual experience; the actual events that move the organization in a new direction.

Administrative agent: the member of a consortium that acts as recipient of the grant and is fiscally responsible for the grant.

Administrative costs: see Indirect costs.

Administrative overhead: see Indirect costs.

Adoption/adaptation grant: a grant, usually small, to assist a school district to implement a project successfully demonstrated by another district or agency; projects which may be adopted/adapted are usually identified by the funder.

Advisory committee: provides suggestions and assistance at the request of the governing or convening body.

Affirmative action: efforts to overcome past employment discrimination; school districts may have a board-approved affirmative action plan.

Alliance: 1. a close association of nonprofits or other resource partners, formed to advance common interests or causes; 2. a connection based on common interests; a bond or tie.

Annual report: a formal account of the proceedings or transactions of a group for the past year. It assists applicants in determining their eligibility by clearly defining funder's goals, mission, and funded projects and grants.

Applicant: school district, agency, organization, or individual seeking funds.

Application Control Center: federal office to which most applications for educational projects are sent.

Application kit or packet: application forms, regulations, guidelines, and other materials needed to apply for a grant for a specific program.

Appropriation: funds appropriated by Congress to support an authorized program; usually less than the amount authorized in the legislation.

Areas to address: see Focus areas.

Assessment: see Evaluation.

Assurances: legally binding statements signed by the applicant in which the applicant assures the sponsor he will do or refrain from doing certain things; federal assurances may include compliance with Title VI of the Civil Rights Act and Title IX (forbids discrimination on the basis of sex) and assurances that the handicapped will not be discriminated against and that human subjects will be protected in research projects.

Authorization: legislation that establishes or continues the legal operation of a program and usually sets limits on the amount of funds that may be available in any given year; authorization of a project does not necessarily mean that funds will be appropriated.

Authorized agent/representative: an individual designated by the board of education to sign legal documents such as applications for fund.

Authorizing signature: the organization representative(s) who must grant authority or power to submit application with all its assurances, guidelines, and restrictions.

Award: a grant.

Award notice: formal notification from a funding agency to an applicant announcing that a grant has been awarded.

Awarding agency: funding agency.

Baseline data: evaluation data indicating the status of project participation prior to treatment or participation in the project.

Benchmarks: reference points for funders and fundees to assure that everything is on track.

Benefits: things that promote or enhance well-being; advantages.

Best and final offer: a revision or modification of the original proposal, generally carried out with negotiated input from the sponsor, usually "best and final offers" are requested from the top contenders for a contract.

Bidders' conference: gathering to train and/or explain the guidelines and concerns of a funding agency. Usually held by government agencies after the application packets have been released to the public.

Bidders' list: a list of qualified organizations maintained by government agencies for the purpose of sending potential bidders' invitations to submit proposals or bids on government contracts.

Block grant: a grant from the government agency to a subunit of government or a school district for broad purposes, largely at the discretion of the recipient; amount determined by a formula (examples: ECIA, General Revenue Sharing, Community Development and Housing Act).

Boilerplate: standard proposal sections that are used repeatedly in different contracts or proposals; includes staff resumes, descriptions of the school district student population, descriptions of the community, and identification of district resources and facilities.

Budget authority (BA): legal permission granted by Congress to enter into obligation generally resulting in outlays; an appropriation for an authorized program.

Budget period: periods of time (usually twelve months) into which a project is divided for budget and reporting purposes; usually a continuation proposal is required each year that the project continues.

Business proposal: the budget and business aspects of the proposal, bound separately from the technical (programmatic) aspects; usually required when bidding on a contract.

Capital outlay: tools, equipment, or apparatus purchased by the fundee for project implementation.

Capitation grant: a grant based on a head count such as school enrollment.

Capture rate: a measure of efficiency in getting proposals funded, usually expressed as the ratio of number funded to number submitted or dollars received to dollars requested.

Categorical funding: most commonly refers to funds or projects limited to a specific educational purpose as opposed to general aid applicable to any school cost (examples: funds for educating handicapped students or another specific group and funds for specified programs such as vocational education).

Clearinghouse: state or local agency designated to review applications for funds in accordance with government regulations; see application guidelines to determine whether clearinghouse review is required.

Coalition: a temporary alliance of factions, parties, and so on for some specific purpose; mobilizes individuals and groups to influence outcomes.

Commerce Business Daily: publication of the Department of Commerce for announcing the availability of contracts and recipients of contracts.

Communications: budget category for telephone, telegraph, and similar charges.

Concept paper: a document prepared by the applicant that describes the rationale for a project or the basic idea that might turn into a full proposal; used by some sponsors to screen proposal submissions.

Conference grant: money to underwrite cost of meetings, seminars, etc.

Consolidation: combining of several into one; usually implies major restructuring effort.

Consortium: several agencies or organizations joined together for the purpose of submitting a single project application.

Consortium grant: funds funneled to one organization that in turn shares the money with other organizations working jointly on a project.

Constituency: the group on whose behalf an agency advocates the initiation or continuation of programs or projects intended to improve the condition or reduce the level of need within the constituency.

Construction grant: funds to be used for building, expanding, or modernizing facilities.

Continuation application: request for funds to continue a funded project that was approved for more than one year contingent upon the availability of funds and satisfactory project operation, requires an annual proposal.

Continuing education grant: funds used to further or to update the training of an individual in a field of importance to the funder.

Continuing resolution: interim funding voted by Congress when a hiatus occurs because Congress did not authorize funds before the beginning of a new fiscal year.

Contract: legal agreement between the funder and a recipient of funds specifying the work to be performed, products to be delivered, time schedules, financial arrangements, and other provisions; contracts (rather than grants) are typically given when the funding agency has identified the need and the activities to be implemented to meet the need.

Corporate foundation grant: money awarded by a commercial enterprise.

Cost overrun: an increase of the total actual cost over the original estimated cost on a cost-reimbursement contract.

Cost-plus contract: contract with a profit-making organization that allows for reimbursing the contractor for incurred costs plus a fixed fee.

Cost proposal: see Business proposal.

Cost reimbursement (CR) contract: contract providing for reimbursement for actual incurred allowable expenditures.

Cost sharing: grant recipient pays a part of the total costs of the project.

Criteria: the points on which the proposal will be evaluated.

Deliverable: to produce or achieve what is desired or expected; make good. Another term for project objectives and outcomes.

Deliverables: the reports, products, research findings, and/or materials that have been promised to or are required by the funding agency by certain dates.

Demographic data: factual information, especially information organized for analysis or used to reason or make decisions.

Demonstration grant/project: grant or specially funded project to support the demonstration and testing or piloting of a particular approach to education or other activity.

Development team: a group of individuals with specific roles and functions, working toward a specific end—a powerful winning proposal and integrated, implemented project.

Direct assistance: grant providing goods and services (personnel, supplies equipment), not money.

Direct costs: total costs directly attributable to the project, including salaries, fringe benefits, travel, equipment, supplies, services, etc.; indirect costs are calculated as a percent of the direct costs.

Direct labor (DL): total amount to be spent on staff salaries.

Discrepancy model: a method used to compare two or more examples. Through this comparison differences reveal characteristics of strong versus weak examples.

Discretionary fund/grant: competitive grant programs in which the applicant designs the project and the funding agency selects projects and determines grant amounts; also called competitive grants or project grants.

Dissemination: making research findings, project outcomes, and products known.

Donation: assistance (financial or in-kind) given to the district by the private sector without any contractual arrangement.

DUNS (Dun and Bradstreet) Number: a number assigned to an organization that identifies it as a nonprofit agency and establishes its fiscal solvency and credit rating.

EDGAR (Education Department General Administrative Regulations): general regulations applicable to proposal submission and project operation for many programs funded by the U.S. Education Department; application guidelines often incorporate specific sections of EDGAR such as community involvement requirements.

Eligible applicants: categories of applicants invited to submit applications, such as institutes of higher education, local educational agencies, individuals, private schools, community-based agencies, and public agencies.

Employee benefits: fringe benefits.

Enabling legislation: a law authorizing a grant-making program.

Entitlement funds: funds allocated primarily on the basis of a formula that seeks to distribute the available funds among recipients in some equitable fashion; funding is not competitive—i.e., all applicants who meet the criteria will be funded.

Evaluation: 1. to ascertain or fix the value or worth of your program, service, reforms, or project; 2. to examine and judge carefully, appraise.

Executive summary: a presentation of the substance of a body of material in a condensed form or by reducing it to its main points; an abstract.

Exemplar: 1. one that is worthy of imitation; a model. 2. one that is typical or representative, an example; 3. an ideal that serves as a pattern.

External funding: funding from a source other than the school district "regular" budget.

FAPRS (Federal Assistance Program Retrieval System): computerized system of information on federal funding.

Federal assistance: financial payments by the United States to third parties which entail conditions to be satisfied by the recipient and are in the form of a grant or cooperative agreement.

Federal projects or federal and state projects: general term referring to all categorical funding coming from federal and state funding programs or from federal programs distributed by the state.

Federal Register: daily publication of the U.S. government that announces opportunities to apply for grants and includes regulations.

Fellowship: a grant awarded to an individual to further his/her level of professional competence.

Fiscal year (FY): the official accounting period, October 1 through September 30 for the federal government. The year that September 30 falls in determines the numerical designation; e.g., October 1, 1982 through September 30, 1983 is FY 83.

Fixed-price contract: agreement to pay a fixed total amount in installments or upon delivery of a product or completion of a scope of work regardless of actual costs of the contractor.

Flow-through money: funds that are funneled through a middleman— e.g., ECIA federal funds are funneled through State Departments of Education; also called passed-through funds.

Focus area(s): a center of interest or activity (e.g., safety, program expansion, curriculum reform, training, staff development).

Fold in: to absorb funds for a specific program into a larger program; e.g., many small categorical programs were folded into the Education Consolidation and Improvement Act (ECIA).

Formative evaluation: conducted during the operation of a program to assess the outcomes of activities, generally for the purpose of providing immediate feedback and if necessary to effect program change.

Formula grant: funds made available to specified recipients based on a formula prescribed in legislation, regulations, or policies of the agency; states are the chief recipients.

Foundation grant: money awarded by one of America's twenty-five thousand grant-giving foundations.

Fringe benefits: amount paid by the employer for various employee benefits such as retirement, health insurance, unemployment insurance, etc.; also referred to as employee benefits.

Full-time equivalent (FTE): combining of part-time positions to show the equivalent number of full-time positions.

General Revenue Sharing (GRS): federal funds given to state and local governments with few restraints on how the money is spent.

Gifts-in-kind: see In-kind.

Goals: the purposes toward which an endeavor is directed.

Go/no go: administrative approval or disapproval of the proposal concept and decision to develop proposal by the agency seeking the grant.

Government grant: usually refers to a grant from the federal government, although state and local governments also make grants.

Grant: any government or private sector financial assistance given to the district for a particular purpose and time period as detailed in a specific application or proposal; used broadly, may refer to a contract, agreement, or other such document.

Grantee: individual, organization, or entity receiving a grant and accountable for that grant.

Grant program: specifically, a project that is funded by a grant broadly used to include projects funded by a contract or agreement.

Grantor: agency (government, foundation, corporation, nonprofit organization, individual) awarding a grant to a recipient; funder.

Grants management officer: official of a government funding agency or foundation who is responsible for the business and financial aspects of a particular grant; usually collaborates with the funder's program or project officer (the grants management officer is the counterpart of a school district's business officer).

Grantsperson: individual responsible for planning, preparing, and marketing proposals.

Guidelines: 1. a statement or other indication of policy or procedure by which to determine a course of action; 2. a set of general principles used in judging proposals.

Hard match: requirement that matching funds be a cash contribution or funds not in-kind.

Horizontal/vertical slice: an extended group of people with similar interests or concerns who interact and remain in informal contact for mutual assistance or support.

Impoundment: situation when the Executive Branch does not spend funds authorized by Congress.

Indirect cost rate: percent of direct costs that has been approved by the government for overhead; a specific formula is used to calculate indirect cost rates.

Indirect costs: overhead; costs incurred in the overall functioning of the institution, which includes providing support services to special projects; costs not readily identified as direct expenditure.

In-kind support: dollar value of noncash contributions to a project by the grantee or another party other than the funder (examples: volunteer services, equipment use, facilities).

Instrumentation: tests, questionnaires, etc., to be used to evaluate the project.

Intervention: to come or occur between two periods or points of time.

Joint powers agreement: agreement between two or more agencies that enables one to make use of the resources of the other(s); frequently does not involve the transfer of funds.

Labor intensive: requiring a large expenditure for personnel.

Labor Surplus Set-Aside: solicitations limited to applicants in areas with high unemployment or underemployment according to criteria set by the Secretary of Labor.

Landscape: portrayed as one would a picture depicting an expanse of scenery ($11 \times 8^1/_2$ as opposed to $8^1/_2 \times 11$).

Letter of commitment: letter from administrator or governing board that confirms they are committed to the proposed idea and the ideas within it and are willing to commit whatever resources the proposal specifies.

Letter of intent to apply: a brief letter or form you submit to the funding agency; it establishes that you will submit a proposal, and gets you in their information loop for subsequent mailings, workshops, or opportunities.

Letter of support: letter from appropriate stakeholders without whose support the proposed project could not be implemented. These letters help to assure the funder that the program is valid and important to the applicants.

Letter proposal: a brief (often preliminary) proposal submitted in letter from, similar to a concept paper.

Level of effort: estimated amount of personnel time required to carry out a project or activity usually expressed in person-years, person-days, person-months, etc.

Local education agency (LEA): school district, County Office of Education, or designated regional educational service agency that will receive and disburse grant funds; in a consortium proposal, one agency must be designated the LEA.

Local government: units of government below the state level such as counties, cities, and school districts.

Maintenance of effort: requirement that the grantee maintain a specific level of activity and financial expenditures in a geographic or program area to ensure that grant funds will not be used to replace (supplant) funds already being spent by the grantee.

Management plan: description usually required in a proposal for how the grantee will relate to the funder and how the project will fit into the district decision-making and government systems.

Manpower loading: proposed schedule of staff/personnel used during the course of the project.

Matching: grantee's required cash or in-kind contribution to a project, usually a percent of the total budget.

Methods: a means or manner of procedure, especially a regular and systematic way of accomplishing something.

Milestones: important events, as in the history of an organization, project, or service, or in the advancement of knowledge in a field; turning points.

Mission: a special assignment or calling by an organization, group, or individual to pursue an activity or perform a service or vocation that addresses a specific need or focus.

Multifunded: a project supported by two or more funders; usually each a percent of the total budget.

Needs statement: a section in the proposal describing and documenting the needs addressed by the proposal.

Negotiations: discussion between the applicant and the funder regarding program and budget changes desired by the funder; negotiations take place before a contract is issued and are becoming more common in relation to discretionary grants.

Network: individuals or organizations formed in a loose-knit group.

New projects: first year of a project.

Noncompetitive follow-on: extension of an already existing, previously completed contract.

Notice of grant award: formal written notice from the funder specifying grant amount, time period, and special requirements.

Objectives: the measurable statements (outcome, deliverables) that demonstrate the growth and reforms being targeted by applicant. Usually describe *who* will do *what* by *when* and under what conditions, and *how* this is measured.

Offeror: organization that is submitting a proposal in response to (or bidding on) an RFP.

Organizational capacity: the ability of your agency to perform or produce; capability. The maximum or optimum amount that can be produced, serviced. Innate potential for growth, development, or accomplishment.

Other direct costs: direct costs other than salaries and fringe benefits.

Outcomes: a natural result; a consequence of your grant and the integration and implementation of its methods, activities, and reforms.

Overhead: see Indirect costs.

Overview: see Abstract, Executive summary.

Padding: adding extra amounts to the budget.

Partnership: a relationship between individuals or groups that is characterized by mutual cooperation and responsibility, as for the achievement of a specified goal.

Passed-through funds: funds that are funneled through an intermediate agency; also called flow-through funds.

Per diem: daily rate for expenses (other than transportation) incurred while traveling.

Performance contract: specifies levels of performance before the work is considered satisfactory or before the applicant is to be paid by the funder.

Person years: a concept by which a funding agency attempts to establish cost parameters by defining the scope of a project as the costs of the number of professionals required to do the job, including support costs of clerical and other assistance.

Planned variation: programs in which funded recipients select from several models which are then evaluated and compared (example: follow through).

Planning grant: supports designing and planning a project.

Portrait: portrayed as a likeness of a person, especially one showing the face.

Positioning: a point of view or attitude on a certain question or issue that aligns you with the funder's mission, values, vision, and goals.

Preliminary proposal: a brief proposal emphasizing the need and program concept; sometimes requested by funders to screen applicants and save them the task of developing a full proposal if it has little likelihood of funding.

Preproposal phase: activities undertaken prior to writing the proposal such as obtaining administrative approval, identifying cooperators, forming an advisory committee, planning, etc.

Prime contractor: agency, organization, or person that directly receives an award of funds with which to accomplish a prescribed scope of work, some of which may be subcontracted.

Principal investigator: usually the researcher responsible for a research project; may be the project director.

Prior approval: approval (usually written) required before a change in the project plan or budget is implemented.

Problem statement: the act of stating or declaring one's needs, concerns, liabilities.

Process objective: a description of the specific ways used by the project staff to monitor the project's activities and management scheme.

Product objective: used by funding agencies in two ways: (1) to refer to the behavior expected of project participants, or (2) to refer to a concrete item to be produced by the project, such as a manual or a film.

Program announcement: press release, booklet, catalog, form letter, or notice in the *Federal Register* telling of an opportunity to apply for a grant or contract.

Program officer: one that supervises, controls, or manages the funds for a philanthropic organization and reports to its governing board. The program officer acts as a community liaison instructing applicants on the guidelines, mission, vision, and values of the funder.

Project director/program director: individual designated by the grantee to be responsible for the administration of a project; the project director is reponsible to the grantee for proper management of the project; the grantee is responsible to the grantor (funder) for submission of all required documents, for maintaining communications between the agencies, and for carrying out all program components as agreed.

Project grant: a general term for a grant supporting a specific project.

Project officer/program officer: the official in a government funding agency or a foundation who is responsible for a grant program, i.e., supervises technical and program aspects of grants; may also be responsible for administrative and fiscal aspects.

Project period: local time over which a grant is to be expended.

Project scope: the amount of effort to be expended in conducting the activities of a project; scope may be expressed in terms of total dollar cost, the size of the target group, project procedures, or manpower utilization including the number of person years to be required.

Proposal: formal written document that provides detailed information to a funder on the conduct and cost of a proposed project.

Provider: an individual or organization who contractually agrees to provide services.

Qualitative: expressed or expressible as a story or narrative that evokes the qualities of the person or situation.

Quantitative: 1. expressed or expressible as a quantity; 2. of, relating to, or susceptible of measurement; 3. of or relating to number or quantity.

Rationale: section of a proposal justifying the proposed solution.

Regulations(s): rules developed by federal agencies to implement laws passed by state legislatures.

Reimbursement formula: formula for providing funds based on population, services rendered, proportion of budget to be provided by grantee, etc.; relates to the methods and activities employed during proposal implementation.

Request for application (RFA): the funder's request that includes guidelines and the forms necessary for the school or district to submit a proposal for funds.

Request for proposal (RFP): the funder's request that includes guidelines and the forms necessary for the school or district to submit a proposal for funds.

Rescission: presidential action to cancel funds previously appropriated to a program; must be approved by Congress within forty-five days.

Research grant: grant to support research in the form of studies, surveys, evaluations, investigations, and experimentation.

Revenue sharing: federal program providing assistance to states and localities for broad general purposes.

Reviewer's comments: ratings and explanation of ratings of the panelists who reviewed a proposal.

Rubric: a score form provided by the funding agency to help readers form an opinion or evaluation of the proposed project and how it positions itself against the agency's guidelines.

Seed money: grants to encourage the grantee to start a new program which the funder expects will eventually become self-sustaining or will be supported by the grantee.

Soft match: matching funds, may be in-kind contributions.

Sole source: agency or organization considered by the funder to be the only available resource to fulfill the requirements of a proposed contract.

Solicited proposal: a proposal that has in some way been invited by a sponsoring agency; a proposal in response to an RFP or a program announcement inviting applications.

Special projects or specially funded projects: used to distinguish those parts of the total educational program supported by special purpose funds from those supported by the general fund; many larger districts have a special projects office or department.

Sponsor: usually means funder.

Sponsored project: specially funded project activity or project financed by funds obtained from applications to a source other than the district budget; externally funded project.

Staff development: continuing professional education sponsored by school, district, or other educational agency; generally refers to training offered to groups of teachers rather than on an individual basis.

Staff loading analysis: estimate of staff time needed for each task.

Stakeholders: 1. the party for which professional services are rendered; 2. a customer, client, or beneficiary; 3. a person using the services of your organization.

Statement of purpose: a declaration of result or an effect that is intended or desired; an intention.

Stipend: payment to an individual, usually to support living costs while participating in a training or fellowship program.

Subcontract: an arrangement whereby the prime sponsor or the direct recipient of a sponsor's funds agrees to use the services of another agency or organization (usually contractually) in carrying out some portion of the proposed activities.

Subvention: federal or state assistance given on an ongoing basis to be used for broad purposes.

Summative evaluation: description or measurement of final program results.

Supplanting: using grant funds to cover the costs previously supported by the school district; most grantors do not allow supplanting.

Supplemental monies: monies appropriated by Congress for programs that were not included in the regular appropriation bill.

Systematic: carried on using step-by-step procedures; purposefully regular; methodical.

Systemic: relating to, or affecting the entire organization, its stakeholders, clients, community, and support network.

Target group: a specified group or category of persons for whom the project has been developed and whose needs are intended to be affected by the proposed activities.

Technical assistance (TA) projects: projects that support the provision of services (usually on a regional basis) to specified agencies or projects; services are usually designed to help practitioners implement a program (example: Desegregation Assistance Centers).

Technical proposal: used by some government agencies to refer to the narrative proposal covering all aspects of the proposal except the budget and business information, which are included in a separate business proposal; this procedure is commonly used in responses to RFPs leading to a contract.

Third party: agency, organization, or individual other than the funder or grantee who is involved in a supported project; often a subcontractor.

Time and material contract: fixed daily or hourly rate for each staff member with direct project expenses charged at cost; periodic payments.

Timeline: a management tool that graphically shows the task to be accomplished, by whom, and over what estimated period of time.

Training grant: supports training of staff, students, prospective employees, project participants, or a designated population.

Unobligated balance: unencumbered amount of a grant remaining at the end of the rant period; funder may require that the unobligated balance be returned or subtracted from a continuation grant.

Unsolicited proposal: initiated by the applicant; not in response to an announcement soliciting proposals or an RFP.

Value: worth in usefulness or importance to the funding agency; utility or merit.

Values: beliefs and priorities of the applicant expressed and reflected in the proposal.

Vision: the central idea to which the applicant is committed through the grant proposal.

APPENDIX C
Sample National Endowment for the Humanities Summer Institute Proposal

Prof. Paul Mariani: "The Modern American Epic: from *Paterson* to *Dream Songs*"

Note: The following essay was submitted as part of a successful application for a summer NEH fellowship. Such programs are highly competitive and, and due to their academic nature, expect the applicants to be strong writers. This essay uses the same principles for effective proposals outlined throughout this book. It is but one part of a larger application, but a crucial part.

Better Git 'It in Your Soul: Poetry of the American Voice

He stood before us waving yet another book, saying yet again that this book was, in fact, the "greatest goddamn poem ever written in America," while he paced the room, smoke from the still-lit pipe in his pocket following him as he went. His name was Frank McConnell and each week he asked us to read another American author for his "Literature and the Environment" class. I was nearing the end of my time at UC Santa Barbara; my psychology classes were becoming increasingly dull compared to the literature classes I had begun to take. By the time he waved *Paterson* around I felt ready to read a three-hundred page poem.

I could say I "got it," but only the arrogance of the twenty-one-year old would account for such a statement. I now realize that I could not have possibly understood the poem's complexity, its subject, its accomplishment. It is not possible to comprehend Williams's *Paterson*, nor his neighbor Ginsberg's *Howl*, nor Wolcott's *Omeros*, nor even Homer's *Odyssey* until one has gone out into the world and found there the death, and love, and songs it offers. You must travel your years to understand and be prepared to argue with Berryman's assertion that:

> Life, friends, is boring. We must not say so.
> After all, the sky flashes, the great sea yearns,
> we ourselves flash and yearn . . .

I left that school, grateful for McConnell's teaching, to "flash and yearn" in North Africa in a small village on the Mediterranean where I spent my days reading and listening to jazz on my Walkman. Two years of reading, writing, coffee, wine, thinking, traveling until San Francisco. Then: marriage to a woman won through Tunisian letters. Two sons. Teaching. My father's too early death. All of this, as Rilke says somewhere, prepared me to write and understand poetry as if for the first time.

If, on the other side of his descent into Hell, Dante looked up and saw "the beautiful things that Heaven bears" and the stars, I arrived at that place—after several years of loss and confusion—and found poetry and the meanings it offers me, which amount to more than the "valiant art" that so bores Berryman's Henry. Somewhere between Berryman and Williams lies my own existence as I live it: not a doctor but rather a teacher who turns to this very computer between classes, much as Williams did between patients, to write what words I can gather in the breeze of my life.

But it is more than their example that draws me to Berryman and Williams. It is the possibilities of poetry that intrigue me. Fiction cannot dream in songs sung in voices so varied as Berryman's. Nor will it easily tolerate the mixing of forms that Williams found possible in *Paterson*. Thus one comes to the study of Williams and Berryman not only for their genius and art but for the chance to study what language can do, how texts can work. Williams tells us in *Paterson*, "there is no truth but in Things"; the novelist Cormac McCarthy writes in *Blood Meridian* that "words are things." I am interested in what can be done with these strange, marvelous "things" in my own hands and those much greater than I.

Which to me raises the question of scale. Is *Paterson* a greater poetic achievement than one of Emily Dickinson's little diamonds just because it is an epic? Is *Dream Songs* a more rare, distinguished whole for the sustained coherence of its parts? Take one of Basho's haiku translated by Robert Hass:

> Insects on a bough
>   floating downriver,
>   still singing.

Is *Paterson*, that long river winding through the poem and all the life it holds, contained within this haiku? Can, as Muriel Rukeyser once wrote, a river contain in its waters all the images of those who ever looked into it and yet still have its truth told in only three lines? Or do you need three hundred pages to examine what the river tells us in all its seasons as each generation from Paterson comes to the river to ask its own questions?

Never mind what the river is asking, though: you want to know what I would bring to your roundtable this summer that would make it a success. I will answer this by telling you about my work with Emily Rosenthal, a student of mine, this year. In September this gifted senior, whom I taught as a freshman in my advanced English class, needed an academic class but found none. On a whim I created an independent study humanities class for her on the condition that she do such great work that I would not need to invest any of my time in this extra responsibility. The problem was that by the end of the first week I myself was carried away by the opportunity to study writers and ideas that don't easily fit into our standard curriculum. The first semester we studied biblical literature and its influences on modern writers (my previous NEH seminar studied the psalms as poetry) and ended the semester focusing on four women poets whom I recommended: Dickinson, Szymborska, Rukeyser, and Bishop.

This study of ours amounted to over three hundred pages of typed correspondence by fall semester's end; it continues apace this second semester. These letters chart a journey of both our minds into territory new to us both. I cannot explain how this experience has inspired my own learning. By the time the NEH summer institute pamphlet arrived, I was finishing Sewall's two-volume biography on Dickinson—while teaching five classes, chairing a large English Department, and being father to two sons—and could only see your seminar in Emily Dickinson's hometown as some partial omen signaling where I should go this summer. Moreover, the subject of your seminar challenges me to return to those works I read in the haze of early adulthood, to "arrive where [I] started/ And know the place for the first time," as Eliot wrote. I suddenly understand the truth of those colleagues of mine who speak of the importance of going back and rereading certain texts again and again, as if to say of books what Heraclitus said of rivers—that we cannot read the same book twice.

To read, however, is not necessarily to know or to understand what writers do, and so I have included a list of those works—poems, essays, articles, and stories—I have published. This seminar offers me, through its themes and format, great nourishment as both a writer and a teacher. My writing has often grown out of my work with students and helped me to be something of a mentor. This work with students as a mentor, and particularly one for young poets, is my blessing, one that yields a steady stream of pride in the words they write and the poets they read. When I find myself facing the skepticism of students who wonder what role poetry plays in our lives, I often think of Seamus Heaney's remarks in his essay "The Government of the Tongue," in which he writes that "no lyric ever stopped a tank." And yet, he goes on, "In the rift between what is going to happen and whatever we would wish to happen, poetry holds attention for a space, functions not as distraction but as pure concentration, a focus where our power to concentrate is concentrated back on ourselves." It is that "pure concentration" found in such masters as Williams, Charles Mingus, Berryman, and John Coltrane that I hope to spend my summer thinking about.

APPENDIX D
Sample Letter
Proposal for
Textbooks

Burlingame High School

Burlingame, CA. 94010-0400

September 24, 1997
Jim Burke
Freshman English
Burlingame High School
San Mateo Union High School District
Burlingame, CA 94010
(---) --- --- -- (Office)
(---) --- --- -- (Fax)
Amount Requested: $550.00

Budget Summary:
World Writers Today
@ $16.75 per copy.

Amount requested: $550.00
to purchase 32 copies of the text.
(BHS English Department to pay
remainder of cost.)

Our freshman Honors English program collaborates with the World History classes to provide a more integrated study of cultures through the use of literature from those countries (and writers from those countries who now live in the US). Specifically, we study in great detail India, China, and South Africa. While the students read major novels from these countries, they lack access to a wider range of voices. Two years ago I was able to purchase one class set of the anthology *World Writers Today*, an excellent, comprehensive anthology that includes poetry, speeches, essays, and stories from major writers around the world. The anthology has a rich offering of authors from those cultures we study and other stories from different cultures that would complement our studies as well. The problem we face is that the class sizes have grown and we now have two teachers dividing the teaching assignment. Thus books we might otherwise read go unused because we cannot afford more, a loss to our course and, of course, to the students. The money from this grant would allow us to purchase an additional thirty books and thus provide a full class set for both classes and thereby enable us to use the books for the current and next semester. When used before, the book proved valuable; the students found the readings by such writers as Nadine Gordimer and Maxine Hung Kingston helped them better understand not only the countries they studied but the people from those countries who often now sit beside them in class here in Burlingame, California.

Jim Burke
English Department

Gerald Arrigoni
Principal

APPENDIX E
Sample
Sabbatical
Proposal

Sabbatical Leave Application Proposal
Teacher: Jim Burke
School: Burlingame High School
Term: Fall Semester

Overview   In light of the growing concern with reading difficulties throughout the district, I propose to study the existing and emerging literature on the subject in order to support those teachers who are running the on-site reading programs. In addition, I will develop materials for all teachers in the district, putting on periodic workshops for teachers during the course of my sabbatical. The final product of this sabbatical would be a concise guide to working with struggling readers at the high school level across the curriculum.

Present   Currently I teach English full-time at BHS. I teach fresh-
Teaching   man honors English courses, which are integrated with
Assignment the advanced World History course. In addition, I teach College Prep juniors.

Future Teaching Objectives

I would like to continue working with juniors, as I find it a fascinating crossroads in their lives and the curriculum. More generally, I want to learn to teach all students to read better and to help other teachers improve in this area.

Sabbatical Objectives

I would divide my objectives between the following domains:

- **Students**: *All* students need to improve their ability to read a variety of texts in different media and across the curriculum. My objective here is to help them develop and expand their capacity to read diverse texts to ensure their success in school and the world beyond our classes.

- **Teachers**: High school teachers, even those who teach English, do not know how kids learn to read; nor do they really have a practical, useful sense of the reading process itself. They need to learn how kids read, why they perform as they do, and how teachers can help students read better on a daily basis in all content areas. Teachers taking on the reading programs at each site will not get the release time they need to research some of these issues; thus I propose to be a resource person to teachers throughout the district in general and all reading program teachers in particular. I would support them through individual conversations—via e-mail, phone, or site visitation— and workshops to which all interested teachers would be welcome. In addition to these reading program teachers, I will concentrate on creating a sustainable, systemic approach at Burlingame; if this model is successful, I would then share it with the other schools through various means, including my web site, which I could supplement specifically to help our district's teachers in the area of reading (http://www.englishcompanion.com/wip).

- **Myself**: In the past seven years I have worked hard to improve myself as a teacher and to learn; the measure of my success is a record of achievement within the classroom, school, district, and profession. More specifically, I have been recognized as Teacher of the Year by students; chaired the English Department for four years; served on several district committees; and, most recently, written a book, *The English Teacher's Companion: A Complete Guide to Classroom, Curriculum, and the Profession*, which will be released in January 1999. I mention all these accomplishments only to demonstrate that, given the opportunity, I will accomplish what I set out to do. Such work will have the added benefit of professional and personal renewal, which is central to sabbaticals. Seven years of teaching English has challenged me to learn how to meet the complex demands of my work; yet these same demands rarely offer the needed time for reflection that we all need if we are to continue to improve in our instructional practice.

Outline of My Plans

What I Will Do

Survey all relevant research and the most current literature to identify those methods that will improve student performance in the area of reading. Such work has the added benefit of showing the WASC teams that our school and district are doing all they can to address the problems of reading.

Create materials and develop strategies for teachers throughout the district, especially those in the reading program, to help them achieve significant gains in student reading ability.

Provide periodic workshops for the reading program teachers to help support their work and meet their specific needs, anchoring these workshops in both their specific requests/programmatic needs and research-based strategies. Additional workshops will be available for all teachers or those with special needs to help them improve student performance in the area of reading. These workshops and other efforts to support the teachers also complement our schoolwide goal in the area of reading; this means there is and will continue to be a sustainable structure for integrating my ideas into the school culture through the time made available to the faculty on Wednesday mornings.

Create and distribute a user-friendly guide to help teachers throughout the district. This guide will include a concise overview of the main findings from research which they can refer to for quick reminders; it will also contain focused activities for different types of reading assignments. The guide will further include other resources they might consult for further learning on their own. This guide could be easily added to my web site (http://www.englishcompanion.com) which I encourage you to visit to further measure my commitment to helping teachers do their work better.

Avail myself to the Burlingame High School and other schools' reading program teachers as they get started in the coming year. Teachers would be able to call me for guidance or to ask for visitations as a consultant or assistant if such requests seemed appropriate to the task. In other words, a teacher could call to say they want to try reciprocal teaching on a particular day and would find it useful if I sat in to observe and offer any suggestions as to how to improve their implementation. They could not, however, say they are just overwhelmed and would really appreciate it if I could come in and work with the kids on the computers.

Other

I plan to attend the California Reading Association convention in Sacramento as well as the National Council of Teachers of English convention in November 1999. My objective at such conventions would specifically be to attend workshops and evaluate materials for use in the reading program and regular classrooms. I also facilitate a national conversation on-line (for several thousand educators) that includes the leading minds in the area of reading instruction and research; this makes it easy for me to tap into existing knowledge and successful models which might benefit our own program.

Endnote

I realize that most people seek time during their sabbatical to take courses and obtain further degrees. I have taken courses and obtained graduate degrees during the past seven years, receiving San Francisco State's Distinguished Graduate Student Award for my work in education during that time. I expect the trustees and the district office like to see people enrolled in courses during their sabbatical as this ensures they are actually doing work for the benefit of the district or their students. Such enrollment holds the teacher accountable. My record of hard work, the evidence of my commitment to helping not only students but colleagues as well, attests to my credibility and my ability to accomplish what I set out to do. The district and, more to the point, our students, desperately need the help my sabbatical could provide. This learning would, in addition, certainly improve my own classroom practice in the process.

I am pleased to include, as part of this application, letters of support from my principal and department chair, both of whom volunteered to write them on my behalf; another letter, by our administrator for curriculum and instruction, is forthcoming. I have also included, as further evidence of my ability to produce quality work, the advertisement for my book.

I would be happy to answer any further questions you might have regarding my plans. Thank you for your time and consideration of my proposal.

Sincerely,

Jim Burke

APPENDIX F
The Ultimate
Source
for Help and
Information:
The Foundation
Center

Note: We debated whether we should include here a directory of different resources, but concluded that information changes so often that it was not efficient to do so. We decided instead to include the following description of The Foundation Center by way of sending you to the ultimate source for all grant seekers and grant makers. Here you will find the latest information on grants. The center's regional offices throughout the United States offer a wealth of wisdom and resources.

The following description comes from the center's Web site, which you can access at www.fdncenter.org, an address that is sure to be valid for years to come.

"What Is The Foundation Center?"

The Foundation Center is an independent nonprofit information clearinghouse established in 1956. The center's mission is to foster public understanding of the foundation field by collecting, organizing, analyzing, and disseminating information on foundations, corporate giving, and related subjects. The audiences that call on the center's resources include grant seekers, grant makers, researchers, policy makers, the media, and the general public.

Foundation Center Libraries

The Foundation Center operates libraries at five locations. These include national collections at its headquarters in New York City and at its field office in Washington, D.C., and regional collections at its offices in Atlanta, Cleveland, and San Francisco. Center libraries provide access to a unique collection of materials on philanthropy and are open to the public free of charge. Professional reference librarians are on hand to show library users how to research funding information using center publications and other materials and resources.

Orientations   Each center-operated library offers free weekly orientations on the funding research process. These orientations are designed to give representatives of nonprofit organizations an overview of the foundation and corporate giving universe and to introduce them to the effective use of the center's publications, resources, and services. Center staff can also tailor orientations to the specific needs and interests of various groups. To learn more about the center's orientations or to schedule a library tour, call the center-operated library nearest you.

Reference Materials Found at Center Libraries
- Forms 990-PF: Internal Revenue Service information returns are filed annually by more than forty-nine thousand U.S. private foundations. These forms are often the only primary source of information on the many foundations that do not issue annual reports. Information provided on 990-PF forms includes fiscal data, grants awarded by a foundation, and the names of the foundation's officers and trustees.

- Grantmaker materials: Each library maintains an extensive collection of foundation annual reports and corporate giving reports, as well as newsletters, press releases, and application guidelines.

- Directories, books, and periodicals: Foundation Center–operated libraries have available for public use multiple copies of the center's publications, in addition to hundreds of other directories, books, and periodicals on such topics as fund-raising, board relations, corporate responsibility, foundation salaries, nonprofit management, and program planning.

- Foundation and nonprofit literature on-line: The center's bibliographic database contains listings for more than sixteen thousand books and articles, many with abstracts, relating to philanthropy and the nonprofit sector.

Congressional Research Service Resources

Since 1985, the center has regularly provided the Congressional Research Service (CRS) of the Library of Congress with eight complementary sets of its core publications. These collections are located in the Congressional Reference Division, in two Congressional Reading Rooms, and in four House and Senate Reference Centers, where they are available to congressional staff responding to constituent requests for grants and funding information.

Cooperating Collections

The center's Cooperating Collections (CCs) are located in public libraries, community foundation offices, and other nonprofit agencies in all fifty states. CCs offer a core collection of center publications free to the public, and their staffs are trained to direct patrons to appropriate resources on funding information. Many CCs also have directories and reports on local funders as well as copies of IRS information returns for private foundations in their state or region. For the address and telephone number of a Cooperating Collection in a given location, click on the hyperlink on the center's website, or call the center at 1-800-424-9836.

Print and Electronic Resources

The Foundation Center annually issues more than sixty publications, among them directories of foundation and corporate grant makers, grants lists, research studies, bibliographies, and authored works on subjects relating to fund-raising, foundations, and nonprofit management. The center also releases annually its electronic funding research tool, *FC Search: The Foundation Center's Database on CD-ROM.*

All Foundation Center print and electronic resources are available for free use in all center libraries and Cooperating Collections.

A Sampling of Center-Issued Resources
• *FC Search: The Foundation Center's Database on CD-ROM* is a comprehensive, fully searchable fund-raising database that covers close to fifty thousand U.S. foundations and corporate givers, includes over two hundred thousand associated grants, lists more than two hundred thousand trustees, officers, and donors, and provides direct links to over six hundred grant maker Web sites.

• *The Foundation Directory* features current data on the nation's largest funders, those that hold assets of at least $2 million or distribute $200,000 or more in grants annually. The volume includes information on more than ten thousand major foundations, which hold combined assets of $304 billion and donate well over $14 billion annually. Designed as a companion volume to the directory, *The Foundation Directory Part 2* covers more than fifty-seven hundred midsized foundations with assets between $1 million and $2 million or annual grant programs between $50,000 and $200,000. *The Foundation Directory Supplement* is issued six months after the directory two-part and provides useful updates to the information contained in those volumes.

• *The Foundation 1000* provides comprehensive, multipage profiles of the one thousand largest foundations in the United States. Profiles include grant maker addresses and contact names, reviews of program interests, purpose and giving limitations statements, application guidelines, and the names of key officials. Also included are in-depth analyses of grant programs, extensive lists of sample grants, and cross-referenced indexes.

• *The Guide to U.S. Foundations, Their Trustees, Officers, and Donors* has current information on every active private grant making foundation in the United States—more than forty-six thousand foundations in all. Arranged by state and local giving, the *Guide to U.S. Foundations* helps users identify both large and small foundations in their geographic area, while the comprehensive trustee, officer, and donor index offers information on the affiliations of board members, donors, and volunteers.

• *The National Directory of Corporate Giving* offers information on more than 2,800 corporate philanthropic programs, including detailed portraits of over 1,900 corporate foundations and 990 direct-giving programs. Grant maker entries include application information, the names of key personnel, types of support generally awarded, giving limitations, financial data, and purpose and activities statements.

• *The Foundation Grants Index* lists grants of $10,000 or more awarded by more than one thousand of the largest independent, corporate, and community foundations in the United States. Containing more than eighty-six thousand grant descriptions, the book is divided into twenty-eight broad subject areas such as health, higher education, arts and culture, and the environment. Within each of these fields, grants are grouped by state.

• *The Foundation Center's Guide to Proposal Writing* offers a comprehensive look at the steps involved in preparing an effective funding request and gives advice on such subjects as proposal formats, budget preparation, and follow-up. It also includes advice from grant makers themselves on the dos and don'ts of proposal writing.

• *The Foundation Center's Guide to Grantseeking on the Web* teaches you how to use the World Wide Web's diverse resources to further your funding research. Filled with tips, strategies, and sample Web sites, this illustrated, step-by-step guide will help you find a wealth of information, including: foundation and corporate giving Web sites, searchable databases for grant seeking, government resources, interactive services for grant seekers on the Web, and much more.

• *Foundation Giving: A Yearbook of Facts and Figures on Private, Corporate and Community Foundations,* a comprehensive overview of the latest trends in foundation grant making, documents the growth of and changes in grant making from 1975 to the present. More than one hundred charts and tables illustrate such topics as foundation grants by subject area, foundation assets and gifts received, and the geographic distribution of foundations and the grants they awarded.

• Research studies published by the center include reports on arts funding and health policy grant making, and a study of program-related investments made by U.S. foundations. Browse the center's publications catalog, or call the center at 1-800-424-9836 and ask for a copy.

Services

Whether they visit a center library to find out about a foundation's giving guidelines, about recent changes at foundations in their region, or about grants in specific areas of interest, people turn to the Foundation Center for information on the foundation field.

Fees

While many center resources and services are available on a complimentary basis, for others a fee corresponding to the cost of on-line time or the amount of staff time required to fill a request is charged. For more information, please call or write The Foundation Center.

Referrals

Among the questions most commonly asked by novice grant seekers are: Which funders might be interested in my nonprofit organization or project? And, Where can I find information about proposal writing and other fund-raising skills?

The Foundation Center encourages people with these kinds of questions to call or visit a center-operated library or Cooperating Collection, where staff trained in the funding-research process can help them get started.

Custom Research and Database Searching

Center staff also provide custom services ranging from photocopying to telephone reference to database searching. Staff consult with customers to identify their needs and determine the most cost-effective and timely way of obtaining the information they require.

The Foundation Center's database contains information on approximately fifty thousand U.S. private and community foundations and corporate giving programs, and records for grants of $10,000 or more awarded by more than one thousand of the largest foundations annually. Center staff can perform database searches for grant makers to assess philanthropic giving in a specific region or state, map funding patterns, or locate grant makers active in a particular field. There is a charge for this service based on the data requested and staff time required.

Research Advice

When people wish to conduct their own research, they often call or visit the center for advice on how to proceed. Center staff can recommend the best on-line and other sources of regional and national information, offering assistance in performing a variety of searches.

Foundation Center Offices

New York
79 Fifth Avenue
New York, NY 10003-3076
Tel: (212) 620-4230

Field Offices

Washington, D.C.
1001 Connecticut Avenue, N.W.
(entrance at K Street)
Suite 938
Washington, D.C. 20036
Tel: (202) 331-1400

Atlanta
50 Hurt Plaza, Suite 150
Atlanta, GA 30303-2914
Tel: (404) 880-0095

Cleveland
1422 Euclid Avenue
Suite 1356
Cleveland, OH 44115-2001
Tel: (216) 861-1933

San Francisco
312 Sutter Street
Room 312
San Francisco, CA 94108-4314
Tel: (415) 397-0902

APPENDIX G
List of Examples
in the Book and
on the CD-ROM

Note: The following list is designed to help you quickly find examples throughout the book.

Appendix H
Sample Winning
Proposal:
Apple Technology
Grant

Note: This grant won $100,000 and was formally recognized as an exemplary proposal by the Smithsonian Institution. The proposal, with its original formatting and with additional attachments and expert annotations, is also available on the CD-ROM.

Roosevelt School Apple Technology Grant

Abstract: In the space provided [on the application cover sheet], summarize your project.

Touch the Future: Teach a Child will focus on the 3 Es: Education, En-vironment, and Ethics. Working with Dr. McCloud and local retirement centers, students will create "Our Town," a Web site that links seniors to our classrooms, our virtual projects, and abundant Internet resources. Computer access will be an enormous psychological boost to these older adults and launch our Service Learning curriculum.

Part I: About the Partners

> *Honor the past, challenge the present, and look toward the future.*
> —*Walt Disney*

The Community: Roosevelt School is a community of learners. Its diverse student population speaks seventeen different native languages other than English, Spanish and Russian dominating all others except English. These 248 students include among their ranks those who make up San Mateo County's Hearing Impaired Classroom. Thus we add to the seventeen languages yet one more, a language many children at Roosevelt school will eventually speak—American Sign Language—thanks to the Signing Club students started up last fall.

Meeting Diverse Needs: Students are also learning to use their hands to communicate through other media, most importantly networked computers. Technology offers Roosevelt's students, who come from very diverse socioeconomic backgrounds, access not only to the tools of the regular classroom, but the knowledge and skills necessary for success in tomorrow's society. Diversity is honored here. The entire school has been focused on a community building theme since the beginning of the year. That theme has been integrated throughout the entire curriculum, and supported by a $23,000 grant from the Shinnyo-En Foundation, which has provided in-service training, an array of books, thematic lesson plans, and student/community assemblies.

Need for Resources: Roosevelt School's existence testifies to the spirit and commitment of its surrounding community. Though Burlingame's other schools benefited from a bond issue passed several years before, Roosevelt was reopened this past September only to find it lacked funding for anything other than the basics. Constructed in 1919, and closed since 1980, the school represented a significant challenge; but where others saw twenty years of deterioration and needed repairs, Roosevelt's teachers, students, parents and volunteers saw only a blank canvas on which they can create a vital community linked to the larger world through the resources available to them in the Bay Area and the wider world of the Internet.

Our Mission: Roosevelt's mission is best summed up by Teddy Roosevelt himself: "The first requisite of a good citizen in this Republic of ours is that he shall be able and willing to pull his weight." Specifically, we are asking our students to devote the full measure of their energy and intellect to The Three Es: Education, Ethics, and the Environment. Our goal is to educate all students to their fullest potential as lifelong learners so they will be able to effectively contribute to a changing society. In turn, the community of Roosevelt nourishes its children. We feel our school is a good school. Dr. John Fischer, Teachers College president, says it best: "A good school is one where children know they are welcome and respected; where everyday they experience some measure of success; and where they are constantly reminded that what they do really makes a difference."

Staff Development: The commitment to caring includes everyone at Roosevelt. Our staff participates regularly in our district-provided professional development days in the area of technology. Several of our teachers have even taught technology sessions to district staff. The district's technology coordinator regularly visits our school to provide on-site training and will be directly involved in the implementation of the program outlined in this grant. Staff development is supported fully throughout the district. The district offers "district" credit toward salary raises as well as stipends for staff presenters.

Current Technology: We have twenty Power Macintosh 5400/180 computers in our lab, and one Power Macintosh 5500-250 for video demonstrations. Each teacher, our secretary, librarian, and principal have a computer on their desk. Our combination third/fourth grade classroom has use of five LC Macintosh models, which are on loan during the school day from the resident childcare facility. A second-grade classroom has a lab of sixteen AppleIIE's that are old but very active. There are three laser printers to service the entire school: one to service the lab; one in the West Hall for the upper grades; and one in the office for use by the office staff, kindergarten and primary grade teachers. There are four ImageWriters and one StyleWriter II in the second-grade Apple IIE classroom.

College of Notre Dame: For over forty years College of Notre Dame (CND) has maintained a reputation for excellence in teacher education and has placed thirty-five hundred teachers since it began in 1953. It has students from around the world and is the only teacher education program in San Mateo County that has established a masters degree program in educational technology. It is accredited through the California Commission on Teacher Credentialing.

Involvement in Schools: The college's mission aligns with Roosevelt's Touch the Future: Teach a Child program to serve the community. Our focus is on better serving adult students through their becoming more involved with the local and Roosevelt community. Our teachers in training will bring new ideas to Roosevelt, especially in networking, telecommunications, in the promotion and use of eMates, and distributed learning throughout the curriculum. These same teachers will be coming back with new ideas and ventures for the college to explore after being exposed to products first hand within a model site and a curriculum setting.

CND's Need for Resources: Our "Mac Lab" was created in 1990 through a $100,000 grant from the Wiegand Foundation—a long time in this, the Communication Age. Our lab needs an infusion of fresh and new technology, so teachers in training can experience the possibilities and tools children need to benefit from for their future success. We see a similar technology need in our partner school, Roosevelt. With the help of this grant and interaction with Dr. David Thornburg, our visiting technology scholar, we will better prepare teachers for classroom 2000.

Part II: The Target Population

Through the struggle to get out of its cocoon the butterfly's wings acquire the strength to fly.
—Robin Williams's character in Dead Poets' Society

Institution Profiles: The 248 kindergarten through fifth-grade students addressed in this project all attend Roosevelt School. Along with Roosevelt students will be the hundreds of district teachers, teacher candidates (CND), volunteers, partners, and visitors to our model technology site. Students at Roosevelt School reflect a diverse socioeconomic mix; some children live in shared apartments, while others live in million-dollar homes. We have the highest percent of English as a Second Language students in the District. Coming from so many different district schools both students and staff have had to make major changes. We have found out that change, though challenging, brings new opportunities. Roosevelt has a unique opportunity to implement the Apple Education Grant with a new generation of learners within a new educational context. CND has a new partner, mentor and model site for coursework reforms.

Student Needs: Touch the Future: Teach a Child has looked to the SCANS Report (Secretary's Commission on Achieving Necessary Skills), the California Standards, and other prominent researched based documents to guide us in shaping our re-vision of what we should be asking from students. We recognize the truth substantiated in the 1991 SCANS Report that "more than half of our young people leave school without the knowledge or foundation to hold a good job." Our efforts are to prepare all students, regardless of diversities, empowering them to enter the world as citizens and workers. As well as wanting all Roosevelt students to gain the more complex competencies to function in the increasingly technological world, we also want students to possess a mastery of basic foundation skills. After long discussions with our students, parents, community members, business leaders, and college alliance, three student goals were designed which embrace our three areas of focus: Education, Environmental Awareness, and Ethics.

Goal 1: To develop in each student the five SCANS workplace competencies to: enhance each students' ability to allocate resources wisely; develop interpersonal skills; interpret and communicate information; design and understand systems; and, select and use appropriate technology to solve a range of problems effectively.

Goal 2: To engage all students in formative experiences that actively contribute to their community and environment by designing local Service Learning experiences that will foster environmental awareness and help students realize that they too, can be contributors to a better planet earth.

Goal 3: To provide opportunities for students, community members (especially seniors) to contribute time and talents to improve and modify our existing educational and volunteer partnership systems and services, building good citizenship, character, and ethics.

Diverse Needs: Roosevelt School encourages all children regardless of age, gender, or handicapping conditions to be active participants in campus projects. The technology "hub's" digital camera, scanners, eMates, software, interdisciplinary lessons, videos, and Internet/e-mail resources await project participants.

Part III: The Curriculum

> *We must be dream makers and create realities out of our dreams and dreams out of our realities.*
> —*Gene Wilder's character in*
> Willie Wonka and the Chocolate Factory

Three months after receiving the equipment, students in Mrs. Connell's third grade class huddle around the computers, waiting to check their e-mail: it is the morning ritual, one they all enjoy. The mail would be coming from their "senior friends" at a nearby retirement home where one of the computers was also installed and connected to the school's network. The seniors, many of whom have trouble sleeping at night, will often write the children letters in the wee hours; their relationship with the children at Roosevelt, combined with their new computer skills, invests them with a sense of purpose some have not felt in some time. Teachers at Roosevelt, including Mrs. Connell, get to school a little earlier to get the system up so it's ready when the kids arrive at eight. They have no trouble doing this as John Geer, the district's technology coordinator, provided several workshops on maintaining their hardware and using the software within the context of the curriculum.

Three months later, six months into the project, the students at Roosevelt have learned to create, edit, and maintain their school's Web site. To this site they regularly add a range of literacy projects reflecting the variety of work and celebrating the accomplishments of the school's students. Their senior friends visit the site regularly, making comments on how nice their work is, posting these comments to them on email. Early links to such local environmental sites as the Coyote Point Preserve allow the students to take "virtual field trips" which their senior friends can also take; these trips allow them to share their observations through writing and the drawings the students make of the different habitats. John Geer and other on-site mentors have, by this time, finished training all members of the staff and all students; in a peer tutoring program, fourth and fifth graders, after demonstrating mastery, teach the students in the lower grades how to use the internet by visiting the Web site of their favorite television show *Kratt's Creatures*, and letting them develop their computer skills through the different activities the *Kratt's* site offers them. John Kim, a third grader with severe hearing difficulties, tells his senior friend, Mr. Hill, about the site; the next morning John has an email from Mr. Hill telling him about the time when he traveled in Africa as a young man and saw his first real lion. Everyone is jealous and wants to read John's email. Mr. Hill also mentions that he, too, wears a hearing aid and tells John that he likes being able to turn it off when he doesn't want to listen to people. John thinks this is funny and shows it to his other deaf friends at school.

By the end of the first year Roosevelt boasts a fully developed Web site that includes links to many different local and distant sites which complement their curriculum. Students in Mrs. Casey's kindergarten class are reading *The Very Hungry Caterpillar* and, after hearing the story, visit the California Language Arts home page where the cyberguide for *The Very Hungry Caterpillar* allows them to visit a number of sites about caterpillars and other insects; this leads them, eventually, to the new National Geographic Web site which features a new page on edible bugs, which the kids find fascinatingly gross. Later on, John's senior friend writes that while in Africa he once ate a small handful of termites to please his tribal host; again, everyone is in awe of John's friend's stories.

Summary of Major Milestones

By Dec. 1998: Students communicate daily with their friends and all other community partners (e.g., the botanist at the Coyote Point Preserve; Retirement Center; Mills-Peninsula Hospital) as virtual projects evolve.

By Feb. 1999: Students update the school Web site weekly, adding to it the featured projects, digital newspaper, and winners of the Students of the Week awards.

Ongoing: School presents its quarterly review of progress in use of technology, its impact on learning and their class Service Learning projects with Bay Area seniors.

March 1999: Seniors at the retirement homes are busy exploring Roosevelt's "Our Town" Web site that links them to many senior resources and activities.

June 1999: Teachers make presentations at district and county meetings and use staff development days to help others learn how to do these same activities thereby creating a collaborative learning environment. The Roosevelt team has completed their evaluation plan. Such literacies are not just purchased, however; indeed, they are the achievement of teachers whose long hours of training and learning culminate in a meaningful curriculum that integrates what students need to know. Successful integration of curriculum and the use of technology depends on time to plan and opportunity to learn. Several units of study exemplify how our students learn; in fact, our school's emphasis is not so much on what students need to learn but how they do and continue to learn.

> *Family Tree:* Students in this fifth-grade class used various tools (what Miles Myers calls "distributed intelligence") to investigate, represent, and present their family trees, the stories of those people, the cultures, and historical periods during which they lived. This was done before we had access to the Internet; we are very excited to imagine what students can accomplish now that we have eMates and are connected to the Internet.

> *Space Shuttle:* While the space shuttle was in space, this fourth-grade class created a simulation that involved using math, science, astronomy, writing, and art to follow the adventure of the shuttle crew. For three days the classroom was turned into a simulated shuttle; during this time all meals were cooked and eaten as they would be on the shuttle. Students kept logs in order to keep track of what happened and how they felt at different times during the experience. Again, this was done prior to the completion of the school's Internet connection; we are eager to do the same simulation involving real astronauts with whom we can communicate directly.

Project Benefits: The chart on page 10 [see Fig. H.2, p. 242] discusses the needs/limitations, benefits, and planned improvements. We have focused on three areas of concern (mobility information management, capacity building) that are both realistic but central to many school technology integration programs. Our site models (Roosevelt/CND) will be both authentic and replicable at other school sites. Other project benefits include: (1) Burlingame District, Roosevelt, and CND will provide professional development, access to technology tools, training and mutual support; (2) Sterling Court, Burlingame Inn, and Dr. McCloud (Mills-Peninsula Hospital) will provide an opportunity for an exciting ongoing Service Learning project; (3) using our new knowledge and equipment we will create our first interactive distance learning "virtual classroom"; (4) Coyote Point will provide opportunities for students to gain formative experiences and enhance their environment; and (5) the Summer Academy will provide on-site pilot classrooms. Each of our project partners bring resources (physical, human, fiscal) that extend Roosevelt's classrooms far beyond their four walls.

Evaluation: Assessment ideally takes place in a variety of contexts and serves diverse purposes. The ultimate objective of our assessment plan is to help both Roosevelt, CND, and seniors better understand where we have gone and where we need to go. Specifically our proposed assessment activities will do the following:

- Measure students' progress toward clearly articulated objectives based on known standards in that domain.
- Provide feedback to educators on successful strategies for technology integration and training.
- Support the development of credible Service Learning technology–based projects.
- Help us make decisions for changing and improving teaching and learning.

Evaluation will address a set of questions derived from each of the Touch the Future goals. It will be both formative, to help articulate the need for ongoing project changes, and summative, to determine the extent to which students, educators and community show desired changes in learning. The evaluation of the new 3 E's will go beyond the use of test scores and support the development of new innovations.

The following are a sampling of evaluation questions related to the established areas of focus:

- *Staff development.* Does the technology training curriculum adequately prepare project participants for a distributive learning environment?
- *Service Learning.* To what extent will our senior projects increase student workplace competencies and increase opportunities to learn and achieve?
- *The 3 E's.* To what extent will a distributive learning environment create a positive impact on systemic change, student performance and community involvement?
- *Technology.* To what extent will technology tools and related institutional changes cause a reorganization of time, systems, services and products from kindergarten through college?

Part IV: Professional Development

I stand on my desk to remind myself that we must constantly look at things in different ways.
                    —*Robin Williams's character in* Dead Poets' Society

Professional Development Needs: One of the most significant elements of Touch the Future is its Professional Development component. Project participants will have the opportunity to work with a variety of instructors to assist them in creating a technology-based, interdisciplinary, student-center environment. Teachers-in-training and veteran educators need coursework that reflects "cutting edge" ideas. Providing instructors who have developed nationally recognized, technology-based instructional strategies is important to us. To this end our project has developed a relationship with Jerry Westfall, creator and program director of TigerNet, a state-of-the-art student-run technology program that began in Oregon and is presently in fifty schools. This year, backed by Intel Corporation, TigerNet is being replicated in five other western states.

Mr. Westfall has been recognized nationally by the Walt Disney and McDonalds Corporations as a winner of their American Teacher Awards and by Intel Foundation for Innovations in Teaching Excellence. As a technology consultant and classroom teacher, he will bring his extraordinary mastery of distributed learning to Roosevelt and CND through a series of workshops and site evaluations. Classes will be conducted at Roosvelt and CND before and after school to attract many California participants. Burlingame district release time, stipends, and/or credit will be available for project participants. Utilizing the resources of our partners and new equipment from this grant will greatly expedite our technology integration plan. Management of the interdisciplinary, technology-based environment will take practice and time, but we are confident that we have the resources we need to succeed. Below is a graph [Figure H.1] showing Roosevelt's staff skill levels and proposed training matrix.

Part V: Impact and Dissemination

The only limit to our realization of tomorrow will be our doubts of today.

—Franklin Delano Roosevelt

Efficient use of grant money requires the sharing of knowledge to increase general understanding of newly available hardware and software. It also means sharing resources. Our labs will be open to interested parties for training, exploration and mentoring.

Because the Burlingame School District has an ongoing goal of working and learning together, there are in-services happening at least ten times a year, organized by our curriculum and technology facilitators. District teachers also advertise and host weekly minisessions on various topics which the district encourages through small stipends. The sessions are well attended. Of particular interest to many will be invitations to the special workshops provided by Jerry Westfall of TigerNet,

% STAFF	RANK	CURRENT	FUTURE
60%	Novice	• Keyboarding Skills • Macintosh Basics • E-mail • Word-processing	• Keyboarding Skills • CD-ROM • Macintosh Basics • E-mail • Word-processing • Simple Internet • Simple Desktop Publishing • Spreadsheet
25%	Intermediate	• CD-ROM • Simple Internet • Simple Desktop Publishing • Spreadsheet	• Advanced Internet • Database • File server • Training skills • Maintenance and Troubleshooting • Complex Curriulum Integration • Presentation skills • Multimedia
15%	Advanced	• Advanced Internet • Database • File server • Training skills • Maintenance and Troubleshooting • Complex Curriculum Integration • Presentation skills • Multimedia	• Advanced Multimedia • Web Publishing • Advanced Database • LAN Management • Trainer of trainers • Innovate Curriculum Integration

FIGURE H.1   **Roosevelt Staff Development Matrix**

Tigard High, Oregon. Roosevelt school will be used as a model visitation site for teaching integrated, student-centered, distributed learning. Our CND students (teacher candidates, education and administration masters candidates) as well as any educators will be welcome to participate in the course work and in-service training program in the Roosevelt "hub" and CND MAC lab.

Our project is centrally located in our state and is easily accessible from the San Francisco Airport and major Bay Area freeways. Three other teacher colleges (San Francisco State, CSU-Hayward and University of San Francisco) have collaborated with our district on grants and educational reforms. They supply many of our Bay Area Schools with student teachers and professional development classes. When appropriate, other Educational and Community agencies will be contacted and invited to participate in our project programs, visit our model classroom sites, or use the course work outlines and materials developed.

Because of the new Web site created by the children, word of this project will spread quickly. The district has a history of piloting and replicating educational reforms. If successful our project will be "cloned" and implemented in four district elementary and one district middle school. We see the opening of similar projects, throughout the district, within a very short time.

Our senior partners will be receiving in-house lessons on how to use e-mail and the Internet. They will also be encouraged to visit the school, work in the "hub," or volunteer in classrooms. BettyJo and Lee Wade, a married, retired couple, active in the Roosevelt School community, have volunteered to teach basic computer skills to the seniors, and coordinate senior activities. They are excited about seeing Roosevelt re-open and involved in Service Learning. This couple's enthusiasm and interest in life make them ideal teachers. Opening up the world of e-mail and the Internet to the senior members of our community is a unique project and necessary contribution to our community.

Part VI: The Use of Technology

Snapshots of Distributed Learning: The Internet, along with other tools present in our environment, teaches students to assign different tasks to different tools. Children learn when it is best to visit the library, and when to search for information on Newsbank, a CD-ROM database the school owns. They also use the scanners and digital camera to integrate different images into their books and reports; some have begun to learn how to copy images off the Internet and incorporate these into their documents. Parents at work can send e-mail greetings to their children during the school day to maintain a connection; in addition, students who pass the mastery test are allowed to visit the senior center and help teach the seniors to use the computers. As computers allow people of all ages to work at all hours, to go anywhere their imagination lets them, this intergenerational collaboration represents the crossing of yet one more boundary. Fourth grader, Jeannie, whose grandfather died when she was very young, is especially excited about the collaboration with senior, Mr. Mangini, whom she finds very funny.

Seniors, free to use the computers for their own purposes, begin to search the Internet for other online communities. Joe Gospacci finds the Veterans of Foreign Wars site and, following the links provided there, travels back to an exhibit on World War II on display at the Smithsonian. Marion Tucker links up with her granddaughter who works in New York; Marion has not seen her granddaughter's new daughter and is thrilled when her next e-mail includes a picture of her great-granddaughter in it. All the other seniors are jealous. Marion forwards this page over to Melissa, her fourth-grade friend at Roosevelt; Melissa had asked her if she had any pictures and Marion had felt embarrassed when she said she did not.

New Offerings: Before computers and other technologies, all classroom research depended on printed materials, many of which were obsolete due to the lack of funding for the school library. Computers, especially those connected to the Internet, provide access to the best libraries in the world and the most current information. Previous simulations, such as those discussed in earlier sections, lacked that "real connection" to the larger world of experience. Space shuttle simulations were little more than amusing though complicated games created and supervised by the teacher; the Internet redefines the teacher's role, making them designers and directors, making them responsible for their own learning in new and powerful ways. The Internet is essentially a living textbook they can use for all their classes.

Student Access: The computers will be placed in a large hallway "hub" right outside the third- through fifth-grade classroom where they can be directly accessed by students once they have completed all mandatory training in their use. Computers and all peripherals will be available to all students at all times throughout the day in order to encourage responsibility and allow for integrated use within the larger school curriculum. This is a new classroom management venture for our staff who has had very limited use of the computers during their assigned classroom technology lab time.

FOCUS AREA	LIMITATIONS	PROJECT BENEFIT	PLANNED IMPROVEMENTS
Mobility	Technology tools not available, integrated, mobile. Not anytime or anyplace.	Technology tools available 24-hour day. Distributive, Service & Cooperative Learning.	Creation of multiple technology "hubs" at Roosevelt School. More teacher skills with hardware and software.
Information	Not fully integrated instructional units.	Abundant, linear, & connected instructional units.	Launch "Our Town" internet Web site.
	No technology tools used for management.	Technologically enhanced student assessment.	Intranet for student assessment record.
Capacity	More communication among educators, partners & community to promote change.	More communication among educator, partners, & community to promote change.	Integrate technology throughout school. Create alliance with CDN, Seniors, Partners.

Organizational Capacity Description

Collaboration: Roosevelt is filled with visitors: seniors, teachers, parents, and students interested in seeing a new learning environment where student-centered, distributed learning has enhanced, accelerated and empowered our community in a special way. Being so close to the San Francisco Airport and major freeways we have guests from all over the country.

Part VII: Organizational Capacity and Administrative Support

Learning has no finish line.
>   —*Roosevelt staff and community,*
>   *Burlingame School District Student*

The Project Team: The first five people on our list are the "official" members of our project team. They will continue to implement, evaluate, refine, and expand the vision of Touch the Future: Teach a Child in the coming years. We would ask Apple to consider modifying its definition of *team* so that we may include Mr. and Mrs. Wade (senior Coordinators #6 and 7) and Ms. Moroney (CND student teacher #8). This would give our major partners equal footing and assist in project implementation.

1. *Fred Heron:* title: principal, Roosevelt School; affiliation: Roosevelt's promoter of "distributed learning"; role: Will provide direction, leadership, and inspiration to the Touch the Future team; responsibilities: implementation and evaluation.

2. *John Geer:* title: district technology coordinator; affiliation: Burlingame Schools "mentor"; role: ongoing assessment, maintenance, and training of Roosevelt staff and partners; responsibilities: coordination, training.

3. *Caryl Brewbaker:* title: Roosevelt second-grade teacher; affiliation: Burlingame Schools; role: grant coordinator; Apple IIE distributive learning classroom teacher; responsibilities: coordinate; facilitate partnerships.

4. *Dr. Diane Guay:* title: College of Notre Dame, chair, Department of Education; affiliation: CND College administrator, curriculum development/training role; Dr. Guay will continue to assess the needs and strengths of College of Notre Dame, Roosevelt, and Service Learning partnerships. She will update and refine CND goals within the parameters of her institution; responsibilities: liaison CND.

5. *Dr. Eide:* title: College of Notre Dame, coordinator, Multiple Subjects Credential Program; supervisor, Multiple Subjects Teacher Candidates; affiliation: CND College administrator, curriculum development/teacher training; role: Along with Dr. Guay, Dr. Eide will assess the needs and strengths of College of Notre Dame, Roosevelt, and Service Learning partnerships. She will work with

student teacher candidates and master teacher candidates in mentoring and coursework reform; responsibilities: liaison CND.

6. & 7. *Betty Joe and Lee Wade:* title: retired members of the community; Roosevelt parent alumni affiliation; active volunteers in senior community and Roosevelt; role: coordinate senior training program and activities. Assist with training seniors in the use of e-mail and the Internet, at Roosevelt and in the retirement homes; relevant experience: both are active computer users and "surf the net" for resources, learning, and pleasure.

8. *Courtney Moroney:* title: student teacher in training at College of Notre Dame; affiliation: active interest in helping to promote technology and distributed learning in our schools; role: to attend trainings, design coursework, pilot units, and evaluate integrated technology activities inside and outside the classroom; relevant experience: intermediate user of technology; time involved: to be determined.

Other Project Partners

9. *Robert Beuthel/Betty Casey:* titles: district superintendent/curriculum facilitator; affiliation: Burlingame Schools; administrative and curriculum support; role: district administration and board representatives; relevant experience: users and promoters of distributed, integrated, and interdisciplinary learning; time involved: as needed.

10. *Bonnie Hasson:* title: School Services coordinator at Coyote Point Museum; affiliation: coordinating scheduling for museum-based programs at Roosevelt; role: will provide the personal link to the students in providing information, environmental education and service programs at Coyote Point Museum; relevant experience: longtime member of Coyote Point Museum; time involved: ongoing.

11. *David Nigel:* title: teacher, Roosevelt School; affiliation: teacher in charge of Student Council; role: assist Student Council with fund-raising to help pay for dedicated lines into retirement facilities; relevant experience: veteran teacher in charge of many schoolwide committee friend-raisers and fund-raisers; time involved: as needed.

12. *Pat Skjervheim/Cheryl Biggs:* title: Roosevelt librarian/technology aide; affiliation: Both staff members are key to smooth execution of distributed learning to its fullest potential; role: available to provide daily assistance in managing software and maintaining technology equipment, available daily when problems occur in computer lab and "hub"; relevant experience: trained in computer use and repair; time involved: as needed.

13. *Dr. Michael K. McCloud:* title: medical director, MedWise Primary Care for Seniors; affiliation: Mills Peninsula Hospital along with Sterling Court and the Retirement Inn bring expertise to our project

as it relates to solidifying the bond between this community and its newest school; role: adviser and link to new resources and senior friends; time involved: as needed.

Hardware/Software Support (5):   Our school has full-time support personnel in technology through our librarian and technology aide. Their responsibilities include managing software; maintaining technology equipment, and staff training. The district has conducted yearly in-service programs to train support staff in maintenance and technology upgrades. Computers needing a higher level of expertise are picked up by Eaton Associates, a computer repair firm contracted by the district.

Site Modifications (6):   The four third/fourth-grade classrooms and "hub" will need increased electrical service, more networking capability, some carpentry, etc. This will be paid by the district as part of the modernization of Roosevelt School. Funding will come from a bond issue passed last year and some state hardship matching funds.

E-mail Capabilities (7):   All staff members at Roosevelt are currently part of the district's e-mail system, which is managed by an outside consultant. The district uses Eudora Lite Software. In the coming year the district is planning to upgrade e-mail to Claris E Mailer.

Internet Capacity (8):   Currently all computers at our school (thirty-two) are part of an Ethernet (LAN) which is part of the district (WAN). All computers have Netscape Navigator 2.02 and access to the Internet through frame relay lines to the district office and San Mateo County Office of Education. As usage increases, the district will "Ramp Up" as needed. Funding will come from lowering of current charges of 40 percent based on the E Rate discount program.

Maintenance/Warranty (9):   After the one-year warranty period expires, computers received from the grant will be maintained and repaired in the same manner as all existing equipment.

Insurance (10):   The district pays fifty cents per computer per year insurance to cover damaged or stolen computers. Buildings containing computers are wired with Sonitrol Security Alarm Systems paid for with district funds.

In the interest of space all our partners share the same goals from these identified needs.

• *Mobility:* the ability to use technology in a distributive way, any time, anywhere. At this time there are no laptop computers, no eMates, no digital cameras, in short, no way for technology tools to leave our building simply and be used at home, on field trips, or in the community.

• *Information Management:* efficient use of technology in students' record keeping and assessment. Most schools use computers only to keep names, address files, and letter grades. Perhaps the most exciting use of technology would be the ability to create "Running Records" about students on an eMate while instructing and have those records available to all the staff that work with those students day to day, year to year. Presently a small written paragraph follows each student in his Cumulative Record Folder updated once a year.

• *Building Capacity:* our focus area, "It takes a village," is an old cliche, however important when trying to reform, restructure, and upgrade educational services and practices. Connecting with CND and other area colleges; beginning a Service Learning program; marketing through our Web site, "Our Town" will lead to an educational environment rich in what we feel are essential elements of creating a visionary school in the information/communication age. Networked, flexible, interdependent and caring of the individual.

Part VII, Question 4: Professional Goals of Project Team

The final test of a leader is that he leaves behind him in other men the conviction and the will to carry on.

—*Walter Lippmann*

Mr. Heron, Principal, Roosevelt School   Thank you for the opportunity to apply to your company for new technology equipment and in-service for our recently opened school. Roosevelt School was closed in 1980 due to declining district enrollment and larger class sizes as a result of cutbacks in state funding. I was the principal when Roosevelt closed and am now the principal for its reopening. I have witnessed the ways in which Apple has played an integral part in building our district's technological capacity and potential over the years—from our first Apple IIe you donated in 1983 to the grocery receipt giveaway and your present nineteenth year of education grants. Our goal is to create a technology infrastructure at Roosevelt. Roosevelt has diverse staff whose teaching would be enhanced by training, and the formation of a student enrichment "hub" filled with opportunities for students and staff to expand and work together through interdisciplinary units. We envision creating our student enrichment "hub" with the equipment and training from Apple and other consultants. We hope, in the next five years, to have technology available to students in every classroom, and accessible, by means of eMates and the Internet. The continued focus, throughout, will be community service, linking ourselves with the senior service learning project that will be a model for others to duplicate and benefit from.

John Geer, Technology Coordinator, Burlingame School District   My goal is to help Roosevelt School implement the 3 E's and create a learning environment that is integrated, accelerated and diverse. The technology "hub" and Senior Service Learning Project will provide students the chance to learn everywhere—classrooms, homes, community, the sky's the limit! As district technology coordinator, I bring expertise to the staff on basic maintenance of systems and applications. My goal is to be available on an ongoing basis for troubleshooting and coming up with creative ways to incorporate technology into all areas of the curriculum. These are much needed skills when starting up a school with new technologies. I have been key in developing labs at both McKinley School and Burlingame Intermediate School. My goal is to create a district model site at Roosevelt, coordinate training, and work toward helping other schools develop similar programs in the Burlingame District.

Diane A. Guay, Ed.D., Chair, Department of Education College of Notre Dame (CND)
Carla Eide, Ed.D., Coordinator, Multiple Subjects Credential, CND; Supervisor, Multiple Subjects Teacher Candidates, CND
CND has long had an interest in making available technology training for its teacher candidates and masters students. The College of Notre Dame has the only teacher education program in San Mateo County, and its Macintosh Lab is in need of an infusion of new computers since most of them were acquired in 1990. My goals for this partnership are: (1) to extend the network of already established partnerships between the Department of Education and public schools to include Roosevelt School specifically; (2) to update the Computer Labs used by teachers-in-training as they complete their credentials; and (3) to extend the use of computer technology to teachers already certificated who have returned to the college for the newly established masters degree in education technology. Working with Roosevelt will be invigorated by the opportunity to have student teachers and staff work hand-in-hand to prepare instructional units that harness the power of new technology through the entire curriculum. Dr. Eide and I look forward to our time at Walker Ranch retreat to meet educators with similar challenges and goals.

Courtney Moroney, Teacher Candidate, College of Notre Dame   This semester I am student teaching at Roosevelt School. Seeing the affiliation between CND and Roosevelt is exciting as I begin my teaching career. I would like to help implement Touch the Future: Teach a Child because I feel that the classroom I will be teaching in can look very different and much more engaging if technology tools and distributive learning were the norm. My goal, if allowed to attend the Walker Ranch retreat and work on this project would be to update my skills, assist in course work reforms, and mentor as many student teachers as possible.

Caryl Brewbaker, Second-Grade Teacher; Roosevelt School Grant Coordinator   I have been an elementary teacher for ten years and have fourteen old but very active Apple IIEs in the classroom. Should this Apple

Training	Teacher Release Time	Source	Cash	In-Kind	Total
4 Days	Release Time for Curriculum Development (3 Teachers, 4 days, $80 per day)	District	$960		$960
2 Days	Release Time for Inservice Distributive Lng. (12 Teachers, 2 days, Per Contract)	District		$1920	$1920
2 Days	Release Time Qrtrly Planning/Evaluation (2 Project Teachers, 4 days, $80 per day)	District	$640		$640
2 Days	Release Time Networking/Dissemination (3 Teachers, 2 days, $80 per day/CUE/CLMS, etc.)	District	$480		$480
6 Days	Release Time for Technology Mentor/Project Project Coordinator, training with CND (2 Coordinators, 6 days, $80 per day)	Mentor		$960	$960
	Training/Teacher Release Time Total		$2080	$2880	$4960

Training	Teacher Release Time	Source	Cash	In-Kind	Total
Materials	Inservice—Distributive Lng/Distance Lng Software, Virtual Classroom Mgt.	Mentor		$2000	$2000
		Roosevelt	$1500		$1500
5 Days	BSD Stipends—Project Staff/Walker Creek (2 Coordinators, 5 days, $80 per day)	District	$800		$800
As Needed	CND Trainers/Mentor	CND		$3000	$3000
3 Days	Jerry Westfall Stipend—Web Site Distance Lng/Virtual Classroom Mgt.	Roosevelt	$1800		$1800
	Support Costs Total		**$4100**	**$5000**	**$9100**

Site Modifications/Misc Expenses	Source	Cash	In-Kind	Total
Bond Funds		$3000		$3000
Telecommunications hook ups/fees	Dist./Partners	$960		$960
Insurance/Travel	District	$1000	$1000	$2000
NECC Conference, San Diego	District/CND	$1200		$1200
Misc. Expenses Total		**$6160**	**$1000**	**$7160**

Budget Summary	Cash	In-Kind	Total
Training/Teacher Release Time Total	$2080	$2880	$4960
Support Costs Total	$4100	$5000	$9100
Misc. Expenses Total	$6160	$1000	$7160
Project Budget Total	**$12340**	**$8880**	**$21220**

Detailed Budget: Touch the Future: Teach a Child

Grant be successful, I will be responsible for getting the appropriate technologies to the teachers who will best model it for others. My goal is to provide the follow-through of finding additional monies to complete Roosevelt's vision of getting a minimum of six to eight computers, and their peripherals, in every classroom. I truly believe in distributed learning and will take an active role in presenting the new technologies that allow for distributed learning to take place in the curriculum.

Part VII, Question 12: Letters of Support

"Think Different"
Apple Computers, Inc.

Burlingame School District
Robert Beuthel, Superintendent of School
Fred Heron, Roosevelt School Principal
John Geer, District Technology Coordinator

College of Notre Dame
Dr. Diane A. Guay
Courtney Moroney

Senior Partners
Mary Janney, Sterling Court
Maeve Reddin, Retirement Inn of Burlingame
Dr. Michael McCloud, Mills-Peninsula Hospital

Environmental Education Partner
Bonnie Hasson, Coyote Point Museum

Enrichment Education Partner
Carol Ann Prater, Summer Academy Program

Note: the following letter of support [shown in Figure H.2] comes from the school district's superintendent. It exemplifies all the characteristics of a compelling letter of support.

Part VIII: Hardware and Software Request and Narrative

Organizing is what you do before you do some things, so that when you do it, it's not all mixed up.
—*Christopher Robin, in* Winnie the Pooh

The chart below summarizes where the hardware we are requesting will be placed. Desktop computers will be placed in third-, fourth- and fifth-grade classrooms and in a large hallway "hub" at Roosevelt School. They will be connected to our existing Ethernet LAN to provide access to the Internet and networked printers. All Roosevelt students will use eMates to extend their learning experiences throughout the school, school grounds, to students' homes, the community, and field trips (outdoor education, etc.). The "hub" will be stocked with resource materials, a digital camera, scanner, printer, desktop computers and eMates for all staff, volunteers, and senior partners to use. The desktop computers placed at College of Notre Dame will be placed in their Macintosh Computer Lab and connected to their existing Ethernet LAN to provide access to the Internet, networked printers, and Roosevelt's Web site "Our Town." The desktop computers placed at Sterling Court and Burlingame Inn Senior Citizen Home will be

Burlingame School District

February 6, 1998

New Connections 2
Apple Education Grants
One Infinite Loop, MS 76-8CA
Cupertino, CA 95014

To Whom It May Concern:

As Superintendent it is stimulating for me to see the excitement created by a group of Roosevelt School community individuals regarding the possibility of a New Connections 2 grant. After having been closed for seventeen years, Roosevelt was reopened last September due to the District's need for additional space as a result of enrollment growth and class size reduction. Roosevelt is a small campus and has already exceeded its space limitations, so as part of the modernization of this over seventy-five year-old building, scheduled next summer, the District will add modular construction units. This will increase student capacity while maintaining quality space for special programs. During the reopening process, the District focused on several enhancements, and one of the key areas was renovation of a room to be used as the "hub of learning in the school", the school library/media center. A limited computer lab has been installed in the media center and the school has been completely networked and connected with the District's wide-area network and the Internet. While the basic infrastructure is in place for technology to be integrated into the fiber of the school, this grant will allow that to occur in a more timely manner, and has the potential of making Roosevelt a model school in the Burlingame community and in the Bay Area.

This grant also interfaces with other District areas of focus including:
- the District's ongoing commitment to staff development
- teachers, administrators and community working together on school programs
- considering/adapting restructuring and/or reform measures to improve instructional opportunities
- systemic reforms through linkage with community agencies/groups with program samples being the District's Integrated Children's Service and Burlingame Together
- integrating academic, social and ethical learning
- focusing on curricular activities emphasizing the environment, service learning and intergenerational collaboration.

I commend the team for their efforts in developing this worthy project and fully support the proposal.

Sincerely,

Robert E Beuthel

Robert E. Beuthel
Superintendent

FIGURE H.2   Sample Letter of Support from Superintendent

placed in the recreation room and have access to the Internet via a modem.

Software required on all "hub" and senior computers will include: ClarisWorks 5.0, Netscape Navigator 3.0, HyperStudio 3.0, and Claris HomePage 3.0. CND will install other software that complements the course work they have developed in the teacher candidate and masters programs.

College of Notre Dame
*2 Desktop Computers

*Peripheral Products

    1 Laser Printer

    1 Digital Camera

    1 Flatbed Color Scanner

    4 EMates

Senior Partners
*2 Desktop Computers (Sterling & Inn)

*Peripheral Products

    2 Inkjet Printers

Roosevelt School Hub
*5 Desktop Computers

Peripheral Products

    1 Laser Printer

    2 Digital Cameras

    2 Flatbed Color Scanners

    10 EMates

Networks and Servers

Existing Ethernet (LAN)

---

*All desktop computers should have at least 32 MB of RAM, 2 GB of ROM, 24x CD-ROM drive, Operating System 7.6, and built-in Ethernet cards.

News Release

January 20, 1999   Name: Fred Heron   Phone: (650) - - - - - - - -

Roosevelt School Community Center

Sponsors
Roosevelt School, Burlingame
College of Notre Dame

Partners
Apple Computer, Inc.
Retirement Inn of Burlingame
Sterling Court
Dr. Michael McCloud
    Mills/Peninsula
Coyote Point Museum

Roosevelt Elementary School at 1151 Vancouver Avenue, Burlingame, CA is holding a Grand Opening for its newly established School Community Center on Friday, February 12, at 10:30 am. The Center, funded by a 1998 Apple Education Grant awarded by Apple Computer, Inc., will provide space and resources for seniors to drop in, share their technological skills or learn new skills. The main goal of this project is to develop a partnership between students at Roosevelt School and seniors in our local community. The hope is to enrich the lives of both our seniors and our children through technology.

Important guests will be on campus during the February 12th Grand Opening. Invited guests include Steve Jobs, Bill Laskey, J. T. Snow, David Lui, Burlingame City Council members, Burlingame Chamber members, School Board members, school principals, PTA presidents and local seniors interested in sharing in our adventure. Roosevelt students will assist in hosting this event.

The Grand Opening culminates Roosevelt's week-long celebration of the National Random Acts of Kindness Week. During this celebration students and parents at Roosevelt will be "creating kindness" with special attention focused on our visitors on Friday.

The program for the Grand Opening includes entertainment by our students. Roosevelt's principal, Mr. Heron, will speak and be available throughout the event for discussion and comments.

FIGURE H.3   Sample Press Release

APPENDIX I
Sample Concept Paper: Summer Academic Program

Note that this concept paper was written as a letter. This is appropriate given the relationship between the participants, but you should consider whether such an approach, as opposed to a more formal paper, is the right one for your situation and proposal.

Mr. Mark Jacobs
San Mateo Union High School District
San Mateo, CA 94402

Dear Mark:

Thank you for spending time with me last week to discuss the Transitions Academy Program and the Multi-media Computer Assisted Learning (CAL) Enrichment/Tutorial Computer Centers. I am writing in response to our conversation and on behalf of the children and families that live in the San Mateo Union High School District (SMUHSD) and its feeder districts. These families feel the need for quality after-school educational opportunities. There are more than 3,000 children in your feeder middle schools whose parents work outside the home. Many of these parents work because of economic necessity. However, too many of their children do not have access to affordable, supervised, academic and constructive activities during the after-school hours and summer. Indeed, experts estimate that there are at least five million "latchkey" youth who come home each day to empty houses.

These youth are at higher risk for drug, alcohol, and tobacco use, delinquent behavior, violent victimization, and injury than their peers who are supervised after school and during the long summer days. Statistics show that the largest number of juvenile crimes and victimization occur during the hours when students are released from school. The nation's police chiefs and educators believe we can no longer ignore the obvious. They overwhelmingly support an investment in quality after-school programming and feel it is the best deterrent against juvenile crime and victimization. Our youth need safe and engaging opportunities between the last school bell and the start of a new school day or school year.

Background Information

The National Report, *Safe and Smart: Making After School Hours Work for Kids*, provides evidence that safe, enriching, and high-quality after-school opportunities can help students acquire new skills and broaden their education. The President and United States Congress call for new investments in youth programs, hoping that every child in the U.S. will be able to take part in Computer Assisted Learning (CAL) classes (Cyber School), and literacy and fine arts courses; receive academic assistance, mentoring, and tutoring; and perform community service. *Providing* evidence, *calling* for investments and *hoping* that quality after-school programs become available do not make them materialize. That takes a great deal of effort, ingenuity, and investment by caring citizens, communities, schools, foundations, and corporations, especially in California, a state whose budget limits summer educational enrichment opportunities to 7% of its public school student population.

Knowing the grim state budget for summer educational programs, how do San Mateo County (SMC) youth fare? Better than most for recreational activities, below the average for academic, literacy, and fine arts activities. That's if they have money. Literally thousands of middle school children are added to the "latch key" roles each summer because their parents do not have the fiscal resources for daily participation in academic or recreational programs over the long ten-week summer period. Graduating 8th grade middle school students, along with thousands of SMUHSD high school students, have *the most limited and inflexible academic program offerings available countywide.* Many just "hang out" after the last school bell rings in June and stagnate. Thousands of future and present SMUHSD students, who were supervised from 8:00 A.M.–3:00 P.M. while attending school, find themselves "on their own" and vulnerable each summer. The county's need for academic enrichment in quality areas such as reading, literacy, mathematics, and the arts is enormous.

The city recreation departments, the YMCA, the Boys/Girls Clubs, and even community churches and synagogues are working hard and playing a major role in planning enrichment activities for community youth, but if you were to review our county's year-round youth offerings during the average year there is still a very poor balance. Few academic, computer, and fine arts programs are available and/or affordable to the middle- and low-income parent or the middle school and high school student. The type of high-quality programming that enhances a child's academic achievement and performance and strengthens effective community partnerships between schools, community-based organizations, law enforcement, and youth groups throughout the year is typically in short supply. Research validates the premise that communities fare better when their young people are "engaged in," not just "supervised in," meaningful, enriching, comprehensive programs, both after school and summers. In light of these findings and our county's need for affordable academic enrichment, the Transitions Academy and Computer Assisted Learning (CAL) Centers were born.

Proposal Narrative

The Transitions Academy program began three years ago in order to "Bridge the Gap" that exists between affordable and available high-quality academic activities for high school students. The goal has been to create more of a balance for families between recreational offerings (usually inexpensive and abundant); and academic and fine arts offerings (usually expensive and/or in short supply). The summer Transitions Academy is open to all San Mateo County Youth entering grades 9–12. Most of its past attendees are or were enrolled in the San Mateo Union High School District (SMUHSD). The Academy presently is a collaborative effort between the San Mateo Union High School District, the City of Burlingame, the Burlingame Elementary School District (BSD) and Academy staff (most are SMUHSD or BSD teachers/alumni). This unique collaborative arrangement keeps costs down, physical resources adequate, and academic offerings challenging. The goal from the start was to offer a quality summer enrichment program that would:

- contribute to raising children's self-confidence,
- enhance their academic retention and skills, and
- raise aspirations for their future.

In so doing we have made teachers and parents happy, and students more successful when the September school bells ring. Our successful three-year track record of continued student growth and superior parent and staff evaluations has attracted local Foundation support and helped us to accomplish these goals. We started with an innovative collaborative of stake holders that had a vested interest in youth—the schools (BSD/SMUHSD), the city (both police and recreation departments), and the funders (parents). The Peninsula Community Foundation and the Bay Meadows Foundation, along with the David and Lucille Packard Foundation, have been key in assisting the collaborative to date, with both operating funds, expansion funds, and scholarship requests. For that we are very grateful.

Six years ago 81 students participated in the Summer Enrichment Academy (SEA) programs offered by the collaborative on two campuses. Now more than 600 students attend enrichment programs on four campuses. Then, as now, the program offerings model the quality outlined in that national research document *Safe and Smart*. What has changed dramatically since 1993 is student thinking. Then, the pervasive thinking among students was that like oil and water, summer, kids, and enrichment learning don't mix. It was thought that summer recreation could not occur in an Algebra, Writing, Reading, Fine Arts, or Science class, only in a swimming pool or on a soccer field. The established summer program offerings excluded ninth graders and echoed this sentiment: high school students only go to "class" in the summer or after-hours to earn credits or make-up work. Then, as now, most "traditional" high school academic programs exclude ninth graders or enrichment learning; rather they exist only for academic credit (gr. 10–12) or remediation (grades 10–12).

A major shift in thinking and momentum has occurred for BSD/SMUHSD students. This, coupled with the fiscal reality that our "collaborative" of Community Based Organizations (CBOs) offers the most cost-effective and targeted academic enrichment program on the Peninsula, has created a 700% increase in enrollment.

Our Request

The summer of 1999 brings us to a new place, a crossroads. One of the significant collaborative partners (Burlingame School District—BSD) is experiencing very difficult financial times. Their ability to provide clerical support, insurance, computer facilities, instructional materials, office space, and other general operating expenses is very limited. On the one hand we have received more requests for Transitions registration materials than ever before, but on the other hand, the program may be scrapped. The reason: the Burlingame School District is no longer able to be the lead agency in this high school academic enrichment effort. They can no longer waive their indirect fees, insure staff/students on the high school sites, and pay SMUHSD's rental and custodial fees. Though interested in all community youth, BSD needs to focus its dwindling resources on the 2400+ Kindergarten–8th grade students who will be returning to their schools in the fall of 1999. Since the Transitions Academy and CAL Computer Centers only have an impact on the academic and social growth of students entering 9th–12th grade, it is a program the District can no longer manage.

In Conclusion

My request to you is twofold. First, I would ask that the San Mateo Union High School District replace the Burlingame Elementary District (BSD) as the lead agency and LEA for the Transitions Academy program and CAL Computer Centers, thus giving SMUHSD the prominent role in supporting and expanding this high school enrichment program. Second, I ask that you would provide access to one or more of your district computer labs this summer and next school year so that together we can build your capacity to assist, remediate, and enrich SMUHSD students in their high school academic course work. New multimedia (CAL-computer assisted learning) software programs in reading, writing, mathematics, and study skills will be site licensed. We will focus on "bridging that gap" between *what students know and what they need to know* to be successful in their high school years. In doing the original research and academic design for the Transition Academy in 1996 I found many SMUHSD high school teachers extremely frustrated at the low reading levels, poor writing skills, and sporadic study skills of entering eighth grade students. The Transition Academy and CAL Computer Centers target these crucial areas, giving participating students entering SMUHSD as ninth grade students a better chance to succeed without costly District remediation and intervention. The program also allows tenth and eleventh grade students to learn material for the first time, obtain remediation, or accelerate. Working with Learning 2000 and Computer Curriculum Corporation (CCC) over the next three years, we would seek to establish on every SMUHSD campus a comprehensive, computer-based, multimedia, remediation, tutorial, and enrichment center (Cyber School) that operates year round, evenings and weekends, to maximize student growth and success.

On the following pages I have detailed the approximate costs (indirect/cash) and issues to your District if, in fact, you choose to replace Burlingame as the Lead agency and LEA.

Thank you for your time and interest in the youth of our county. If you need additional information about the Transitions program, the multimedia CAL Computer Centers, or budget projections, please feel free to contact me.

Sincerely,

Carol Ann Prater
Director, Summer Academy Programs

Projected Budget—Summer 1999

Transitions/Multimedia Computer Center for Computer Assisted Learning
One site: Burlingame High School
Income: 150 students @ $300 tuition   = $45,000
Expenses:

9 staff members @ $2750	=	$24,750
Director (C. Prater)	=	$4,500 (10% Gross)
Software/Site license 1	=	$8,500
Instructional materials	=	$3,000
Office supplies	=	$1,750
Rec. dept. fees	=	$2,250
Credit card fees	=	$250
TOTAL		$45,000

Projected Budget—Fall 1999

Two sites: Burlingame High School and Mills High School
Income: 100 students @ $300 tuition   = $30,000
Expenses:

4 staff members @ $3500	=	$14,000 (2 per site)
Director (C. Prater)	=	$3,000 (10% Gross)
Software/Site license 2	=	$8,500
Instructional materials	=	$1,750
Office supplies	=	$1,000
Rec. dept. fees	=	$1,500
Credit card fees	=	$250
TOTAL		$30,000

Benefits to the SMUHSD, staff, and students

- Assistance with transitioning middle school students successfully.
- Assistance with supporting students with low reading/academic scores by providing targeted and cost-effective remediation.
- Expanding capacity to enrich students and accelerate learning.

- Unique opportunity to harness computers to enhance academic success for a majority of SMUHSD students.
- Building capacity to provide flexible and accessible instruction that will support all students and assist staff with curriculum delivery and student assessment.
- Moving SMUHSD into a CAL instructional format that would provide the groundwork for Cyber School course offerings for official district credit. These courses would be accessible by all district students at a future date.

APPENDIX J
Sample Letter
Proposal

September 23, 1993

Mr. Charles Sopp
Bay Meadows Foundation
San Mateo, California 94402

Dear Mr. Sopp:

Not many years ago the San Mateo Union High School District decided to close Burlingame High School. Low enrollment and parent concerns about the "open" campus made it an easy target. Thanks to a new administrative team, a "closed" campus, and many new and challenging programs, the high school is again thriving at full capacity with a waiting list of students. One of the many programs that has contributed to this "turn-around" is the Theatre Arts program. For many years Burlingame High produced exciting productions but then, as budgets got tighter, the Theatre Arts program and the theatre were much neglected.

Over the past four years a new Theatre Arts director and a dedicated parent support group have worked diligently to bring the Theatre Arts program to a level of excellence equal to the talents and needs of the students. The problem that remains is a facility that has been virtually neglected for twenty years.

The rebuilding of the Theatre Arts program began several years ago with the students ambitiously scheduling both a fall drama and a spring musical, complete with pit orchestra. Students have since played to "sold out" crowds. They have also taken their talents "on the road" and donated their time to take one-act plays to all the neighboring elementary schools.

Amidst the late-night rehearsals, homework, and donated time for performances for children, senior citizens, and civic groups, the theatre students and parents have actively worked to help gather the funds to begin the journey of getting the Burlingame High School/Community Theatre "back in shape." The facility does not meet the basic needs of staging our many school and local community productions the students, parents, and local citizens work so hard on each year.

The lighting system is at the top of the renovation list and needs to be replaced. There are gaps of illumination with the present lighting system and in some areas the wiring is unsafe. Our technical theatre program at Burlingame High School has grown so dramatically that in recent years our graduates have gone on to two- and four-year colleges majoring in lighting, sound, and other areas within the technical theatre umbrella. The equipment they encounter at those schools is more modern and State of the Art. We also have students that are going right out into the professional theatre workplace. It is our responsibility to better equip them with the technical experience and information to be hired and successful.

Our program is a "hands-on" curriculum where the skills of the students are immediately applied in our theatre. This fall marks our fifth season of fund raising. It was our dream that for this fifth anniversary a new lighting system would be installed for our fall comedy, *You Can't Take It with You*. To this effort the students and parents have raised $22,000, the cost quoted last spring by several companies to be up and running with a new lighting system this fall. Unfortunately when the contract went out to bid last summer, which is required by California law, the lowest bid submitted was $9,500 higher due to some electrical complications. It seems we now have enough money to purchase all the lighting equipment but we do not have the funds to pay electricians for installation.

The lighting equipment is destined to sit in boxes for a year or two more until parents and students are able to raise the additional funds. We are asking the Bay Meadows Foundation to help us realize our first major facilities dream and provide funds for the installation of the new theatre lighting system at Burlingame High School/Community Theatre. After the Herculean task of raising $22,000, we are so close yet so far. The new system could be installed in a week if we had the last $9,500.

The new lighting system will provide students and community groups a beautiful facility for many years to come. It will complete phase one of our theatre renovation project and will bring hours of wholesome activities and entertainment to the citizens of this and neighboring communities. Unlike the theatre in San Mateo, the theatre in Burlingame is small, available, and appropriate for most school and community events since it seats less than half the amount of people as the San Mateo Performing Arts Center. Like the Performing Arts Theatre we have come to realize that theatre renovation and theatre arts productions are supported by more than ticket sales and parent booster clubs. From time to time there is a need to ask for assistance from local foundations. We feel this is one of those times, for we have reached a benchmark in our four-year effort.

Please consider our request for $9,500 to install the new lighting system at Burlingame High School/Community Theatre. Your gift would be greatly appreciated and make the 1993–94 Theatre Arts Season long remembered by students, parents, and community.

Sincerely,

APPENDIX K
Contents of
I'll Grant You That
CD-ROM

A Note from Jim Burke and Carol Ann Prater

Annotated Sample Grants

Apple Technology Grant

Lincoln-Galiban Literacy Grant

Work-to-School Grant

Resource Directory

Links to Web Resources

Name and Address Directory

GrantSAT

Interactive Version

PDF Version

Software

Adobe Acrobat Reader®

Inspiration®

Index

What You'll Find on Our CD-ROM

Certain resources lend themselves to digital format rather than paper. Programs such as Adobe Acrobat© or the Internet's hyperlinks allow us to offer select documents in more interactive, functional formats to better help you through the process described in the book. On the enclosed CD-ROM, you will find the following information and tools to help you write the best proposal you can:

Annotated Sample Grants

In addition to the prize-winning Apple Technology proposal, we have included proposals from two other areas where people seek funding: literacy and educational reform (e.g., School-to-Career programs). The examples are annotated to direct your attention to those aspects of the proposals that will help you write your own. These annotations discuss the style and content, as well as the form and function, of the documents themselves. They are in Adobe Acrobat, which allows us to highlight certain passages and make notes in the margins which, if you click on them, reveal the message.

Resource Directory

Here you will find a list of elite resources organized into the following categories:

- funding and grants
- corporate giving
- education
- standards and reform
- books, libraries, and literacy
- magazines and journals
- technology
- news and research sources

Carol evaluated resources for both quality and quantity of content, and determined these to be the most useful, according to their ability to help you:

- locate materials and resources needed to write your proposal;
- learn more about and take advantage of the vast resources available through the philanthropic world;
- find and use the best support materials available online and through certain books to help you write a winning proposal;
- navigate the vast network of resources and agencies available through the government's different departments; and
- utilize the most current research and data to support your arguments.

GrantSAT (Grant Self-Assessment Tool)

This interactive evaluation tool was developed by the U.S. Dept. of Energy and the Westinghouse Electric Company to:

- assist U.S. educational institutions and nonprofit organizations in writing winning grant proposals; and
- provide U.S. educational consultants and businesses with a commercial tool;

using one hundred core characteristics of a winning grant proposal. We have taken the GrantSAT idea a step further by making the 75-item instrument interactive so you can create a final evaluation to print and use to improve your proposal.

To Start the CD-ROM

On both Windows and Macintosh computers, the program should launch automatically when the CD-ROM is placed in the CD drive. If it does not start automatically, simply open the CD-ROM and double-click the icon labeled "Start."